FROLICKSOME WOMEN & TROUBLESOME WIVES

WIFE SELLING IN ENGLAND

Barb Drummond

Copyright © 2018 by Barb Drummond

All rights reserved.

No part of this book may be reproduced in any form or by any electronic or mechanical means, including information storage and retrieval systems, without written permission from the author, except for the use of brief quotations in a book review.

Bristol Broadside reproduced with permission Bristol Library Services.

Author image by Gareth Jarvis

978-1-912829-06-4 ebook

978-1-912829-07-1 paperback

978-1-912829-08-8 hardback

By the same author:

Mr Bridges' Enlightenment Machine: Forty Years on Tour in Georgian Britain

The Midas of Manumission: The Orphan Samuel Gist and his Virginian Slaves

ACCOUNT OF THE

SALE of a WIFE, by J. NASH,

IN THOMAS-STREET MARKET,

On the 29th of May, 1823.

This day another of those disgraceful scenes which of late have so frequently annoyed the public markets in this country took place in St. Thomas's Market, in this city; a man (if he deserves the name) of the name of John Nash, a drover, residing in Rosemary-street, appeared there leading his wife in a halter, followed by a great concourse of spectators; when arrived opposite the Bell-yard, he publicly announced his intention of disposing of his better half by Public Auction, and stated that the biddings were then open; it was a long while before any one ventured to speak, at length a young man who thought it a pity to let her remain in the hands of her present owner, generously bid 6d.! In vain did the anxious seller look around for another bidding, no one could be found to advance one penny, and after extolling her qualities, and warranting her sound, and free from vice, he was obliged, rather than keep her, to let her go at that price. The lady appeared quite satisfied, but not so the purchaser, he soon repented of his bargain, and again offered her to sale, when being bid nine-pence, he readily accepted it, and handed the lady to her new purchaser, who, not liking the transfer, made off with her mother, but was soon taken by her purchaser, and claimed as his property, to this she would not consent but by order of a magistrate, who dismissed the case. Nash, the husband, was obliged to make a precipitate retreat from the enraged populace.

Copy of Verses written on the Occasion:

COME all you kind husbands who have scolding wives,
Who thro' living together are tired of your lives,
If you cannot persuade her nor good natur'd make her
Place a rope round her neck & to market pray take her

Should any one bid, when she's offer'd for sale,
Let her go for a trifle lest she should get stale,
If six-pence be offer'd, & that's all can be had,
Let her go for the same rather than keep a lot bad.

Come all jolly neighbours, come dance sing & play,
Away to the wedding where we intend to drink tea;
All the world assembles, the young and the old,
For to see this fair beauty, as we have been told.

Here's success to this couple to keep up the fun,
May bumpers go round at the birth of a son;
Long life to them both, and in peace & content
May their days and their nights for ever be spent.

Shepherd, Printer, No. 6, on the Broad Weir, Bristol.

CONTENTS

Introduction	vii
1. Origins	1
2. Sources	9
3. The Legal Position	19
4. The Contract	32
5. Crossed Wires	48
6. Punishment	64
7. Alternatives to Sales	71
8. Rituals	87
9. Women as Victims	102
10. Scolding Women	121
11. A Wife's Worth	134
12. Children	149
13. Friends and Family	158
14. Missing Men	167
15. Mobs and Crowds	174
16. Beyond Smithfield	182
17. Extraordinary Cases	193
18. On Shame	203
19. (Un)happily Ever After	218
Appendix I Notes	225
Appendix II Timeline	245
About the Author	257
Untitled	259

INTRODUCTION

A woman was sold in Sheffield Market Place with a halter round her waist. A man asked: 'What do you ask for your cow?' When told a guinea, he replied: 'Done!'

This account reads like an old vaudeville sketch, but it is from *The Doncaster Gazette* in 1803. How do we read it? More importantly, how was it read at the time? Was the paper mocking the people of Sheffield, as a rival northern city, or were those involved mocking something else?

Examples of English — and occasionally Scots and Welsh — men selling their wives are scattered through newspapers from the early eighteenth century. From the mid-nineteenth century these accounts were unearthed by editors and reprinted as examples of the backwardness and primitiveness of their ancestors, to show how great Britain had become. The press condemned the men who sold their better halves as 'brutes', and the taking of a woman to market in a halter and selling her to the highest bidder as degrading, humiliating and shameful.

Yet the same accounts often noted how meek the women seemed, with few showing any signs of opposition or shame. There were instances where women clearly approved of the transaction, and even some who seem to have initiated the event or demanded the sale go ahead. Some wives were fresh faced teenagers; others well past the first bloom of youth. Whilst the press claimed they were all ignorant and poor, a few were dressed in silk and lace, and one departed the scene in a fine carriage. Buyers and sellers sometimes shared a meal, a farewell drink, or spent the sales money and more on 'a spree'. Prices varied from a few farthings to hundreds of pounds. There were even a few instances when church bells were rung in celebration.

The French often claimed that any Englishman tired of his wife could legally dispose of her at London's Smithfield Market. This helped encourage the widespread view that the eaters of 'bifsteaks' were a nation lacking morality and religious beliefs. The practice was mocked in print and was included in plays to indicate the brutishness of a male character. Sales continued throughout the Victorian era, when Britain was holding itself up as a beacon of enlightenment and Christian morality. And yet when the matter was raised in the House of Commons, the Home Secretary denied any such thing ever happened.

Sales often involved rituals and commercial practices which people believed made them legal. Documents were drawn up and signed, sometimes by attorneys. The auctions were held in open markets, and wives taken through tollbooths and tied up in pens in order to ensure the contract would 'hold'.

The press often claimed the practice was illegal, though failed to mention on what grounds. Occasional punishments were handed out, with the use of stocks, prison and the treadmill.

What on earth was happening?

1

ORIGINS

The English are an ungovernable race.
 Voltaire (attrib.)

In 1814 officers of the parish of Effingham in Surrey tried to sell a poor woman of their parish, claiming it was 'in accordance with the old system'[1] but failed to explain what this 'old system' was. Did they mean some local practice or were they merely acting on rumours, attempting to rid themselves of the responsibility to support a poor woman and her children?

Many accounts of wife sales claimed it was based on ancient custom. The only book dedicated to the subject is by Samuel P. Menefee who described a wide range of traditions such as trial marriages which allowed couples to separate and which he suggested were of ancient Celtic origin. These rituals are interesting enough, but most of those cited by Menefee were in Scotland and Ireland, places where wife selling does not seem to have been common outside the realms of folklore. He was an American, so was unlikely to be aware of the immense diversity of language, culture and traditions across geography and of time in these islands. The Romans and Normans suppressed local customs and the Reformation caused further social problems so local culture suffered. The Black Death, Wars of the Roses and the Civil War wiped out huge swathes of the population, reducing the numbers of people able to preserve and pass on knowledge and traditions. . The founding of new towns as a result of the Industrial Revolution, and movement of people from the countryside to urban centres and emigration to the various colonies further disrupted the local transmission of information and shared memory. When Alan Lomax was making field recordings of songs in the U.S.A., he found many that had died out where they had originated from in Britain. Could wife selling have survived all these upheavals into the modern age?

Most accounts of wife sales have come from local and regional newspapers, but until the relatively recent establishment of professional journalists, articles were written by the office-based editor/publisher. Some pieces were sent to them by members of the public, but were often unattributed, so may not have been first hand. Some may have been provided as examples of moral laxity, so emphasised certain elements at the expense of others. Accounts by French visitors seem to have been written by officers who were allowed limited freedom as prisoners of war. H. Rider Haggard was astounded by a request to be taken to Smithfield Market by a French visitor who hoped to witness such a spectacle. Many French visitors believed the practice was normal. This may have caused the English to mock the reports as propaganda, or to have inspired them to investigate the curious practice themselves.

Those who could afford to move to healthy suburbs abandoned the dark, dirty towns and cities from the eighteenth century, leaving their centres to fall into decay. By the mid-nineteenth century when sales and interest in them seems to have peaked, inner cities were no longer mixed communities where rich and poor worshipped under the same roof and the poor were supported by more affluent neighbours in times of need. High levels of poverty-driven crime further drove the physical separation of rich and poor. Claims were made that the better off had more knowledge of distant parts of empire and often campaigned for charities there, whilst ignoring problems at home. This lead Dickens to coin the term: 'telescopic philanthropy'.

Thus, when wife sales happened, the middle class were unlikely to be present; they did not relate to the people who participated, so the sales were mostly reported negatively.

In the early eighteenth century Sir Richard Steele complained of the indefensible practice of throwing cocks, and observed:

> 'Some French writers have represented this diversion of the common people much to our disadvantage, and imputed it to a natural fierceness and cruelty of temper, as they do some other entertainments peculiar to our nation... I wish I knew how to answer this reproach. The ladies of the present day will probably be surprised to hear, that all, or the greater part of these barbarous recreations, were very much frequented by the fair sex, and countenanced by those amongst them of the highest rank and most finished education.'[2]

It seems the people of England were often a mystery to themselves as well as to tourists from across the Channel.

Some historians challenge the supposed age of many traditions: often, they were invented in the Tudor or Stuart periods following the suppression of the Church of Rome with its many allegedly idolatrous and ignorant practices. Assumptions were often made that traditional behaviour was fixed, whereas country people were constantly adapting to weather and a wide range of circumstances to survive. It makes sense that they were likewise flexible in their social behaviour. Authorities — often driven by religious beliefs or the need to control the terrifying eighteenth century creature, 'the mob'— could encourage or condemn practices. Something as apparently simple as the arrival of a new priest — whether he was traditional or progressive — could have a major impact on local traditions. When a new ritual replaced an older one, the former was often soon forgotten and its new form gained the patina of tradition with surprising speed.

There are also problems in the various elements of the wife sale. While a few written accounts can be found in the mid-sixteenth century, it was not until well into the eighteenth century that accounts mentioned elements such as a public auction or the woman wearing a halter. So, does this imply continuity, adaptation, or a series of coincidences?

Rituals and practices generally arise in response to a need, and vanish when that need is gone. It seems that wife selling aimed to solve the problem of a broken marriage, which in turn required that the concept of a marriage for life existed, and that there was no other recourse when it failed.

For most of Britain's history, people lived in small agricultural communities where they negotiated amongst themselves how to behave and solve disputes. Whilst the parish church was the centre of most communities, by the eighteenth century, many clerics were either absent or negligent, especially in isolated areas. People tended to marry people they grew up with. so knew them well; they were given advice and support from friends and families so they were likely to be compatible and able to live and work together. This may not have required a formal contract, but such unions were a force for good in communities, so were often celebrated, and a range of rituals grew around them.

Until modern times, a marriage could be the simple exchange of vows, even without a witness. Until the middle of the nineteenth century, marriage in Scotland required merely a declaration from the couple. Few people saw the need for any official involvement as many believed that 'marriage was marriage, even when performed by a barber on the open moorland.'[3]

But in the eighteenth century, the economy expanded, and the population became more independent and mobile. Many young people had already left home for work and had little support or advice on their choice of partners, so marriages increasingly went wrong. But the absence of affordable divorce meant that they were trapped in their relationships till death took one of them. Men about to go to sea often married in haste to protect their girlfriend's reputation and provide financial security for her if he failed to return. Guardians of young heiresses lived in fear of unscrupulous men seducing their charges to acquire their fortunes. Some couples married outside their own parishes to avoid the embarrassing and expensive rituals. But this could later cause problems if they needed proof of their marriage but were unable to track down witnesses, so they did not know if they were married or not. Further confusion followed the introduction of the 1704 Test Act which declared dissenters' marriages to be void. 'Fleet marriages' were commonly made when sailors were leaving their sweethearts to go to sea. They were mistakenly believed to be legal by the young couples and were hoped to protect the young women if they later fell pregnant.

The 1757 Marriage Act was passed to establish a clear definition of legal marriage. It required a church service by an Anglican cleric, the details of which were entered into the parish register. Scotland continued with its traditional laws, hence the popularity of fast, discreet marriages by the English at Gretna Green, and the lesser-known border crossings at Coldstream, Berwick and Lamberton. Shaming continued in Welsh Nonconformist chapels into the nineteenth century. Apparently Bibles were thrown at women who misbehaved.

Before the Reformation, England's church had courts for punishing breaches of moral behaviour. Its punishments mainly involved public shaming of the convicted, such as having to publicly admit to their crime and to stand in their underclothes in front of the congregation. In extreme cases, people could be denied the holy sacraments or excommunicated. When other religious groups were formed, they built their own places of worship, and developed their own systems. The Anglican authorities became weaker after 1660 as they became nervous of enforcing punishments for fear of people turning to the various Nonconformist groups.

The earliest known example of a wife sale involved a cleric being paraded round London for selling his wife.[4] It dates from 1553, the year Queen Mary began the return of England's church to Roman practices. The parson was from St Nicholas Cole Abbey, the first church to celebrate the revival of Catholicism. The timing suggests the so-called Parson Chicken had married in the Protestant church, but was returning to the practice of celibacy. His marriage was nullified, so his wife became surplus to requirements and was sold. He was pelted with refuse, but it is unclear whether this was for changing his faith, or abandoning his wife. Yet this is curious, as his marriage was nullified, so he was never legally married. How did he have the right to sell the woman? It seems the driving force in many cases was the need to have a man responsible for the woman to keep her out of the Poor House.

In 1581 the Vicar of Gamlingay convinced Edmund Scayles to sell his wife Isabell to Christopher Upchurch for sixteen shillings, but a churchwarden reported him to the consistory court in Ely.[5] This was after Queen Mary's death, so the country was once more Protestant under Queen Elizabeth. This incident is incomprehensible, but it again shows clerical involvement. The high price means the matter was serious, but why the sale was forced is a mystery. As in the majority of cases, there is no information on the wife. Was Scayles living with two women and forced to sell one of them? As with Parson Chicken, if there were two wives, one marriage was illegal, so how did the man have any rights over the other woman? More sales were referred to consistory courts in the years 1584, 1585, 1613, 1638 and 1696,[6] which covers the reigns of the Tudors through to William of Orange, but not surprisingly, there were no courts held during the Civil War when people seemed to have managed their own affairs locally.

The Church of Rome was a huge transnational organisation, so many church leaders in England had close ties with the continent. Thomas More wrote fluently in Latin and his writings were widely read abroad. But when Henry VIII declared his independence from Rome, he also deprived English scholars of access to the written word, much of which was in Latin. This language was used to impart mystery and ensure priests controlled the laity's access to the very Word of God. Many books and manuscripts were lost in the iconoclasm, which put the brakes on education and early science. But it also meant England was no longer subservient to Europe, or specifically to the southern countries which retained their links with the Vatican. Severing England's ties with Rome made her more isolated, but the English became more independent, as they debated how to read the Bible free of priestly interpretation and intervention. Such independence of thought, of thinking on the fly, was evident in several cases of wife selling, with witnesses debating the correct procedures, aware of the need for the sale to be seen as legal and supported by neighbours should problems later arise. It would be interesting to discover if such independent thinking was found in other Protestant countries.

Europe's Reformation was very different to that of England. Their objections to the Church of Rome were triggered by Luther's outrage at the corruption of the church and the huge sums raised by selling indulgences to shorten a person's time in purgatory. But in England, the church was still popular. The population was mostly rural, far removed from international politics. They paid for the decoration and maintenance of their churches and shrines, they participated in festivals and enactments of Bible stories, and left legacies for prayers in their memory which helped pay for church schools. When churches were ordered to be vandalised, especially under Edward VI, some images were rescued or painted over, and objects for masses were hidden, to reappear under Mary.

A major downside of the separation from Rome was that England became the only European country that did not reform its divorce laws. England alone continued to make it impossible to divorce. In the wake of Henry VIII's marital problems, there had been hopes for change, but his son was a conservative, so this failed to happen. Mary tightened the rules, and Elizabeth had no interest in the matter. As a result, marriage was often embarked upon as a source of happiness and mutual support but became an inescapable trap when problems arose.

If a marriage failed, the church could grant a separation 'from bed and board', but this did not allow either party to remarry. Marriage continued to be defined as lasting till the death of one of them. In 1603, it became a criminal offence to marry while a spouse still lived.[7] It seems that, by then, people were already making their own arrangements. The high cost of divorce, of having to argue through three courts before obtaining an Act of Parliament made it almost impossible. The 1857 act transferred marital affairs from the ecclesiastical courts to the state and removed the need for an act of parliament. The New Court for Divorce and Matrimonial Causes which was begun in 1858 managed all aspects of divorce. Before this, virtually the only divorces granted were to wealthy men whose marriages had failed to produce a viable male heir. Only fifteen divorces were granted by this date.[8]

It seems likely that before the Tudors, marital arrangements were mostly negotiated amongst communities; it is possible that the notion of the union was less rigid, so when relationships failed, local solutions were found. Or perhaps the belief in a better world after death made life on earth bearable.

2

SOURCES

If only one could unmarry again if it didn't suit! Only one couldn't
  Edward Lear[1]

The practice of wife selling was surprisingly widespread, both in place and time, and covers people from the very poorest ranks of society to the upper classes, so it is surprising to find so few mentions of it in modern print. Its origins are unclear, but traces can be found in church records from the late seventeenth century, with the most recent being 1920. Witnesses to sales were recorded for local history societies well into the twentieth century.

The only book to date that has been dedicated to it is *Wives for Sale* by Samuel Pyeatt Menefee,[2] whose 'scholarly examination of an informal institution' was published in 1981 but is now out of print. This is extremely well researched, ranging over newspaper sources, court records and folklore, but it is flawed by the author — an American legal historian — focusing on numbers and failing to question the veracity of some of the cases. He also had little knowledge of England and its people, so he often fails to understand the variety and complexities of their behaviour.

E.P. Thompson's *Customs in Common*[3] does an impressive job in placing wife selling within a cultural and social context, discussing English crowds, local justice, and the wider field of marital relations, as they were seen at the time, and in the decades since. He also writes well on the problems encountered in researching and analysing the subject, and attempts to understand why it has been largely ignored by writers.

Prolific author/historian/cleric Sabine Baring-Gould relates a tale in his *Devonshire Characters and Strange Events*[4] from when he was a young boy, and the local poet returned from market with his bought wife. He has left us a valuable first-hand account of a sale, the community's response and — perhaps best of all — the outcome. He devoted a whole chapter to wife selling, which includes a number of other incidents, from various sources, providing an indication of how widespread the practice was in rural Devon, and how it was perceived there.

He also provides a challenge to the French perception of English wife selling:

'It is, so far as my experience goes, quite useless to assure a Frenchman that such a transfer of wives is not a matter of everyday occurrence, and is not legal: he replies with an expression of incredulity, that of course English people endeavour to make light of, or deny, a fact that is "notorious"... I heard a country curé once preach on marriage, and contrast its indissolubility in Catholic France with the laxity in Protestant England where "any one, when tired of his wife, puts a halter round her neck, takes her to the next market town and sells her for what she will fetch." I ventured to call on this curé, and remonstrate, but he answered me he had seen the facts stated in books of the highest authority, and that my disputing the statement did not prove that his authorities were wrong but that my experience was limited.'[5]

It is unclear how the French could be so much better informed on the matter than the English, but they show the same stubbornness as the wife sellers did in insisting the practice was legal and morally sound. It seems the folklore of English wife selling had created a French folklore of it being widespread and socially acceptable.

A French officer, General R. Pillet spent a decade travelling in England, most of it as a prisoner of war at the time of Napoleon when wife selling seems to have been flourishing. He wrote a book of his observations which included a chapter called *Divorces among the Common People*[6] which may have served as a primary source of French information or — as the English authorities would call it — misinformation.

Centuries of religious and political rivalry may well have been a major factor in the widespread fame of wife selling in France, and the apparent hypocrisy that a country famed for its enlightenment should be reducing its own women to the status of chattels. Similar criticism — or perhaps bemusement — was shown by North Americans who were unimpressed by the English objecting to the selling of African slaves whilst allowing the sale of Anglo Saxon women, so the abolition movement acquired an air of both arrogance and hypocrisy.

Scouring the indexes of English history books unearthed a rare mention in Christopher Hibbert's large tome *The English A Social History*,[7] where he claimed, like Menefee and many newspapers, that it was an ancient custom. He provides no examples, but cites the sale at Weydon Priors Fair in Hardy's *The Mayor of Casterbridge* set in the 1840s which caused such scandal when published in 1886. Recent research has unearthed Hardy's private notebook which reveals the famous account of the sale of Henchard's wife was based on a real incident. Hardy began the notebook in 1883 and it includes items from the Dorset County Chronicle. An account from 1829 of a sale in Stamford, Lincolnshire, was noted by Hardy as being 'used in the Mayor of Casterbridge'.[8]

Most accounts used in this book are from the British Library's online newspaper archive, but early papers were frequently printed in whole or part in italic, so examples often fail to be picked up by the search engine. There is also a problem in the dearth of first-hand accounts: the author only found three detailed descriptions of the sales, one of which involved interviewing those present, so it seems they were not deemed worthy of record either by the press or by private journals or letter writers. Perhaps they took place covertly so left no trace.

It could be that there are accounts to be found in unexpected places, as E.P. Thompson refers to the pioneering work of Jeanette Neeson with reference to food rioting. Opposition was expressed in many forms other than riots which were recorded in contemporary court records, and ranged from lobbying to harassment and arson, some of which could continue long after the events.[9] In some accounts of wife sales, the initial event was unrecorded, but details emerged in later court cases over inheritance and even in baptism registers. Some accounts may have had more value in the material they were written on, as happened to Boswell's diary after his death. Some of his papers were found used to wrap goods in a market in Boulogne.[10] Some of Bach's works were used to wrap butter.

Because wife selling was not a crime in itself, events fail to appear in court records as punishable incidents. But they formed the background to some cases of assault against the wife, in public disturbances, riot due to the crowds they attracted, or in parish records in relation to the support of a wife and children.

Neeson also suggested that local law enforcement may have left no traces, as she described how riots over enclosures sometimes involved calling out troops. But this was often time-consuming, and was usually a last resort. She described a group of local gents gathering for a meal who were notified of a riot. They rode to the site, settled the dispute and returned to their port, so no official record was made. Another record of a riot was found in War Office records, so accounts can appear in surprising places.[11]

It is hard to imagine any wife sales requiring a mounted response. But they were sometimes held at the time of the local assizes or quarter sessions, which increased the risk of legal intervention. Sales often only lasted a few minutes, which further lowers the chances of any record having been made.

The eighteenth century was a prolific time for the writing of letters and journals, but many were destroyed or lost; some authors requested their destruction at their death. If published, they could be heavily edited to show the author in a better light. Given how many people, including the Home Secretary in the late nineteenth century, believed wife selling did not happen, it is possible that accounts of them have been destroyed or ignored due to their lack of credibility. Menefee cited a broadside from Bristol in 1822 which he suggested was adapted from some other case and adjusted to be sold locally. He claimed this was given further weight by it not having been reported in the local press. But there are a lot of reasons for it to be missing from the press, the most likely being a lack of space. One of the most important events of the nineteenth century — and one that should have been immensely important to the people of Bristol — was the passing of the Abolition of the Slave Trade Act in 1807. Yet the Bristol press was silent on this momentous event; even in the capital it rated only a paragraph or two This is because the trade had declined to the extent that it was no longer of much interest to the public.

In Latimer's *Annals of Bristol in the Nineteenth Century*, a wife sale was noted as one of the first sales in 1828 at the new St. Thomas's Market, but there is no suggestion that this was a novel event, which raises questions as to how many incidents preceded this, and where they were held. Latimer only mentioned it in passing in relation to the market; the event is not listed in the index, suggesting that he, like many of his peers, failed to take the event seriously. Most papers at the time seemed to delight in condemning the wife sales, or highlighting them as curiosities which Felix Farley's Bristol Journal often reported. Or it may be that, accounts were believed but were censored to prevent copycats, as Latimer states of food riots in Bristol in 1801: 'No account of the disturbances was published by the newspapers supporting the Government, on the pretext that such intelligence was likely to have a bad effect.'[12] But corporation accounts recorded expenses for dealing with the market riots.

Newspapers began as sources of political and commercial information for governments and merchants, so would never have been interested in such events. Till well into the eighteenth century, they were funded by advertising or, occasionally, by wealthy patrons with vested interests, such as Robert Walpole, so they continued to provide a narrow range of information. Censorship was also a problem, but it collapsed completely, along with commerce, courts and much else, from 1640 to 1660. This allowed an explosion in the market of broadsheets and ballads — the internet of the age — some of which have survived. They were printed on demand and did not have to fit into the newspapers' printing cycle, so could respond more quickly to events.

To encourage literacy, Queen Anne failed to renew the London Stationers' Company's monopoly on publishing. Yet the Stationer's Company was the only 'Guild' which grew dramatically in the eighteenth century. By registering your work at the Stationer's Hall, you reinforced your copyright. They were thus the forerunners of the modern Legal Deposit Agency. The 1710 *Statute of Anne* was the first Copyright Act, which encouraged the tentative emergence of provincial newspapers. But to combat satires of his corrupt government, Walpole passed the Chamberlain's Act in 1733, which censored publishers and performances By the middle of the eighteenth century, literacy was widespread and the economy improved which created a reading audience that demanded more variety, and was prepared to pay for it. In 1750 shorthand reporting was introduced into divorce courts which allowed detailed — often scurrilous — accounts of the upper classes to be published, bypassing the censors in the name of public interest. But there were still no professional journalists as we understand the term. In Dr Johnson's era , the 'Grub Street Scribblers' were in competition with each other, and the press — like today's tabloid papers — competed to outdo each other in shaming the rich and famous.

Papers — especially in the provinces — filled space in slow news weeks by including items of local interest. Some, such as *Felix Farley's Bristol Journal,* claimed to be repositories of the arts and sciences. They reported the latest scientific, agricultural and medical discoveries, so were important sources of information sharing, encouraging people across the country to research and experiment. These papers also included poetry and curious anecdotes, and it is in the latter category that wife selling is often found. But as they were seen as oddities, especially of the 'lower sorts' of people, they often featured unusual or appealing elements, such as a pretty young wife or an old or brutish man. They were designed to arouse readers' sympathy for the woman and outrage at the man. But this raises questions as to how many less remarkable couples were involved in wife selling, and never deemed curious enough to attract the editor's notice. Newspapers were printed on hard-wearing paper made from rags, so could be collected. Inns, coffee houses and libraries held not only a wide range of current papers, especially from London, but also collections of back copies for their readers such as Hardy. The downside of this interest in curiosities in the press was that unusual items were cut out and saved in scrapbooks, or even mounted on screens as collages, so the most interesting items may have been lost in this way.

Libraries, both public and private, often included collections of curiosities, globes and maps as well as books, to cater for gentlemen pursuing their interests and as an aid to any research they carried out. Bristol's library received a collection of rocks which claimed to prove the truth of Noah's flood. From the mid-eighteenth century new national publications emerged which catered for this hunger for knowledge and provided a forum for discussion and clarification. The first of these was *The Gentleman's Magazine*, which published articles on a wide range of topics, encouraging its readers to comment and sometimes reprint them again. They appealed to the growing numbers of letter writers, amateur scientists, historians, antiquarians, and the socially curious. Others titles included *Chamber's Journal, The Book of Days, The Annual Register* and, for a time, *Notes and Queries*, which was purely for gents — and occasionally, ladies — to discuss news and views, so was an early — though of course very slow — version of a blog. Wife sales occasionally appeared there and were discussed, but seldom with any resolution as to their legality or what should be done about the so-called problem.

From the mid-nineteenth century, when Britain had conquered much of the world and investigated many so-called 'primitive' societies, polite society turned its attention to the primitive folk at home. England had expanded from a nation made up of small communities where rich and poor lived close to each other, to a nation where the rich had escaped to the healthy suburbs and country houses, becoming completely oblivious to the poor and their ways of life. Within London, claims were made that the denizens of some slums were as mysterious as people on tropical islands. Newspapers began trawling their own archives and reprinted items about wife sales to highlight the curious customs of their primitive ancestors, demonstrating how enlightened and advanced the editor and the readers had become, so bringing the printed records closer for historians to search. Against all this, there are problems of the survival of the original papers, of where they were stored and how prone they were to damp, decay, floods, fires etc.

As newspapers grew more numerous, more frequent and larger, the accounts of wife sales, in turn, were able to become longer and more detailed, though only one, from c1833 at Wednesbury in the Black Country, has been found to show a complete and well written account of the event, including interviews with witnesses, providing a colourful record of what was involved. Probably the most reprinted, so best known, is that of Farmer Thompson of Carlisle who gave a witty, seemingly honest account of why he and his wife chose to separate. But the authors have questioned the reliability of these two accounts, as there is no sign they were written down at the time, but they lived in a culture not cluttered with trivia, their minds not forced to remember PIN codes and follow storylines in soap operas, or who won the football. Their world was still largely an oral one, so, especially when they witnessed an exceptional event which they would discuss and re-tell over time, these accounts are probably close to the truth. There is also a detailed witness account from a man who, as a young boy made a bid at a wife sale and for a time feared he was about to become the woman's owner. Questions have been raised as to whether the man would be able to recall the event in such detail, but the extraordinary event must have seared itself onto his memory, and the story been told repeatedly over the years, often to the same people who could correct him if his memory wandered.

Wife selling cannot be seen as an isolated practice. People of all classes were unhappy at the cripplingly high cost of divorce and the lack of rights for women. These high costs reflected the hypocrisy that the rich could solve their matrimonial problems by legally separating, but the poor were treated as beasts, ordered to endure their unhappiness.

The British generally blamed the French Wars on unruly peasants being able to write, allowing them to distribute radical ideas, so the poor were often taught only to read. This explains why many people could read, providing a huge market for ballad sheets and the effectiveness of broadsides, yet many marriage certificates were marked with an X rather than a signature. British authorities were terrified of the disturbances crossing the Channel, so it seems there was less tolerance of riotous behaviour, which seems to have brought wife sales into the public view when they attracted crowds. There were also occasional problems when the couples argued over the sale, or when those involved adjourned to a local hostelry and the celebrations got out of hand. There were rare cases where the man tried to force the woman to be sold, so faced charges of assault, and cases are also found in parish records of the wives and any children becoming the responsibility of the overseers of the poor, so the original husband was tracked down and held responsible for her.

A final problem with these accounts is, even in the most detailed of them, we are denied the social context. Most of the women are not named: some of the men have named professions, and their clothes and behaviour can point to their social status. The crowds are sometimes mentioned, and their response can suggest much, whether shouting — whatever that expressed — or cheering; throwing mud at the couples, intervening to prevent a sale, or preventing the authorities from stopping it. In one case, there was only silence. Was that shock, surprise, disapproval, or were they trying to understand this novel event?

In almost every account, we are left hanging, not knowing what happened next, which is a problem with the press by its very nature: news has to be new. It has no time or resources for follow-ups unless these are also newsworthy. This is why there was so much opposition to young eighteenth-century women reading the new literary form of the novel. It was not just its novelty that was the problem, but it was widely believed that it gave young, inexperienced women false expectations of the reality of married life. It provided no understanding of the complexities and compromises necessary for a life long commitment. Romantic novels all ended with the marriage, the handsome young couple sailing off into the sunset. The 'happily ever after' was always assumed but the route to it never explained.

3

THE LEGAL POSITION

St Augustine of Hippo, though repeatedly questioned on the matter, had provided no authority for the admissibility of divorce ... but Augustine Averred: "That 'tis lawful for a man to dismiss a wife for ... adultery — does not admit of doubt."
    Francis Watson[1]

Wife sales were variously described as being 'a disgraceful transaction', 'a most disgraceful scene', 'repugnant to our own sense of moral decency', or various combinations of immoral, illegal, scandalous, barbarous or indecent. Husbands were accused of being 'a monster in human form', or — most commonly — a brute. But *The Lichfield Mercury of 1933* showed refreshing sympathy towards the practice, claiming that before the 1857 Divorce Act many people were forced to live miserable lives, with only a few being rich enough to make use of this legal solution.[2] This goes to the very heart of wife selling, and is a theme that recurs time and time again in history. Many people assume that because an action is barbarous or crude through the eyes of modern, so-called civilised people, that those who were involved were ignorant, brutish, or whatever. Without the context of the behaviour, such accusations cannot be accepted as reality.

The authorities often urged disputing spouses to go home and live quietly, but it was much harder for the poor than for those who wrote the laws. The rich generally have a better quality of life. That's why being rich is so desirable and is so often defended by those fortunate few. If their marriages went wrong, they had options. They had larger houses, so they did not have to share a bed with a person they had come to loathe. Rich people could travel, they could live apart. They could have affairs, so long as they were discreet and the women avoided becoming pregnant. This sounds like a cliché, but it generally holds true: to the rich, marriage was a word; to the poor, it could cause such endless misery, it became a death sentence.

It is ironic that England's Reformation had been triggered by a monarch's need to end his marriage, but the country was the only Protestant nation that retained its unreformed divorce laws. Marriage was incredibly easy; it could involve merely the exchange of vows, even without witnesses. But escape from it was impossible. Throughout the eighteenth century, women such as the poet and royal mistress Mary Robinson compared the lives of women with slavery, of being birds in gilded cages. This may seem an exaggeration from women who were not homeless or starving, but some of them lived with the constant fear of domestic violence and homelessness.

When wife sellers were brought before justices, the response varied from being told to go home and make the best of it, to a London alderman claiming: 'if husbands and wives were allowed to separate Smithfield would be too small.'[3] He was joking of course, but it does suggest there were a lot of unhappy couples about, most of whom seem to have suffered more or less in silence, at least for modern researchers. Perhaps this was why so many men chose to spend their evenings in pubs, and why gentlemen's clubs became popular as refuges from their unhappy home lives.

Although it seems that wife selling declined in the late nineteenth century, claims were made that it continued — flourished even — in isolated regions, especially in mining districts. In 1881, T.D. Sullivan, an Irish Nationalist M.P., raised the matter in the House of Commons by asking the Home Secretary Sir William Harcourt, why nothing was being done to convince the lower classes that wife selling was not legal. The reply was: 'Everyone knows that no such practice exists.'[4] It seems the French, Irish and Americans knew more about the common people of England than those sitting in parliament. This could in part be explained by the fact that Harcourt was an expert on international law, so the Home Secretary may have been genuinely ignorant of events in his home patch. But it seems the rest of the house was likewise in the dark, which highlights how unrepresentative were elected representatives were at the time. The electorate at the time was also a very small class of people before the 1843² Reform Act.

The judiciary was much better informed, especially in the capital, as they were confronted with many cases of wife selling. In 1819 Judge Edward Christian in his *Charges to Grand Juries*, called for prosecutions against the 'shameful and scandalous practice' which he claimed was so prevalent by then. He suggested both buyer and seller should be sent to the pillory, but this was a problem, as the pillory had been abolished in 1816, before this was printed.[5]

General Pillet was a French prisoner of war who wrote of his sojourn in England. He witnessed a wife sale and asked a magistrate why he failed to intervene. He was told that it was difficult to establish on what grounds the law could take action unless the sale participants were disturbing the peace. The magistrate claimed that it was a custom of the people, and that it would be dangerous to deprive them of it. This was during the French Wars, so the British authorities were wary of any form of disturbance, but after peace was declared, the courts and press became more condemnatory of the practice, leading to more sales appearing in the press and being broken up. But that still left the authorities with a dilemma as to what to charge the sellers with. If any law was broken, it was that of bigamy, but that was by the wife. However, since the husband approved, this made him responsible. But 'in the eyes of the law the rite of wife sale was a non-event. Legally, the parties might have been taking part in a pantomime.'[6]

And yet it was sufficiently well known and of concern to the authorities for a public warning to be published in 1799 to the many lower-class couples who believed wife selling to be legal. It claimed that 'by a determination of the courts of law in a former reign, they were declared illegal and void.'[7] This 'former reign' was unnamed, but in any case, this was simply untrue. Intriguingly, the article further claimed that sales were a cover for adultery. Again, this seems not to be true, but if it had been, it would have been counter productive, as in effect, such a public ritual would draw the attention of the authorities to the crime, bringing the risk of arrest.

Part of the dilemma faced by the authorities was the lack of clarity as to which area of law should cover wife selling. Traditionally it was a moral matter, so should have been dealt with by the ecclesiastical courts, but they had lost most of their vigour in the late seventeenth century and were unwilling to prosecute for fear of driving parishioners into godlessness or the competing chapels. But even within the clergy, there was a lack of clarity, as at least one believed sales were legitimate, as shown by a christening that was entered in the parish register from Purleigh, Essex, in 1782:

> 'Annie daughter of Moses Stebbing by a bought wife brought to him in a halter'.[8]

Possibly the priest included it as a curiosity, or in an attempt to add legitimacy to the event. If he was, like many local priests, poorly paid, he may have needed the money and seen no harm in such an entry. But if he believed the child was not born into a legitimate marriage he was more likely to have listed her as 'base born'.

The sale was a contract, so it should have been dealt with by common law, but most sales followed legally acceptable practices, such as payment on delivery or in some instances various forms of credit, so this would have caused no problems. The Court of Chancery dealt with the care of widows, orphans and inheritances. It was mostly concerned with trusts and wills, but unlike canon law, was not limited by precedents, so was often an alternative to it. But demand for this court rose spectacularly in the eighteenth century, and it became agonisingly slow. At times, proceedings continued beyond the deaths of the beneficiaries and trustees. As a result, most people went to great lengths to avoid this route. People wrote incredibly detailed wills with chains of inheritance to ensure the intentions of the benefactor were respected.

This left only the criminal courts to deal with wife selling, which meant that the case had to cause some form of public-order offence or, in a few cases, contend with a husband who was violent towards his spouse. Thus, when wife sellers were brought before the authorities, it was unclear what to do with them. At a local level, justices of the peace dealt with minor infringements of the law. They were local gentry. Though often well meaning, only some were trained in the law, and they were unpaid, so there were limits as to how far they would become involved. It is possible they could put the husband in the stocks to cool off and hopefully change his mind about the sale, but it is difficult to see what more they could do beyond warning participants as happened in several instances. They had considerable freedom in sentencing, so sales could be punished as general misdemeanours.

In 1849, Punch provided a rare, enlightened insight into the problems of marital law, and how it failed to serve the poor, i.e. the majority of the population. The article described a man who was convicted of bigamy and — like so many — refused to obtain a separation from the church courts, then obtain a legal separation and then a divorce via an Act of Parliament as it 'is always to be had on proper evidence given — and yet the poor will not purchase their remedy.'[9] Nothing to do with the poor being poor, then.

The Matrimonial Causes Act of 1857 set up a secular divorce court which aimed to speed up the practice of divorce and bring it within easy reach of most people. It was alleged that men saved up for years to be able to afford their freedom from an unfaithful wife.[10] Divorces could be obtained for as little as thirty pounds as opposed to the thousands of pounds under the previous system. If a couple could declare their income was less than fifty pounds per annum, even these fees were waived so divorce was at last within easy reach of all people.

But the only grounds continued to be that of the wife's infidelity, which was humiliating to the woman, and in many cases was not true. With only one court in London, anyone outside the capital had to take time off work, find the money for travel and accommodation and perhaps arrange childcare, so it still excluded the majority of those it was designed to help. Even today, attending court is for most people a terrifying prospect, so for provincials to go to such lengths was still a huge expenditure in time and money.

There was a rare occasion when the law did intervene in a wife sale that caused a dispute between two parishes in Lincolnshire over who was liable for the support of the children of Prudence who had been sold to Joseph Holmes many years earlier. Their three children were entered in the baptismal register as legitimate. But the court claimed that children born in a marriage belonged to their legal parents, so Prudence's first husband was declared to have been their father. The court agreed

> 'it would be monstrous to admit of a husband's coming forward to bastardize the issue of his own wife'.[11]

This seems utterly absurd, ignoring the reality of people's lives. The children had no connection with their mother's first husband, and none of his genes, but courts could only enforce existing laws; they did not write them. The law took no interest in intervening in pantomimes as they were described earlier.

Reports appeared in the press that many soldiers returned from the French Wars to find their wives had remarried and had children. The problem was often resolved by the first husband selling the woman to her new partner. It was claimed that sales happened virtually every market day in the industrial areas through 1815 and 1816.[12] The fact that local authorities failed to intervene helped confirm the public's belief that the practice was legal. Of course it was not, but the alternative was to break up the second families, force ex-soldiers to raise the children of a stranger, and to prosecute the wife for bigamy. The husband had been away, so could not have given his consent, and could not be held responsible for the wife's behaviour. But the courts were always unwilling to prosecute women, so any action would benefit nobody and cause immense social and personal damage. Such informal arrangements resolved the situation, kept families together and saved vast amounts of legal time and public money.

England has traditionally been defended by its 'wooden walls', i.e., its ships. Many men went abroad, especially during the eighteenth century when the country was so often at war with various European neighbours, often in America and the Caribbean. Some fled unhappy marriages or unemployment; some may have found new partners and established new families and never returned. For those wishing to come home, they could be shipwrecked, captured by pirates or enemy ships, or stranded by poverty. The problem was exacerbated by the fact that sailors were paid on their return, so their families often ran out of funds and were forced into the badly holed safety net of the local poorhouse.

Such problems were well known, and Captain Coram established the Foundling Hospital in London — not for orphans as we understand the term — for children who were often handed over by their destitute mothers. A married couple were seen as being yoked together through life, so the death of one brought about the destruction of the family unit. A common image on funeral monuments for a father was of a broken pillar; which deprived a house of its support. They left tokens such as a scrap of cloth cut in half with them retaining a piece as proof of the exchange, buttons or paper, all of which were duly catalogued, but almost none were ever redeemed. These records survive in the Foundling Museum and are utterly heartbreaking. These children were fed, clothed, educated and apprenticed, but the fate of their mothers is not recorded. They may have found work, probably as domestic servants which made it impossible to care for their children. Others were forced to move in search of work, or were forced into the poorhouse and/or died. If their husbands returned, they may not have been able to find them, so many families were destroyed in order to establish and defend the British Empire.

In 1859 The Birmingham Journal announced that the divorce court in Westminster Hall was running at full capacity as soldiers divorced their wives prior to going into battle. This may have been to release their wives from the pain of having to wait for them, so a reverse of the many Fleet Marriages of the previous century when many weddings were held in haste on the eve of soldiers' and sailors' departures. But this wholesale divorcing may have been something more sinister, perhaps forced on the servicemen by the government in order to deny their wives the ability to claim pensions on their demise.

One of William Cobbett's most passionate rants was against the starving poor whilst what he called the 'Dead Weight', i.e., war pensions, continued to increase. Any returned serviceman — young or old — acquired a pension for life, which made him attractive as a husband. 'The man, who under such circumstances, does not marry, must be a woman-hater.'[13] When a husband died, his wife and children were still supported by taxpayers, so Cobbett claimed 'she is our widow, not his'.

Several of the sold wives were noted as young and pretty, with old husbands who seem to have made an odd match. It is possible these men were pensioners who had attracted young women in need of a secure future. The famous case of 'Rough Moey' at Wednesbury in particular fits this as he had a wooden leg, and his face was scarred with gunpowder burns.

The legal system has long hesitated to wade into the swamps of personal relationships, but its hand was forced when public funds were involved, such as when the woman was abandoned by her husband to become dependent on her local parish for support. This is often when the case appears in public records. If her second husband failed to support her: — by fleeing, becoming sick or dying — then the first husband would be expected to maintain her and any children. If he failed to do so — probably due to having his own family to maintain — he would be charged and imprisoned for abandoning her, and her second family would be forced onto poor relief. But this arrangement was often cause for complaint as it prevented the man from supporting either his current or previous family, it ran up legal costs and may have caused him to lose his job on release from prison, so plunging two families into poverty, possibly for life.

Yet another reason wife selling did not warrant legal intervention was the many instances where overseers of the poor conducted the sales. Their accounts were meant to be approved and signed off by local priests, which means that the Anglican Church itself could be charged with these offences. This would not only have been embarrassing, but — given the number of bishops and their supporters in the House of Lords — such a law could never have been passed. Bishops were also seen as hypocrites as they often juggled their sacred and secular hats by opposing reforms to the divorce laws whilst voting for the passage of individual acts for divorces.

There was a wider historical objection to changing English laws, even when they were clearly unworkable. After the Civil War, any change to the constitution made politicians very nervous. England led the European Enlightenment, so the English felt the national laws were of a high standard, even when they caused problems. The one area that was closely watched was the balance of power between the king and parliament. Local laws, which could have dealt with the problems of wife sales, were left alone as

> 'James II's attempt to meddle with them was one of the main causes for his fall. Property rights were considered the basis of society.'[14]

If women were seen as property, this may be why wife selling was seen as legal. In other words: 'if it ain't broke, don't fix it', and though dealing with wife selling could occasionally become a problem for local authorities, it was clearly not a big enough problem to justify the huge effort and expense of enacting controls on it.

Britain was changing fast throughout this period with its expanding colonies; it must have seemed that ruling the growing empire felt more like holding onto the reins of a carriage drawn by bolting horses. The House of Hanover was not popular or secure, and with so much instability in Europe threatening to spread to these islands, changing any law could only be undertaken if absolutely necessary; wife selling, by its nature a personal matter, could never rise to such prominence where authorities that the were driven to intervene.

The 1704 Test Act excluded Catholics and the various Nonconformists from holding office, and it declared their marriages void, so a growing proportion of the population were forced to effectively behave outside the national laws, though they were still at risk of fines for not attending divine service on Sundays. Despite having such outsider status, many became wealthy industrialists who were then involved in establishing improvement trusts via Acts of Parliament as the result of a local petition. They were concerned with building bridges, improving roads, building and maintaining assembly rooms, market houses and public libraries. Parliament merely authorised local people to act.[15]

This may seem to have little to do with wife selling, but it points to a number of similarities as well as a shared mindset. The exclusion of non-Anglicans from holding office did not prevent them from making significant improvements and valuable contributions to their area. In many towns, Nonconformists were the wealthiest groups and many factory owners built housing for their employees which allowed them to place strict controls on workers' behaviour in return for giving them a home. Some banned the consumption of alcohol; some refused to allow licensed premises in the town. A landlord in Wales even insisted on workers wearing clothes made only of local wool. If a tenant in such circumstances was involved in a wife sale, they could lose their employment and home. In these conditions, legal proceedings were not necessary, and such activities were unlikely to appear in any records.

In England — especially the Midlands and the North — such industrialists played important roles in keeping the peace as many towns lacked councils which were able to keep up with the exploding populations. Many towns were based on a single industry, so the factory owners — often one family — had huge power over their workforces. When a wife sale took place at Haverside near Manchester in 1835, their employer discharged them all[16], though it is unclear whether this was due to the sale or the fact that the buyer was the wife's brother-in-law, suggesting this was a case of incest, which was of course illegal. A more active intervention scuppered a sale at Little Horton, near Bradford in 1858. A crowd gathered, but the factory owner threatened to sack anyone who participated, and he kept the intended buyer at work, so the sale fell through.[17] Given such instances, it is possible other sales were likewise prevented, and failed to leave any record. They also show that the factory owners were engaged with their employees and concerned about their morals, so they could be more proactive in keeping the peace than the established law enforcement.

Northern industrial towns and cities were often seen by the London press as some form of amorphous mass, but they were all very different in their origins, development and the type of people who made up the population. Bradford stood out for having a high population of Quakers, but also a large German community who founded music and literary clubs. Though the Quakers may not have participated in these, they recognised their importance for the workers. Mayor Samuel Smith praised the opening of St George's Hall for staging entertainments for the upper levels of society, but there was also a level of self-interest, and it served a very practical purpose: by providing an alternative to pubs, it reduced the number of hangovers which lowered efficiency in the workforce. Halifax was the first English town to build a temperance hall, showing similar concern for the workers' behaviour.[18] In such an environment, heavy drinking was probably controlled without any legal interventions. Wife selling may have likewise been dealt with informally.

At times, the interface between English local custom and established law becomes blurred. In parishes where churches had no bells to be rung, such as Pensham and Pinvin in Worcester, alternative traditions were established to celebrate a marriage. Locals gathered round the home where the bridal supper was being held, and discharged their many firearms. Sometimes accidents happened, such as the thatch catching fire. But in 1845 a hole was blown in the front door of the house during the bridal feast. The accused defended himself by citing ancient custom, but this failed to protect him from being forced to pay damages and costs.[19]

This shows that local practice was tolerated so long as it did not cause harm to persons or property, i.e. it strayed into national law enforcement. From the same source and only two months later is a fine example of local people hijacking the established law for their own means. A man of Bassbury called William Kendrik impounded the horse of a neighbour, Richard Jones. The owner was so outraged that, with a few friends held a mock trial and sentenced Kendrick to sit in the stocks. It was during the local wake, so probably involved the consumption of industrial quantities of alcohol.[20] Both the above cases and many of the wife sales demonstrate how willing locals were to enact what they saw as legal practices in order to solve problems.

In late eighteenth century when food rioting became widespread, especially in the West Country, Tom Poole wrote of how local people patrolled the area to keep the peace, so

> "we see the people doing what the government dared not do, and the government permitted them to do it."[21]

A Mrs Dening is on record as having witnessed a sale in the Kingston district of Somerset in about 1857. The man led his wife by a halter to the centre of the village and asked for bids. Mrs Dening's father and the local squire acted as witnesses to the agreement, so even at this late date, it seems that the practice was still seen as legal. Or did they — like so many other local justices — treat it as a pantomime, a harmless incident where objecting or intervening would only cause trouble?[22]

A retired policeman told this author that if he was called out to deal with a drunken man being violent to his wife, reporting it as domestic violence involved a lot of paperwork and lots of accusations and counterclaims which may never be resolved. In fact, when the man sobered up, he might treat his wife even worse. A much simpler solution was to ask the man to step out into the street where he could be arrested for being drunk and disorderly and dragged off to the local police station to sleep it off.

The Legal Position

In the absence of any law to deal with wife selling, the authorities seem to have used similar stratagems. When sales were held in open spaces and attracted large crowds, those involved could be charged with public order offences, and cases are on record of men being sent to the pillory, the treadmill, or — as a warning to others — to prison with hard labour. Some participants were let off with a warning not to re-offend. Hence it seems that the punishment was dealt with by local justices of the peace and magistrates without the mess and cost of passing a specific law. So much easier for the politicians who could continue to pretend it wasn't happening.

4

THE CONTRACT

Marriage itself was a contract, although an agreement ambiguous as to purpose.
   S.P. Menefee[1]

Napoleon allegedly claimed that the English were a nation of shopkeepers, and much of the country's history is linked by its merchants and overseas trade. Wife selling is often called a ritual, and there are ritualistic aspects to it, but at its heart, it was the practice of commerce. There was no general law of contract until the seventeenth century, but most exchange was local, so continued to follow established local traditions.[2] But commerce preceded the development of written language, and it followed the same basic principles that are in use today. The major difference over time has been that it has segued from a largely verbal to a written transaction.

For a contract to be valid, it required mutual assent, so needed some actions as proof of this, which could be ritualistic in form, such as a declaration of the facts in the presence of witnesses. A woman became legally invisible on her marriage, so the notion of her consent in a wife sale becomes debatable. But this is to miss the fact that a wife sale involved two different processes. In order for a wife to be sold she had to be 'un-married', which involved the consent of her husband, her legal guardian for the contract to be undone. Once free, she was then able to give her consent to be remarried, just as she had done at her first marriage.

Observers often noted how submissive the wives seemed to be, but this does not necessarily mean they were in agreement with the sale. If a relationship had broken down to the extent that a sale was suggested, it had probably reached the point of no return. When a sold wife and her purchaser appeared at the quarter sessions in Truro in 1820, she claimed her husband had mistreated and threatened to sell her,[3] a theme that appears in several other cases. But she had cohabited with her purchaser before the sale, which leaves us wondering what came first. Did she leave her husband because he was violent, or did he become violent when she showed interest in another man? Or was she trying to inspire sympathy in the justices?

The often-mentioned element — that the wife must be willing, as in any legal marriage — was generally upheld. This flies in the face of claims that the woman was treated as an animal or a chattel. The requirement of the sale to be held in public allowed the public to witness that all parties were willing participants, so made the matter legally binding. If the woman was seen as being coerced or bullied into the agreement, witnesses could intervene and call off the sale. There were a number of instances where — driven by outrage at the sale itself — the public intervened to protect the woman, or. An ugly example of both these elements was in Cheltenham in 1830 when a woman was lured into the market by her husband who tried to place a halter round her neck, and the crowd turned on him.[4] The objection here may not have been to the sale but to the assault on the woman.

In Birmingham in 1823 an ex-soldier sold his wife against her will, after allegedly being brutal to her. She was sold to her brother, so her family rescued her from a violent marriage.[5] Baring-Gould wrote of a case in the early 1860s when a man sold his wife in Chagford for a quart of beer by private agreement. But when he came home and presented her with her future spouse, she left them, only returning for her first husband's funeral.[6] The purchaser seems to have assumed the husband had her agreement, or perhaps this is yet another instance of late-night drinking producing unfortunate outcomes.

E.P. Thompson claims that the notion of a woman being treated as a chattel fails to stand up as even the most ignorant and poorest women would have been aware of the existence of magistrates and justices, so could have reported their purchaser for rape. If this had ever happened, the authorities would have punished the man with the utmost severity, but there is no record of a single case.[7] But if she accepted the sale, she accepted that rape was not a crime within marriage until very recently. Men in authority were often distant, intimidating figures, not the sort a vulnerable woman would be at ease relating her domestic problems to. Men could legally 'discipline' their wives, though how far this could go was never made clear. Men accused of what is now recognised as assault, rape, kidnapping, imprisonment and even murder were often not prosecuted. Even if the husband was convicted, he received little if any punishment, so prosecuting a violent husband was unlikely to help the wife. The husband may have been angered by her action and abused her even more. Houses had thin walls, so neighbours would have heard the arguments which could spill out into the street where people could intervene. If abused by employers, servants could lose their jobs, their reputation and any hope for a future. So, unless the victim had male friends and/or family to defend her, and to take her and her children in for protection, such men often went unpunished, and their crimes unrecorded.

Thompson was writing before the scandals of powerful men abusing young women sent shockwaves through the modern media. Many of these recent victims of abuse reported their experiences but were not believed. If the husband was abusive, the buyer may have provided a respite, so the woman would have been better off with him.

In 1838, a woman was led to a Gloucestershire village after the beast market with a halter round her neck. Locals asked if she was to be drowned, hanged or something else, so the practice of selling her was clearly a novel one. When told she was to be sold, she was asked if she was willing and on her confirmation, the sale commenced.[8] So even where wife selling was a new practice, the woman's agreement was believed to be necessary.

A sale that appears to be utterly opaque in both the mechanism and motivations is one from 1766 when a private contract was made at Midsomer Norton by a gentleman to purchase Ann Parsons, the wife of a clothworker for the large sum of six guineas. But it was one of the few cases where the husband really was, as was so often claimed, an ignorant brute. The case appears on the public record because two years later, Ann was forced to appeal to the justices of the peace for protection from her first husband as he was demanding more money and threatening to kill her. She produced a bill of sale, claiming her husband had breached a contract which she believed the court would accept as legal, whereas it was merely the background to threats of violence.[9]

Ann was so certain her second marriage was valid that she appealed to the authorities to enforce it. She was still legally married to her abuser, so should have been arrested for bigamy, and her first husband forced to support her and her children, but here the risk of violence must have been the main concern of the local justices.

There were several instances of police involvement when husbands tried to force their wives to be sold. In 1817, a man was seen at Smithfield Market trying to force a halter round the neck of a beautiful woman who struggled against him. The crowd drew the constables who took the couple to the magistrates' court.[10] At Wigan in 1895, Peter Tyson was charged with assault for tying a string round his wife's three times, almost strangling her. He claimed he had bought her but was dissatisfied with his purchase, so wished to sell her.[11]

If this was a standard commercial matter, he should have returned the 'goods' for being unsatisfactory, but many sales included some form of caveat that the wife purchased would be taken for all her faults and failings. Markets by their nature drew buyers and sellers from far afield; it is possible that tracking down the husband to demand a refund was too much effort. This case also raises questions as to how many serial sellers there were, and how many wives were repeatedly sold. Some authors suggest wives must have been too terrified or simple-minded to resist, so were effectively treated as chattels or slaves. Or perhaps they lacked an independent income, so had no other option.

Several sales were the result of drunken domestic arguments, and some men regretted them in the harsh light of day. In 1764, a husband demanded the return of his wife, but his wife refused, saying: "a sale is a sale, not a joke".[12] This again confirms that the wife's consent was respected. If the first husband was determined to have his wife back, he could have reported the wife to the local overseers of the poor who would have retrieved her.[13] But it seems this never happened as it was unlikely to produce a happy ending; it rather served to confirm the original sale was justified.

One of the arguments made in support of the indissolubility of marriage was that it ensured the husband always maintained the wife. When a woman surrendered her legal rights to the husband under the law of coverture, she gained his lifelong protection and support for her and her children. The law itself fell into disuse, but the notion of a man as the stronger partner protecting his family continues to hold moral force. One of the worst examples of abuse of this concept is also the only oral account found, in Shepton Mallet in 1848, when a man married in order to get the woman's house, then tried to sell her. Neighbours rescued her and took her to her parents.[14] This story is odd as it is unclear how she could own a house if her parents were alive, which suggests she was a widow. Like many other women in this book, she was not the submissive creature her husband expected.

Several examples show the women to be more than in agreement, that they may even have initiated the sale, with one waving to the crowd and being condemned as a 'hussey'. An account in Blackburn from claimed: 'the woman persists in carrying the contract', and in Gloucester in the 1830s, the husband lost his nerve, but his wife flicked her apron at him and said: 'I will be sold. I wants a change.'[15]

The attempted 'Wife Sale Extraordinary' at Plymouth in 1822[16] was described in great detail; the woman seemed to have been the initiator of the sale, and was determined it continue despite several obstacles. When taken before the authorities for causing a disturbance, both she and her husband argued that the matter was perfectly legal as they were both in agreement. They were astonished that anyone might think that they had done anything wrong, so they seemed to think that the basis of law was that of mutual agreement. Here we have a clash between commercial practice, under which the sale was accepted, and the legal system, where it was not.

The site of the sales often suggested women were being treated as livestock, especially at the famous Smithfield beast market in London. In 1832, The Times reported that a wife was sold for ten shillings with two shillings commission to the drover who must have been paid for the use of his pen. This seems to have followed standard commercial practice. The sale was private so would not appear in any market toll books, raising the possibility that other such incidents have been lost to the record.

Commentators claimed that choosing the market as a venue showed wife sellers were treating women as beasts, but more likely they were exploiting a loophole in market law. In 1826, a Mr. Hilton of Lodesworth sold his wife for thirty shillings plus a shilling toll. The magistrates sent for the toll keeper, who referred to a market bylaw which stated that any article not enumerated by law is to pay that toll.[17] This was probably an ancient law that allowed the sale of animals other than the types in which the market specialised.

Tolls were paid for wives and entered into the market records at Edgbaston (1773), Sheffield (1796), Smithfield (1805) and Cornwall (1836), suggesting the practice could have been widespread. In 1800 at Stafford, a woman was offered and, after spirited bidding, handed over for five shillings and five pence, with the toll ticket handed over as proof of ownership. A wife was taken through a turnpike, the reason for which is not stated; a receipt was collected for the toll paid, to confirm this part of the contract had been honoured. This may have been a confused version of paying the market toll.

In 1790 parish officers paid the toll at Burton Fair, which gave it the appearance of legality, and in Canterbury in 1820, a local salesman refused to sell a woman as he only dealt in cattle.[18] The husband purchased a pen, paid the sixpence toll and sold her himself. Yet again, this shows the flexibility of the ritual and contract to achieve the required outcome.

There are numerous examples of wife sales involving documents, so they were accepted as legal transactions. One such agreement, from the above sale at Edgbaston in 1773, ended with the phrase 'to take her with all her faults'.[19] This was the equivalent of a no-returns policy, which made the sale irreversible, leaving both parties free to remarry. It was signed by all three and witnessed by another. In Stamford in 1786, a contract was drawn up between a tailor, Thomas Hand, and cordwainer Thomas Hardy, who had a written memorandum signed by three witnesses.[20]

At Bolton market in 1833, the parties adjourned to a hostelry where: 'purchase money was paid after a stamped receipt had been given' and the wife 'duly delivered'.[21] It seems that by moving indoors, the sale became more formal. The publican or innkeeper was a man of substantial business acumen and local influence, with some serving as mayors; his premises had to be licensed so he was unlikely to put his business at threat by allowing illegal activities under his roof. This in turn must have given support to the notion that sales were legal. Allegations were also made that public houses encouraged such sales to increase their own sales through the wedding celebrations or drunken sprees that often followed.

In 1881, a Mrs Dunn of Ripon showed that she knew of the wider importance of the contract when she claimed to have been sold, adding 'I have it to show in black and white, with a receipt stamp on it, as I did not want people to think I was living in adultery.'[22] And yet in 1822 in Bristol, knowledge of the law was mixed, as a broadside claimed that a husband assaulted his wife for her drunkenness and profligacy, and decided to sell her, but the wife was fully aware that she could not be disposed of by private contract, so agreed to public auction.'

A sale at Maidstone in 1815 was claimed to have been conducted in a very regular manner, with a deed and conveyance witnessed.[23] The term 'conveyance' suggests parallels with property dealings rather than with beasts, which reflected the rising importance of property crime rather than crimes against the person which had occurred from the early eighteenth century. Yet this was from a man who turned up on the wrong day for the market. But the contract he made was unusually generous, as he offered to take her back any time, so there were clearly no hard feelings involved.

Other fair dealers were noted, such as Thomas Jones in Caerleon in 1822 who sold his young wife for threepence, then offered to take her back and return half the money if the buyer changed his mind.[24] So several sales allowed various forms of sale or return.

There is a widespread assumption that few people were literate before compulsory education for children was introduced in the mid-nineteenth century, but from the mid-eighteenth century, many people were functionally literate, i.e. they could recognise words in a similar way to travellers navigating in strange countries. Many were literate enough to sign agreements. Chapbooks and printed ballads were sold in great numbers, and many people learnt to read from their family Bible, which also served as a source of family history.

But oral culture remained strong, and the poor often continued to conduct their business in public in the presence of witnesses. In 1837 John Allen sold his wife to James Taylor at Wirksworth market when his wife would be delivered 'according to the law'. Allen passed the end of the halter to Taylor and made a formal declaration asking if the purchaser would buy his wife; the buyer agreed and handed over the money and a man was called to witness the return of the ring and the agreed payment.[25]

This is extraordinary not just because of the verbal agreement, but also in the way that Allen's distress at losing his wife seems to have been assuaged by the contract. It was carried out in a marketplace, so there must have been other witnesses beyond the man named, who could be called upon if the agreement was challenged. The language that Taylor uses is also interesting: *bereaved* is more often related to death, which suggests the man had suffered by the loss of his wife.

Sabine Baring-Gould wrote of 'an old poacher and fisherman' from his parish in Devon who described a woman being taken to market in a halter. 'On being asked whether, in such instances, the neighbours generally considered the transaction legitimate, [he] replied in the affirmative; he declared that the vendor was held to be free to wed again, and the purchaser to be liable for the maintenance of the woman, but not till the money had changed hands over the bargain.'[26]

There was also an example from 1814, when the master of Effingham workhouse took a woman to Croydon market and made out a receipt 'to publicly seal the bargain'.[27] The fact that a parish officer could do this in public again adds weight to the sense that this sale, and hence others, were legal contracts. The deal was sweetened by the donation of a leg of mutton for the wedding feast. In 1875, a labourer sold his wife at Blackburn, and a written agreement with witnesses was produced. The husband was described as drunk at the time, sot he could have tried to claim that he was in no fit state to agree to anything. The woman persisted in carrying out the contract, so it seems drink was only part of the problem. In 1841 near Penkridge, a wife was sold in the marketplace, then 'all went to an inn to ratify the transfer', but did this mean they were completing a written document sharing drinks or both?

Town criers or bellmen were employed by local officials to summon the public to courts, with the aim at ensuring they were held in the open, public space to ensure honesty. Criers provided public announcements of national events and celebrations as well as for sales and auctions. They used formulaic terms for specific subjects, and to draw attention and encourage sales. As parish officers, they were expected to abide by strict rules. When they were employed to make announcements of sales, they added another layer to the perception of legality and acceptability.

But in 1849, the bellman at Blackburn was taken before the magistrates for crying "all fish that come to the net"[28] to announce a wife sale. He was given a warning, forced to pay costs and promised not to offend again. In 1774, the Leeds town crier announced a rare event: the sale of a husband who was described as a good carpenter and devoted husband.

Scattered through eighteenth-century newspapers are notices announcing runaway wives, placed by husbands to warn that they would not be held responsible for any future debts. In 1831, The Manchester Times reported a case from Bolton when a woman was sold for three shillings and sixpence and a gallon of ale. The next day, she was delivered by her husband to her new beau, 'according to contract'. The day after, the bellman announced the husband was no longer responsible for any of her debts. This sale is unusual for being spread over several days. The men involved were condemned as brutes, as the buyer was a former lodger, so had betrayed the trust of his landlord by seducing his wife.[29]

The 'Wife Sale Extraordinary' in Plymouth mentioned above makes for confusing reading, as the sale was announced three times at Medbury, and at Plymouth where the sale was held. The famously humorous speech praying for deliverance from 'troublesome wives and frolicksome women'[30] given by Farmer Thompson at Carlisle in 1832, possibly part of the general spirit of reform that year was also announced by the bellman. More town crier announcements are recorded at Liskeard (1823), Market Harborough (1859) and Honiton (1879). An incident at Shearbridge near Bradford in 1858 is another oddity, as it was announced by the bellman, but held outside a beershop. Apparently, they had already tried to make the sale, but had not followed the rules — whatever they were perceived to be — and were fearful of intervention by the authorities. In 1878 a time-consuming case at West Riding magistrates involved a violent husband who allegedly had the bellman announce he would not be responsible for his wife's debts and that she was for sale. He claimed the last part was added by his friends for a joke.[31] Yet again, those involved had failed to drink responsibly.

Few people carried cash beyond what was necessary for their immediate requirements, in part due to the risk of being robbed, so there are a few cases where a deposit was accepted to seal the wife sale, similar to the 'fasten-ha'penny' for hiring servants and the infamous 'king's shilling' used to entrap men to enlist in the army. But most sales were of such low values that this was seldom necessary. In Grasmere, Yorkshire, in 1807, a man bought the wife of an innkeeper for a hundred guineas and gave one guinea to seal the contract. But when he returned the following day to pay the remainder the wife refused. The deposit was not returned, which was a breach of contract.[32] In 1789, a sale was made at Yarlington Fair for five shillings, with sixpence 'paid in earnest'.[33]

In Wrexham in 1885, a 'Lilliputian collier' returned home 'in drink' and had an argument with his wife, the result of which was she was put up for sale. There was little interest, but eventually, she and her baby were knocked down for the reserve price of two shillings and six pence. After the deed of sale was drawn up and signed, the buyer requested credit, with a shilling on account, but was refused and the sale fell through.[34]

In 1790, a man led his wife on a string to Thame market as he had been told by neighbours that the sale he had made two or three years earlier would not stand because it had not been in a public market. It seems a long time to realise this, or at least to take action to fix it. It is also unusual as it shows the husband was still in contact with his wife, suggesting the community supported the arrangement.

It also shows his willingness to take advice from his neighbours to ensure the legality of the contract.

Some sales were held at fairs, but the venue's legality for holding the sale was doubted at Lansdown Fair in 1833; the group moved to Bath market where they were arrested.[35] And yet in another example, the magistrates in West Kent claimed: 'the crime would have been greater if in open market'.[36] What did they mean? The crime in this instance was a minor misdemeanour, probably causing disturbance, so a side effect of the sale rather than it being a crime per se. It seems the legality of a wife sale often only became an issue for established law if the authorities were concerned with it causing public disorder, so police could intervene. If it took place within a building, it was defined as on private property, so deemed a private matter for the landlord. This echoed the police attitude in dealing with domestic violence mentioned at the start of this book.

Central to the sense of legality was the insistence on being sold in open market. Richard Gough's *The History of Myddle* describes a messy account of an ancestor of his being imprisoned for refusing to pay what he perceived to be an illegal tax. The bailiffs offered him four nobles as compensation for the injustice, but only if the exchange was done privately. The victim declared he had not been taken to prison privately, so demanded payment was made in the open street where he called out to neighbours what was happening so they could witness the exchange.[37] Gough's ancestor understood fair dealing in an open space and his neighbours knew how to witness it.

But as the population expanded in Victorian times, traffic increased in towns and cities and marketplaces were encroached upon. The construction of covered markets and market halls added to this, and also led to the demise of markets in smaller towns, so finding an open space for the sale became an increasing problem. Some towns had young idlers who were keen to cause disturbances, but another source suggests that if the wife was young and pretty, there may have been men who were angry at missing out on a bargain, so they also caused trouble, adding to those who were outraged by the immorality of the event.[38]

Legal contracts also involved a level of trust, so goodwill was often a part of contracts. This could be shown by sharing a drink or a meal, as with several examples of farewell, celebratory and/or wedding dinners. Some of the sales involved part-payment in alcohol, which may have been another side of this social aspect.

Some accounts noted participants shook hands as a means of sealing the contract, to show goodwill and that there were no hard feelings, as is still common after a sports match. A person refusing to shake hands represented a lack of 'closure', perhaps serving as a warning that revenge was possible.

A sad tale is recorded from Ashton in 1849 when a wife eloped with most of her husband's property whilst he was in the infirmary. He tracked the couple down, and they agreed to the sale. As the new couple departed, the husband held out his hand to her, saying 'Give us a wag of thy hand, old lass, before we part.' But her response was to claim she had raised more than he was worth and she left him 'in high glee'.[39]

Perhaps the practice which causes the most confusion was that of refunding part of the purchase price, as *luck money*. Menefee claims this was a gift, again implying friendship or good will, a shared bond beyond the money involved.[40] But luck money is explained in an article about farming practices in Drigg, Cumbria as recently as 1965:

> 'When a farmer sells an animal not intended for slaughter he will give about one shilling in the pound back to the buyer in *luck money*, to ensure the animal's good health.'[41]

It seems extraordinary that this gesture of goodwill or good luck continued well into the modern age.

Near Rotherham in 1775, a procession was led by a cuckolded husband, which attracted a crowd of about a thousand. The wife was sold for the huge sum of twenty-one guineas, with a guinea returned for luck.[42] In 1821 at Boston a wife was sold for a shilling [twelve pence], with eleven pence returned for luck.[43] In 1832 at Horncastle and in 1831 in a sale at Stockport market both asked for a pound, and returned two shillings and six pence, or half a crown, for luck. So luck money seems to have been a widespread practice over time and region. It also defies many sources who claim that wives were sold purely for money. In many sales — perhaps the majority — the money was a means of sealing the contract.

In any financial arrangement, there is the risk of fraud. In 1870, a young husband described as an idler, rang the church bell in Clithero with his friends to announce the sale of his wife, but when the crowds appeared, he failed to show. A sale at Swindon Fair in 1775 seems to have been a fraud from the outset, but the circumstances leading up to it are incomprehensible at this distance. A wealthy shoemaker agreed to buy the wife of a cattle dealer for fifty pounds the following day. But when he returned the couple had vanished.[44]

At St. Thomas's Market in Bristol, a sale turned nasty when the first offer was accepted, but it was claimed the bidder was a proxy for the wife's favourite swain (how many did she have?) so this was a breach of the principle of an open sale. Finally, a sale at Mansfield market in 1822 was caused by the wife being 'not a votary at the shrine of Diana'.[45] This term was apparently common in the Regency period in reference to lesbians, so it seems she was in breach of her marital vows. If the marriage had not been consummated, the marriage could have been annulled. But this would still involve having to prove in three courts that the woman was a virgin, so this expensive and embarrassing route was not an option. Instead, the sale was called off when the husband, after a parting drink with his wife, decided to keep her and was accused of carrying out a mock auction.

Despite the many similarities between wife sales and established contracts for sales, there is one glaring difference: that of supply and demand. Throughout history, women have outnumbered men, so logic suggests they should have been the buyers. There is no evidence of competition to enable purchasers to compare goods, so standard commercial practice was inverted. The crucial factor at the heart of wife selling was that until recent times, women became the legal responsibility of their husbands when they married. This was at the heart of the various Poor Laws that were enacted from Elizabethan times. By the late Victorian period, tens of thousands of temporary desertions were being dealt with by magistrates who had to issue maintenance orders.[46]

Unlike a wife sale, abandonment of a wife *was* a criminal offence, and the man was often imprisoned for it. Hence when a man sold his wife, he had to be certain the agreement would stand, otherwise he could be held responsible for her and any future children she might produce. By ensuring the contract stood, the man believed himself to be free to remarry and start a new family. This explains why there were cases of overseers of the poor who sold wives or forced men to sell their wives to men of other parishes, which freed them of responsibility for the women in future.

Until the 1857 reform, divorce involved three actions, in three courts, the second of which involved the husband obtaining a prosecution against the wife's paramour for *criminal conversation*. (The third was obtaining a divorce by act of parliament) This was to compensate a man for the loss of his wife's contribution to his household, her companionship and housekeeping, but in reality it was more a matter of pride and to prevent any future liabilities. On one level, this is bizarre as upper class women brought a dowry to the marriage, but contributed little more to the family income, whereas lower-class women often contributed to family finances via paid work or in the maintenance of the household. Criminal Conversation and the demand for financial compensation was more about injured male pride, and some sources claim it provided an alternative to fighting duels.

At the very least, many of these contracts show that money was not the primary motivation, any more than in the criminal conversation cases of the wealthy. It is likely that the money was only the most visible part of the process. It was more that the marriage was formally ended, that all parties were able to find what we now call 'closure', and move on.

5

CROSSED WIRES

The marriage rate, the Lancet reported, was in fact falling... The Times declared that thousands were living in sin with little thought for the consequences.

Francis Watson[1]

When Reverend Sabine Baring-Gould (born 1834) was a child, he saw the local poet Henry Frise return from Giglet Fair at Okehampton with his bought wife; his account provides us with a unique insight into how locals responded to the unusual event. News preceded the couple's arrival, and a curious crowd had gathered. Baring-Gould's uncle was the local vicar and his grandfather the lord of the manor and justice of the peace. They informed Frise that — based on the Bible and the justice of the peace's reference manual — it was not a legal transaction. But Frise was adamant:

> "I don't care... her's my wife, as sure as if we was spliced at the altar, for and because I paid half a crown, and I never took off the halter till her was in my house; lor' bless yer honours, you may ask any

one if that ain't marriage, good, sound and Christian, and every one will tell you that it is."²

Frise's claim to legitimacy was echoed in many accounts of wife sales. But it is the defence of it in the face of the authorities that comes closest to short-circuiting the brains of most commentators. How could so many people (aka ignorant brutes and female victims) hold and defend the belief that wife selling was legal when confronted by authorities who could prove it was not? Were the masses really as ignorant as writers claimed or are we missing something?

English law is an incredibly complicated and convoluted beast. At no point was there a group such as the USA's Founding Fathers or the leaders of Revolutionary France who put in immense time, effort and discussion to codify it. Instead, English law's origins are mostly lost in the mists of local custom and common practice, with much of it devised to fit specific needs. When laws are changed, the previous ones are seldom removed, so like many computer operating systems, a lot of space is taken up by antiquated and irrelevant content. Some authors claim that the massacre of nobles by Henry VIII removed many great leaders and made the rest nervous about change. Or it could be that after the turmoil of the Reformation and Civil War, nobody in power was interested, or brave or reckless enough to change a system which had become the basis for such civilised society. 'Enthusiasm' in any form was seen as dangerous.

Before the Reformation, the church dominated local communities. It was the major landlord, so received rents and punished those who defaulted. It maintained the church building and churchyard, roads and bridges, ditches and drains, conduits and parish pumps, as well as educating children, and caring for the poor, sick and infirm. When the religious houses were closed, some of these functions were adopted by parish councils, but where this didn't happen, urban centres sank into congested squalor. For water, people dug their own wells, which were often contaminated by nearby cesspits and graveyards, spreading diseases such as cholera.

Religious houses were celibate communities, and people outside would usually marry when accommodation became available, so the population tended to be stable. When Henry VIII was crowned in 1509, the population of England was about three million, but by about 1590, it had soared to four million. From the 1560s, there was a huge increase in vagrants, especially in London. The early 1590s saw bumper harvests, but this was followed by five years of wet summers and ruined harvests, which led to the creation of a series of Poor Laws to try to care for and control the expanding underclasses. Pre-Reformation religious houses had cared for the poor, but no arrangements were made to adopt this role, so the soaring population created a perfect storm of unemployed and unemployables, and many orphans.

The first law was the *Act for the Relief of the Poor and the Suppression of Rogues* which was passed in 1597. It was repeatedly renewed but was almost unchanged until 1833. Its wide-ranging aims included care for the vulnerable and the education and training of orphans. It sheltered those unable to work, provided employment for those who where able, and punished those who refused.[3]

Able-bodied poor were given 'outdoor relief' to keep them in their own homes. The 'impotent poor' i.e. the old, disabled and sick were placed in poorhouses or almshouses, but the able-bodied unemployed were labelled as rogues and vagabonds, a large and varied group that included 'tinkers, gypsies, begging scholars, palm readers, musicians and actors".[4] These laws explain why Shakespeare and his fellow thespians required the patronage of the wealthy for protection.

The concept of 'settlement' was introduced to make parishes responsible for the care of those born in, or who had valid claims on, the area. This prevented itinerant rogues and vagabonds from exploiting what was at best a limited source of assistance paid for by poor rates. But it had the disadvantage of keeping unemployed people in areas of high unemployment, hindering people without resources from travelling in search of work. It also depended on the presence of an active and committed group of gentry to administer the Act. To minimise the strain on Elizabethan charity, children were billeted with rich neighbours, loans were made to help young tradesmen set up businesses, almshouses and hospitals were founded, and corn dealers were forced to sell at a discount to the poor, and many of the poor were sent to the colonies. By 1640 poverty had declined, and vagrants were no longer seen as a danger.[5]

Poor rates were administered by overseers, who were unpaid citizens, but the care they provided varied hugely. Ideally a parish was a small community where people knew each other, and there were sufficient wealthy people to support the poor. The parish of Saints Phillip and Jacob in the east of Bristol stretched half way to Bath, a huge region which included the impoverished underclass that worked the coal mines, of Kingswood but very few gentry to serve as parish officers or to donate to good causes. When the future landscape designer Humphrey Repton moved to the tiny parish of Susted in Norfolk, he had to serve as the churchwarden to maintain the church fabric, overseer of the poor, surveyor and lord of the manor.[6] So if he fell ill or was absent, none of these roles would have been fulfilled. Though in such a small community, locals must have been used to managing their own affairs.

When overseers of the poor were recorded as having sold wives, their accounts should have been signed off by the local clerics. This suggests parish priests were either negligent or absent, or that the official church either encouraged or condoned the practice. Menefee claimed one was clergyman personally involved in an affair as late as 1832 when John Penson, a carpenter was charged with bigamy. He claimed a clergyman had drawn up an agreement for Penson to separate from his first wife who then paid him two pounds to remarry. All those involved considered the matter to be legal. The story was even more extraordinary as Menefee further claimed his first wife was living with the clergyman.[7] With such low standards of behaviour from shepherds, it is little wonder their flocks also strayed.

Many clerics in the eighteenth and nineteenth centuries were more interested in their own advancement than their parish duties. Cobbett described the abandonment of parsonage houses near Warminster in Wiltshire whilst the tithes to support them were still being collected. A peripatetic parson preached at three or four churches of a Sunday, while the official priest was paid a third of the tithes, which allowed him and his family to live in the capital or to visit the various spas. The overseers of the poor — often local farmers with little time for, or interest in, unpaid parish duties — failed to collect the relevant funds, so the poor were managed as they saw fit. Cobbett complained of the region having huge areas of fertile farmland and plentiful game from which the poor were excluded; they were starving in the midst of plenty.[8] As huge estates were established from the mid-eighteenth century, largely paid for by money from the colonies, this had a huge impact on the rural poor. Some of the biggest landlords owned hundreds of parishes, and they were free to allow housing to fall into decay and to demolish homes, forcing the tenants to seek housing elsewhere. This allowed them to declare the parish 'closed', where no rates were paid. In adjoining parishes where the poor were forced to move, this led to soaring poor rates.[9]

In towns too small to have purpose-built court houses, criminal trials and inquests were held in inns and public houses, in addition to these being venues for entertainments, public sales and auctions. They were often mentioned as venues for wife sales. Landlords were men of strong physical, financial and personal stature, sometimes serving as justices of the peace, magistrates, mayors and auctioneers or in drawing up or witnessing agreements. Claims were made that wife selling moved from the open market to public houses to evade the law, especially after Peel's police forces were established. This echoed the movement of public markets indoors when market houses, or covered crosses were built from the eighteenth century. But it may have been to escape the open — sometimes chaotic — public space of the streets to a venue recognised for legal transactions. When couples chose such places, they were seeking more than a venue in which to celebrate; they were hoping to add legal validity to the proceedings. Several publicans and innkeepers bought or sold wives themselves, which further led people to believe the process was legal. Some publicans were accused of encouraging the practice as the sales were often followed by a celebratory dinner, sharing drinks to seal the deal or by spending the sale money on a 'spree'.

Baring-Gould described how a local stonecutter advertised his wife for sale by posting written notices in several public places. Yet again, there is no sign of condemnation from the reverend author. He describes how the proceedings — probably a first for all those involved — were discussed and negotiated to ensure the sale was accepted: 'the foreman of the neighbouring granite works remonstrated, and insisted that such a sale would be illegal. He was not, however, clear as to the points of law and he believed it would be illegal unless the husband held an auctioneer's licence, and if money passed. This was rather a damper. However, the husband was desirous to be freed from his wife, and he held the sale as had been advertised, making the woman stand on a table, and he armed himself with a little hammer. The biddings were to be in kind and not in money. One man offered a coat, but as he was a small man and the seller was stout, when he found that the coat would not fit him, he refused it. Another offered a "phisgie", i.e., a pick, but this also was declined as the husband possessed a "phisgie" of his own. Finally the landlord offered a two-gallon jar of gin, and down fell the hammer with "Gone".'[10]

This example provides so many elements that were echoed in many other sales, yet it was all decided on the spot. From the outset, those gathered seemed to think wife selling was legal, so had perhaps heard of it, but they were all clueless as to the correct procedure. So the group attempted to create a ritual that would stand up to later scrutiny and to prevent problems arising after the fact. The refusal to take cash also echoes many other events in which payment was either in kind or the amount seems to have been derisory. No attempt was made to represent the value of the wife, but the price was more a token to confirm the sale. Holding the event surrounded by other people provided witnesses if the transaction was ever challenged. This was incredibly widespread, from the use of godparents at christenings to animal sales and property contracts. It was also part of many marriages before the passing of the 1757 Marriage Act which made crowds of witnesses largely redundant through the creation of parish registers. Thus Baring-Gould's account of what was claimed to be a ritual carried on by ignorant peasants provides a fascinating insight into the process of mainstream English legal practices.

In Boston, Lincolnshire, in 1853 a large crowd gathered to see a wife sale, but the auctioneer had doubts about the legality, so refused to act and the sale was called off.[11] This again shows how the sense of legality was not fixed. Such behaviour was often described as degenerate, illegal and outrageous, but it followed standard practice for auctions, and those present seemed to approve of and support it. If they had not, they would have made their opposition known and the innkeeper risked losing custom. But the main purpose of law is to keep the peace, as a broken marriage could lead to disputes and even violence between the couple.

A labourer named Clayton in Warrington in 1876 made an offer for the wife of Wells, a foreman who had been separated from her for two years. Clayton was determined to do the right thing, so asked Wells if he would 'hurt' him if he married her. Wells replied that he wouldn't hurt either of them, and that they could marry that night. As a further sign of goodwill, they shared drinks and Clayton accepted Wells' little girl as well, so the ritual again followed sound commercial practices.[12] It is not clear what 'hurt' meant in this instance: whether this implied personal insult or physical assault, but as with many other wife sales, Clayton was determined to do the right thing and be free of retribution or repercussions at some later date.

Baring-Gould claimed

'the remarkable feature in these cases is that it is impossible to drive the idea out of the heads of those who thus deal in wives that such a transaction is not sanctioned by law and religion.'[13]

Yet they were following established practices which *were* accepted by their communities as being legal, so it was only a small step in their reasoning to believe that this made the process legal. The problem here is that the law as understood by common people was flexible, able to be adapted to their needs at the time, so was seen as a tool to achieve their goals. The law as recognised by Baring-Gould and other literate people was written in books, so was fixed and so less adaptable to adapt to different situations.

When wife sellers were condemned for not knowing the law, how could they? The sale described by Baring Gould was openly advertised, so justices of the peace and clerics such as himself could have known about them, and yet there was no intervention. Did they not visit the local shops or did they see it as some form of local pantomime, of no interest to them? There is nothing in the account to suggest Baring-Gould made any attempt to clarify the legal position. Perhaps he was treating it as folklore for his collection so was happy for it to continue. Or did he know from his childhood experience that such intervention would be futile and fear it might endanger his research? As in so many other cases, the process was open, and since there was no opposition or intervention those involved quite reasonably believed the sale was legal and Christian, just as Henry Frise claimed. Were the authorities so completely absent, as suggested by Cobbett, their estates run by agents who were solely interested in maximising income from the estates, or did they just not care?

People who sold wives were sometimes well enough informed to be able to make use of the official law when needed. A woman who had been sold in Birmingham market and who subsequently outlived her seller, purchaser and a second [legal] husband had a surprising victory. When her first spouse died, she successfully defended her right to his legacy against his relatives, who claimed the sale had constituted a legal divorce.[14] But since her second marriage was not legal, she was still married to her first husband, so the relatives were in the wrong. Interestingly, there is no mention of her being charged with adultery, which might have led to her being punished, though perhaps her late husband may have been held responsible for her straying. The situation — like many others — was complicated.

There was a widespread belief that when a wife fled her husband, he could place an advertisement in the paper warning that he would not be responsible for her debts. This was not legally enforceable, but it warned people not to trust a truant wife, so in the local community it had the same effect. If it didn't work, it would not have continued.

A more unusual belief was that if a wife married wearing only a shift — i.e. her underclothes — she and her new husband would be free of her debts. This seems to have been a garbled transmission of the pre-Reformation practice of shaming people in church in the same state of undress, in some cases described, confusingly, as being naked. In Saddleworth Chapel in 1774, the widower Abraham Brooks married the widow Mary Bradley; he forced her to be married in her shift. But the church was so cold that her shivering led the minister to cover her with his coat while the ceremony was concluded.[15]

There is no suggestion that the vicar agreed with the strange attire or its implications, but he could hardly have demanded she go home to dress more sensibly. Since he raised no objection to the strange practice, it probably confirmed their belief that the practice was legal.

Time and time again, one finds accounts of people using the law — or whatever they perceived it to be — as a means of solving their problems; as long as it was accepted by their neighbours, it was thought to be sound. This principle lies at the heart of the sale of wives. Most of these people were not ignorant. They were often hard-working, practical people, accustomed to solving their own problems. Country people were often described as conservative, but they worked long and hard, dealing with the risk of floods, fires, storms, pests and wild animals. When there was work to be done, such as the harvest being brought in ahead of an approaching storm, they worked till they dropped. If they needed a tool, they used what was at hand, adapted another or made a new one. They discussed their problems, asked each other for advice, and made decisions that were supported by their neighbours. In many of Shakespeare's plays, the protagonist addresses the audience, thinking out loud, asking for advice.

But they could also be resistant to change and could seem to be completely unreasonable. In Syd Tyrrell's account of his life in Northamptonshire at the dawn of the twentieth century he described a furiously independent old woman, Sally Dancer who was opposed to anything new, having lived through the introduction of machinery that had replaced agricultural workers. She insisted that mushrooms never grew after the grasscutters had passed, so Syd offered to bring her a plate of fried mushrooms to prove her wrong. He compares her with many characters from Hardy's Wessex novels, with 'the same blind obstinancy, the same clinging to the old ways when the better ways had dawned.'[16] It was no coincidence that Hardy had written of the 'hungry forties', when Sally was a teenager. Survivors of famines, especially when they were young, tend to be deeply scarred, to cling to the safety of what they know rather than embrace untried novelties.

This echoes the reality of the age. People had to be flexible in order to survive, and as so many lived in small communities, they also had to be flexible in relation to their neighbours. When they married, they often had few choices, so again, often had to make do with what was at hand, as a strange incident from Holmes Chapel in Cheshire, in 1777, suggests. Two young farmers obtained licences for their impending marriages, but the names of their spouses were accidentally swapped. The article suggested they were drunk with love or something more potent, probably to firm their resolve on embarking on such an expensive, life-changing step. Both were illiterate, so the mistake was not noticed till the clergyman queried it at the ceremony. The couples were confused, but as they were all friends, agreed to proceed with the marriages as stated on the licences.[17]

In this case, the parties probably knew each other well, and were physically strong and healthy so could support each other, but it also suggests they were driven by a need to marry rather than the specific charms of their intended, as is more common now. It is also interesting as these couples were not wealthy, yet they chose the great expense of marriage by licence. This was often condemned as foolish, but they thus avoided the public embarrassment of the cheaper public reading of the banns in church and the boisterous wedding celebrations. It also shows that marriage was increasingly seen as a private affair, rather than an opportunity for the wider community to celebrate.

Such flexibility could happen en masse, as an expedition to Malta in 1800 found the many soldiers' wives to be a burden, so sent most of them home. But en route they stopped in Minorca where they fell for an Irish regiment. Their husbands were reported as being wiped out, so they married their new beaus, but when the report was discovered to be untrue, only a single man took his wife back, and was mocked for doing so.[18]

These conflicts between local and official law happened during the long eighteenth century, when many draconian acts were passed to punish property crime rather than crimes against people. Since the rich had property and the poor did not, laws increasingly served the wealthy to the exclusion of the majority of the population. Walpole's Back Acts in particular, together with the Riot Act, established a wide range of punishments which were more suited to terrorism, and which were later used against various uprisings in England, Scotland and Ireland.[19]

These new laws — usually known for sending starving bread thieves to the colonies — were only possible because law makers had lost all contact with the people they ruled, especially the poor, who were generally assumed to be rogues and vagabonds. And yet this happened when society was becoming more civilised; diversity in forms of worship was increasingly accepted, there was great emphasis on manners, bear baiting and cock fighting were being condemned, witchcraft ceased to be a crime, and campaigns for women's rights ran in parallel with demands for the abolition of the African slave trade. In earlier times, those responsible for the laws would have called the poor neighbours.

The religious houses' valuable contents sold by Henry VIII — fine metalwork, delicate embroideries and much more were treated with contempt, as:

'Halls of country houses were hung with altar cloths; tables and beds were quilted with copes; when the knights and squires drank their claret out of chalices and watered their horses in marble coffins.. it went hard with the sacred vestments; a generation or two of domestic wear and tear, and what was left of them?'[20]

Rather than living within their means or creating new industries as the sensible Netherlanders did, the English aristocracy clung to their passion for wealth and became unscrupulous in their search for it. The Tudors became pirates Much of their new money came from the North American colonies, where the labour was initially carried out by indentured servants and kidnapped children, who died in huge numbers from overwork and mistreatment, so were slaves in all but name. Servants were bought and sold; when they died on board ships they were listed as cargo and were named in wills as items of inheritance alongside buildings and animals. This abuse of the poor caused such outrage that the practice was made illegal, but it carried on for many years forced underground, with adults and children kidnapped from the streets of London and major ports by 'spirits', hence the term 'spirited away'.[21]

Many of the poor who were sent to the colonies of Virginia and Maryland were indentured apprentices from the poor houses. Thus overseers of the poor had form in treating their charges as chattels to be bought and sold. Though they were expected to be trained as per usual apprenticeships, there was no control or supervision of their welfare once they left Britain, so it took many years for the abuse to be acknowledged and stopped, but of course the abusers were never punished.

Public outrage eventually put an end to the kidnappings, but by then the Caribbean colonies had become dependent on the labour of African slaves. Their owners often abused their workforces with impunity, and by the mid-eighteenth century, the planters began moving back to England, leaving managers in charge. When they purchased huge estates, they also imported their callous attitudes to their workers. Just as colonists saw unfarmed areas of the colonies as wasteland, in need of improving; much farmland in England maximised profits by eliminating areas of woodland which had allowed locals to forage and supplement their low incomes.

The worst abuses in the slave colonies occurred when owners returned to Britain, leaving managers to extract maximum profits. The same pattern happened in Britain when these rich planters became owners of multiple estates, spending most of their time in London, the spas or abroad, and having no interest in the welfare of their tenants. It has been suggested this inspired the practice of fox hunting, to try to bring the wealthy estate owners into contact with local people and lead them to show sympathy for their needs, and to distribute alms and justice to their tenants when in need.

Newspapers of the eighteenth and nineteenth centuries printed notices offering rewards for information leading to the prosecution of people who damaged fences and wildlife owned by lords of manors. Such offences were not necessarily indicative of a rise in crime, but could have been a protest at the behaviour of the landlords who had enclosed common ground or inflicted an unfair punishment on a local.

The clash of central law and local justice helps explain why highway robbers were often seen as heroes when they went to the scaffold. These men were skilled horsemen, so not from poor backgrounds, and they often behaved as gentlemen, returning valued keepsakes, or accepting a kiss from a young lady and allowing her to keep her property. Their feats of horsemanship and of evading the law made many of them popular heroes, and demonised the thief takers who pursued them.

It is no surprise that such a system was incomprehensible to ordinary people, just as the brutality of sentencing horrifies us today. To equate a human life with the theft of a loaf of bread or even of a fine horse suggests our ancestors were monsters.

This same sense of disbelief was shown by many wife sellers when taken before the authorities, and in the case of the poet Frise, when confronted by Baring-Gould's uncle and grandfather. Most of these were not ignorant yokels, but the disagreement over the law represented a very real clash of cultures, the process of local customs being swept away by central government, as part of the cost of building an empire.

This incomprehension was also seen when Joshua Jackson was convicted at West Riding Quarter Sessions in June 1837 for selling his wife, and sentenced to a month in prison with hard labour, when 'a good deal of surprise was felt in many villages of ignorant members as a result of the law.. it was generally and firmly believed that he was acting within his rights.'[22] This pattern of incomprehension being blamed on ignorance appeared in many accounts, but itshowed yet again how divorced from the lower classes the law makers and enforcers had become.

In Ronald Blythe's brilliant local history, *Akenfield* a magistrate in the 1960s Suffolk village described instances among the poor when a wife was worn out by constant childbearing, was ill or dead, and her husband would 'turn his attentions' to their eldest daughter who became responsible for the household. The law only became involved when the relationship was reported to them, or when the girl became pregnant. The magistrate spoke of their 'Strange form of innocence.' Yet again, this was not ignorance; this was a long-standing practice which continued below the radar of law enforcement. By today's standards, this was abuse, and the man would be put away for a very long time for it. But the magistrate continued:

> 'Then you realise that what he'd done and what we were saying he had done were two quite different things. We had strayed into the dark, into the deep — the hidden ways of the village.'[23]

Time and time again, it seems that people involved in wife selling tried to do the right thing, to make things legal as they and their neighbours conceived it. They tried to make the sales 'hold', to allow both parties to move on, and to prevent husbands being held responsible for destitute wives and another man's children at some later date. There are even instances where attorneys were employed to draw up what purported to be legal contracts. In 1749 a wife sale came before the great judge Lord Hardwicke, who later steered the first Marriage Act into law; he described it as 'a scandalous prostitution of the law' since 'the bond looked as if drawn by a lawyer'. So if a lawyer didn't know the law, how on earth were ordinary people expected to know it? At least they tried.

But lawmakers were not above the law. Lord Erskine travelled to Gretna Green dressed as a woman to marry his housekeeper, was in breach of Walpole's Black Act which criminalised men parading in women's clothing, and he could have been executed for it. Though how a man past seventy got away with this is yet another mystery.

In 1767, two women and a man — the husband of one of them — asked a Bristol magistrate to attest to the husband changing owners for ten guineas. 'The magistrate naturally pointed out that such a barter was invalid, and the parties left much dissatisfied."[24] This case reversed the legal concept of a man owning a woman, but then, this was Bristol. But in terms of supply and demand, it makes more sense than most of the sales. If he was not a breadwinner, what was his attraction? They went instead to a local hostelry where a crowd was attracted to witness the completion of the ceremony, so as in many other cases, they sought legitimacy from the landlord in lieu of the official lawmakers.

As towns expanded, and especially after the establishment of police forces, sales in public became increasingly difficult. In 1845 a sale was stopped by police at Banbury Market Place, and when legal advice was sought, those involved were told to go further away.[25] So even the legal profession treated the official law more like an obstruction in the road to be navigated around, rather than a means of stopping their behaviour outright. In the minds of many ordinary people, there was no great conflict between the two legal systems;

the official one was a tool made for the use of the law; when it didn't work, they chose one of their own making. This is why the practice seems so difficult to understand in our modern age when we are so used to obtaining everything ready-made. We are used to instant gratification, to being able to obtain all our needs, rather than to plan, to 'make do and mend' like the wartime generation, to design and to execute items custom-made for our needs.

6

PUNISHMENT

This and no other is the root from which a tyrant springs; when he first appears he is as a protector.
   Plato

Selling a wife was often claimed to be a crime, with one newspaper stating it was banned under a previous — but unnamed —monarchy. It has apparently never been a crime in the UK, so there has never been a legal punishment for it. Other sources made accusations that it served as a cover for crimes such as adultery, abandonment, bigamy and public-order offences, which were punishable. Until the Reformation, the established church dealt with matters of personal behaviour and morality. Immoral behaviour was punished by forcing the offender to stand in a public place, i.e. church or market place, in a white sheet, holding a candle, to be shamed in front of their community and serve as a warning to others. The earliest account of a sale is very confusing and dates from London in 1553 when Parson Chicken was forced to ride a cart around the city for selling his wife to a butcher.

In 1581 the Vicar of Gamlingay persuaded Edward Scayles to sell Isabell his wife to Christopher Upchurch for sixteen shillings, a very large sum which suggests it was some form of compensation. But the case was referred to the ecclesiastical court at Ely. In the 1696 churchwarden's accounts from Chinnor, Oxfordshire, Thomas Heath, a maltster was ordered to do penance for selling his wife.[1]

But the ecclesiastical courts collapsed between 1640 and 1660, which left control of moral matters to whatever civic or military local authorities survived. Or not. Punishments were still based on public shaming, but were moved from the church into civic spaces. Instead of penance, miscreants were punished in the stocks or pillory; in criminal cases, they were whipped in the centre of a town, often at the High Cross on market days to maximise the audience and provide plenty of missiles for the crowd to express their contempt for the offenders. There is a single instance of a couple in Loughborough in 1826 being sentenced to the treadmill for a wife sale so there were various punishment options for local authorities.

Unlike modern justice, punishment was partly handed to the public, which ensured the judgment was accepted by the community and prevented retaliation against the authorities. But giving such power to the crowd could have unpredictable outcomes. There were cases of thief takers, rather than the thieves, who were almost battered to death, as they were seen as traitors in the pay of corrupt rulers. Some had to be removed from the stocks before their sentence was served. Defoe was sent to the pillory in 1703 for a satirical article but was allegedly pelted with flowers. In 1794 political radicals Thomas Hardy and Horne Took were loudly cheered and carried from the stocks in triumph. Even executions were not always assured as there were attempts to rescue those who were seen to have been unfairly condemned. If such a rescue failed, executed bodies were sometimes stolen to prevent them being handed over to surgeons for dissection.

Before the Reformation, most people lived in small communities which were largely self-policing, with the large religious establishments caring for the sick and disabled. When these institutions were closed, the state struggled to fill the void in terms of charity and dealing with moral behaviour. When the poor were involved in moral crimes such as premarital sex, Elizabethan Poor Laws empowered overseers of the poor to force men to marry the mother of their alleged child, or if this couldn't be established, to remove a woman to her place of settlement, i.e. the home of her husband, which could result in her being dumped in a region far from the support of friends and family. But if that parish was struggling to deal with the poor, it could refuse to accept her, so even the most basic of care was not guaranteed. If a man abandoned his family he faced prison, but this was often condemned as counterproductive because it prevented him from supporting his family, making the parish effectively responsible for the result of his crime.

A sordid incident from 1828 involved a couple and their lodger sharing a Poor Law cottage in Kent. The wife and lodger became lovers, causing a local scandal. The Poor Law authorities ordered the lodger to leave. But instead, the trio tried to resolve the problem by selling the woman to the lodger, naively believing this would be acceptable to the church officers and that the ménage à trois could remain in the cottage.[2] Instead, they were all arrested, with a claim made that the offence would have been greater had it happened in an open market rather than by a private contract.

This is utterly opaque, though suggests the offence of public disorder did not apply on private property. In a massive overreaction, perhaps so the case would serve as a warning to others, they were all charged by a grand indictment, similar to those used against early trade unionists for being depraved, accusing them of encouraging 'adultery, wickedness and debauchery.'[3] Despite being presented as violent insurrectionists, they were sentenced to only a month in prison, but they were probably homelessness and unemployed on their release.

When the agricultural workers who became the Tolpuddle Martyrs were convicted in 1834 for making unlawful oaths, the 1749 Mutiny Act was invoked. Their sentences of transportation triggered widespread protests and riots, but the sentencing judge claimed: 'part of the object of all legal punishment was to offer an example and a warning'.[4] This again suggests there was a high risk of their crimes being emulated by others.

In 1819, the Rector of Clipsham indicted a parishioner for punishment at the Rutland Quarter Sessions for purchasing a wife. 'The purchaser was selected for punishment, as the most opulent, and fittest to make an example of' is an incomprehensible detail. Was there some major outbreak in this small community made up of only thirty-three houses and a population numbering one hundred and seventy-three?[5] There is no information on what punishment was applied.

In 1868, William Cross was charged with making his wife chargeable on the Dudley Union poor authorities after he had sold her. The full story is unclear but probably the sale fell through or the new marriage was unsuccessful. He was sentenced to twenty-one days in prison, the same as for abandonment.[6]

Joshua Jackson was sentenced in 1837 at the West Riding Sessions for one month in prison with hard labour, a punishment which again seems to have been made as a warning to others, as 'a great deal of surprise was felt in many villagers of ignorant peasantry at the result of the trial'.[7] By this date more newspapers reported the sales, but even the radicals and Chartists condemned the practice, though they did show sympathy, as they suggested such scenes would be ended if a cheap form of separation was available.[8] This suggests such behaviour was common in this small community.

The punishments for wife selling thus ranged widely, which reflected the confusion as to the legal status of the practice, as mentioned previously. Some reports detail long discussions by the authorities as to how to deal with the incidents. In 1847, a sale at Barton market came to light when the purchaser refused to honour the wife's debts. The woman claimed she had been bought 'in the usual way',[9] which dumbfounded the judge and again suggests the practice was widespread and well known by all except the authorities.

In 1833, when James Stradling was taken before magistrates at

Bath, no prosecutor could be found; it seems they could not decide what to charge him with, so he was given a reprimand by the mayor.[10] A similar case comes from 1865 at Grantham market concerning a seventeen-year-old mother; the crowd attracted the police who stopped the sale. The newspaper claimed it was gratified that the authorities intervened, but had found insufficient grounds for punishment, possibly because the sale had not actually been completed.[11] When a teenage wife was arrested at Smithfield in 1841 after an attempted sale, the alderman warned her of the dangers of continuing to see her purchaser and that her husband could refuse to support her if adultery could be proven. This shows that the authorities were not merely punishing miscreants, but were also concerned about crime prevention and the welfare of those involved. This further suggests there may have been similar cases where the sale was interrupted or prevented and those involved given similar legal advice. A man was sent to Andover jail in 1818, then on bail to attend the quarter sessions, when he was discharged as 'he was entirely ignorant of committing any offence',[12] a claim that would not stand up today.

Some sales attracted large crowds, which in turn attracted the attention of the press and the authorities who charged those involved with causing public nuisance. In 1834, George Faulkner was ordered to post a surety of twenty pounds to keep the peace or go to jail.[13] In 1835, an unruly mob disrupted a sale in Suffolk; the party were arrested and fined ten shillings at the Guildhall.[14] It seems wife sellers needed to be flexible, prepared to flee the mob and make alternative arrangements, either by retreating to a local hostelry or trying another town at a future date. A couple in Rochdale in 1856 were advised to 'go home and live comfortably' to which he wife replied ominously: "Nay, I shanno".[15]

A man in Leominster was sentenced to six months in prison for selling his wife in 1819, seemingly another case of the punishment serving as a warning to others.[16] In Birmingham in 1823 a former soldier accused of brutality against his wife sold her against her will. Assuming he was then legally free, he remarried in a church but was convicted of bigamy and sentenced to seven years transportation.[17]

This confirms again that the participants believed the sale to be legal, and that they were attempting to behave within the law. When the man remarried, someone in the congregation should have raised the question as to whether he was free to enter into the marriage. But perhaps the marriage was in a parish where he was unknown, a common practice for couples to avoid boisterous locals joining their celebrations, and not challenged by local vicars who were often poorly paid so welcomed the extra income.

In 1895, Peter Tyson was charged with assaulting his wife by trying to get a string round her neck in order to resell her, and fined five shillings. He wrapped the string round her neck three times, which suggests some sort of debased ritual was involved, but this is unlikely at this date.[18] Middlesbrough was a boom town based on iron smelting, so was an area with little work for women where they tended to marry young and have little independence. This fine seems to have been a lenient sentence, suggesting there was little risk of the sale being emulated, and a jail term would probably lose him his job and home. The authorities may even have been his employers.

All these incidents suggest a breakdown in the domestic relationship, but it seems the most miserable was that of a publican named Hansard, of Boston, who sold his wife for a mere penny and a half and was reproved by magistrates. He claimed he could no longer live with her because she was a hardened alcoholic who often stole from him to feed her habit. As evidence of this, she was before the same bench for stealing, and trembling, so she was clearly ill. It is hard to imagine how he could manage his business, in which his wife should have been his helper, whilst he had to be constantly keeping a watch on her behaviour. In desperation he offered to pay for her to be kept in the local workhouse, but this was refused as she continued to be his responsibility, for better or for worse, till death did they part. He was fined five shillings for her theft plus twelve shillings and sixpence costs. Mercifully for them both, she died a week later of alcohol poisoning.[19]

There was a rare example of a woman being punished, though this was for the after-effect of the sale. In Spilsby, in 1821, a woman was sent to the house of correction for threatening to set fire to her former husband's home.[20]

Two husbands received unexpected punishments for selling their wives: one in 1810 failed to find a buyer locally at Bewcastle so went to Newcastle. But on arrival he was taken by the waiting press gang. The local paper claimed this was pre-arranged by 'a modern Delilah'.[21] In 1856, an abandoned husband in Retford had the town crier announce his wife for sale, but when he tried to lead her away by the halter, he was attacked by her, and suffered extensive bleeding for which he received sympathy from the crowd. But he was then arrested for deserting his militia, who had probably been alerted to his presence by his advertisements for the sale.[22]

With some — perhaps many — sales being announced by the town crier, in 1849, the Blackburn bellman was warned by magistrates. He had believed that it was legal to cry: "all fish that come to the net". He was forced to pay costs and promised not to offend again.[23]

When couples were ordered by the authorities to go home and behave themselves, some may have been frightened enough to do so. It is possible that the shared trauma and shame of their arrest may have brought the argumentative couples closer together. In 1822 a man took his wife to Mansfield market where he put her on sale, claiming she was not a 'votary at the shrine of Diana'.[24] Complaints were made by several young men that the sale had been a fraud. But it may have made the couple realise the value of what they were about to throw away.

But all these punishments — with the exception of the press gang and the transportation — were of short duration, whereas living with an estranged partner was to the death, a harsher punishment than anything the courts could inflict on them.

7

ALTERNATIVES TO SALES

Marriages go bad not when love fades — love can modulate into affection without driving two people apart.
   Phyllis Rose[1]

A marriage that lasts 'till death us do part' is a rare thing now, but centuries ago, it was both the ideal and the norm, as it formed the bedrock of social stability, and was integral to the idea of a fixed universe. The Christian God was at the apex of a social pyramid which descended and expanded down through the pope, kings and aristocrats to the humblest of peasants. The expectation that the relationship should be long-lasting led friends and family to invest great efforts into trying to ensure that young couples were well suited to each other and that they were prepared for a life of co-operation and compromises.

But this system was badly shaken by the upheavals of the Reformation and Civil War. The English king replaced the pope as head of the church; he executed bishops and many nobles who opposed him. The Civil War caused the execution of the king, so for decades the English perceived their world was turning upside down. When England expanded its colonies, there were further disruptions as the economy expanded, people became more mobile and the young increasingly chose life partners on impulse without the advice of older, wiser friends and family. This freedom meant that more mistakes were made, and as divorce was impossible for all but the very rich, it seems there were growing numbers of people for whom the dream of a happy marriage became a nightmare from which they could not awaken.

One of the conundrums in researching wife selling is how it became so widespread. Throughout most of English history, people lived in tiny settlements, some unworthy of the term hamlet. The royal court and some clerics were highly mobile, and shared information, but most people had to rely on travellers. This was why — beyond the recreation they provided — events such as markets and fairs were so important. They brought together groups from great distances, and allowed trade but also gave potential marriage partners the chance to meet. This prevented local communities from becoming inbred, just as the purchasing of fresh livestock kept their animals robust. Some professions such as the building trades, malt brewers and drovers travelled for much of the year, often returning home in winter. In earlier times, soldiers were allowed home to help with the harvest as the intention of wars was not to starve the enemy. Of these professions, it is only the drovers who were strongly associated with wife selling, suggesting the practice had its basis in cattle sales.

Railway navvies had a reputation for hard drinking and immoral behaviour. Women who gravitated to their camps were often accused of being prostitutes. Some camps were like the Wild West where riots and violence were common, especially when the workers got paid and went on drinking sprees in local towns. On one occasion in Penrith, four navvies raped and assaulted two women. They were prosecuted by a magistrate who claimed it was the worst such case ever tried in England.[2]

But the camps were also home to women who were respectable wives, mothers, nurses and teachers, so the men were not all bad. They tended to live in crowded huts, and their hard lives attracted the attention of missionaries who tried to control their drinking, provided education for their children, and encouraged couples to marry. But their women often found they were better off in less formal arrangements, due to the instability of the work, and the accommodation which was linked to it. If a man was sacked, he was forced to 'go on the tramp' in search of work, leaving his family in limbo. He may have intended to send for them, but this could take weeks or months. In the meantime, his family could only stay on the site for two weeks. The family would be forced into the not-so-tender care of the local workhouse, but the hard-working, independent women often refused this. Instead, they would find a new partner. Many women managed to survive via a series of common-law marriages, raising children with different fathers and earning money from lodgers. One missionary complained that they could divorce for a mere thirty pounds, and in the 1880s some agreed to do so, but this did nothing to improve the security of their incomes and often resulted in a lot of guilt and the risk of being charged with bigamy.[3]

But even in settled communities such as the steelworkers in Middlesbrough, marriage was not always the best option, especially for the woman. Lady Bell visited a home where a woman cared for the child of her youngest daughter; who was unmarried. 'A good job too, she's got the child and she's not got the man/he was worthless, and she is well rid of him.'[4] Lady Bell noted that in many cases, that as long as the woman was free to leave, she had a hold on the man. She described a woman who was encouraged to marry, but it turned into a disaster. By giving up her freedom, she left the man free to ill-treat her, and he no longer cared about his behaviour because he knew she was trapped. So if many women found marriage did not suit them, then they probably just left if things became unbearable. This seems to suggest it was those who were married who were sold. But in the above case, it seems the man enjoyed the power he had over the woman, so would be unlikely to sell her, unless he found a woman to replace her.

Even Charles Dickens — the man so often associated with the ideal Victorian family — had marital problems. His wife became worn out by the constant cycle of childbirth, child rearing and managing their large home, and the great author lost interest in her.

But he author had options. He could throw himself into his work or leisure pursuits, he could travel and pay for women to provide for his intimate needs. But advice from sensible friends was that marriages were often unhappy, and they suggested he improve his own behaviour and make amends with his wife. It seems his marital problems were similar to other self-made men whose lives had drastically changed, with their wives failing to keep up. Eventually, Dickens moved into an adjoining bedroom and covered the doorway between them with bookshelves.

Wife sales were often described as a cheap form of divorce when divorce itself was still illegal in England. Henry VIII is often claimed to have set a precedent by divorcing Catherine of Aragon, but this is an error. He and his mistress Anne Boleyn studied church law to allow them to claim his first marriage had been illegal based on the *Book of Leviticus* which claimed the resulting marriage which would be unfruitful, so Henry fudged biblical teachings to obtain an annulment. The Pope had given Henry a dispensation to marry Catherine so he claimed the pope did not have the power to do this. Henry passed several acts to remove papal authority over the English church, taking charge of it himself. He declared his first marriage void via an Act of Parliament, and until the 1857 Marriage Act was passed, England remained the only Protestant country to retain pre-Reformation divorce laws. The second divorce in England was not granted until the 1690s, and there were only fourteen in the first half of the eighteenth century. As with Henry VIII, these were all driven by a need to provide a legitimate heir to inherit a title, property and wealth, as until 1747 'no divorce was granted to a man who had a living legitimate son, and petitioners played up the dynastic elements of their case.'[5]

In the highest social levels, especially in the military, where a man's honour and sexual prowess were traditionally interwoven with his social status and wealth, the insult of cuckoldry was of paramount importance to him and his family. It could cause revenge killings or duels. And yet there is no record of a man murdering his wife's lover in England after 1700.[6] The French blamed this on the nation's lack of passion, but it was more likely common sense, a Protestant respect for their own lives. The practice of duelling seems to have been replaced with court action called criminal conversation or crim.con in which the lover was sued for stealing the wife's affection. This legal option was often compared with wife selling, so when the French claimed that the English men profited from their wife's infidelity, further confirmed that England was a nation of shopkeepers. After winning a case for criminal conversation, the husband was generally able to obtain a divorce by Act of Parliament, to cut off his wife's income and access to their children, and for both to remarry.

The process of criminal conversation had much in common with wife selling. Both were seen as degrading to women, both were highly public sources of embarrassment, and both were connected in the minds of the European lawyers. Lord Lansdown in 1857 described crim.con in the House of Lords as being based on the assumption 'that the affection of the wife is to be treated as the loss of an ordinary chattel, and is to be compensated in pounds, shillings and pence.'[7] It should have been an embarrassment to a nation at the height of its powers, as the self proclaimed moral guardian of the world, spreading Christian values whilst not always practising them.

In many wife sales, the woman had already left the husband and set up home with a new partner. So the sale was more a means of formalising the end of the marriage contract, and attempting to ensure the first husband was not held legally responsible for either the woman's future debts or her children.

Whilst newspapers ranted about the immorality of the sales, there is no sign of any clerics publicly condemning them, which is odd, as is the fact that bishops sat in the House of Lords condemning divorce but voted for individual cases to be passed. Following the collapse of ecclesiastical courts and decline in church attendance by the late seventeenth century, a corresponding collapse in morality could have been expected. But this seems not to have happened. Many Nonconformist groups and later evangelicals helped maintain moral standards within their own circles and could eject anyone who offended their morals. In the absence of state welfare provisions, marriage continued to be the major source of mutual support, especially for women with children. Communities seem to have become largely self-policing, but scattered through Richard Gough's *The History of Myddle* — concerning a town in Shropshire at the turn of the seventeenth century — are tales of drunkenness, deceit and debauchery that seem to have gone unpunished. Perhaps the worst was that of William Tyler who debauched a man called Hussey's wife, which ended the marriage. The wife moved away but he visited her and had a child — Nell Hussey. When she was grown, he took her as his housekeeper and had a bastard by her. Gough notes 'I need mention noe more of his villanyes.'[8] There is no mention of any punishment or shaming of this man who seems to have become a successful local businessman.

The English of the eighteenth century — especially the later decades of it — are often seen as misbehaving, debauched and drunk. But marriage was still the basis of civil society and most couples managed to live respectable lives, working hard, paying their taxes, and raising their children as best they could. They were couples on a physical level, but also as financial units; the man was the main provider, but the woman was still expected to provide a dowry and to pull her weight within the family unit. Thus physical strength and the ability to compromise with others were of immense importance in the choice of a lifetime partner.

Local communities supported and defended marriages, and they could be condemnatory in response to wife sales, as in several cases of wife selling when those involved were pelted with mud or snow. Several wives were condemned for appearing to be a 'hussy', for not showing shame at the humiliation of the sale and, by default, shame at her adultery. But some crowds cheered the new couple, or were noted for their silence. Interventions were made to stop some sales, but other crowds stopped the authorities from interfering. A few husbands fled the mob's wrath; one staged a fake sale with a friend dressed as a woman as a decoy, while the real sale proceeded elsewhere.

E.P. Thompson claims that it was impossible to change partners within communities without causing a scandal as it disturbed the social fabric. He suggests that wife sellers would be forced to move elsewhere but some were unable to find suitable work.[9] This assumes communities were stable and shared common values, but this was not always the case, at least not in the many new industrial and mining areas. Such settlements often brought together a wide range of people with different beliefs and social practices. Until communal belief systems could become established, there was probably considerable tolerance of unusual behaviour. This is where wife selling seemed to find its home, as well as among mobile communities such as boat people on the canals.

A woman lost all legal identity at marriage, so a legal separation meant she lost everything: her property, possessions, dowry and access to all her children. Husbands had complete control over their wives — they were allowed to discipline them — but this term was poorly defined, so even extreme violence was seldom punished. In extreme cases, it allowed husbands to imprison, starve, assault, rape or murder their wives with impunity. As the eighteenth century progressed, the notion of marriage being based on companionship became more widespread and women were allowed more rights. But for a broken marriage there were still few options. If a couple in conflict were brought before the magistrates — usually for disturbing the peace — there was nothing the law could do to remedy their situation.

In the absence of legal resolutions, communities could intervene to protect or rescue the wife, especially if the man was unpopular and/or known to be violent. In the early eighteenth century, a Wokingham cleric married a woman for her money but when she refused to hand it over to him, he assaulted and threatened to kill her. Several neighbours became worried enough to teach him a lesson. One man dressed himself as a woman and accused the reverend of assault. The cleric was then dragged through a forest and scared within an inch of his life before he was abandoned with threats of further visits if he did not treat his wife better.[10]

We can only guess at how many couples were forced to stay together whilst despising each other. Some may have sought solace in religion, and wives may have moved back to their families. But if children were involved, their options were limited. Until mechanics institutes, libraries and music halls became common, the only escape for the men was to a local inn or tavern. It is no surprise that they sometimes came home drunk and became violent, which is where couples become visible on the records of either the courts or newspapers. Sadly, there were also incidents of men murdering their wives, sometimes after threatening to do so.

There was a near miss in 1829 in Anstey Leicestershire. A sale was made between two stocking weavers, but when the seller saw his wife happily at work afterwards, he became jealous and was about to shoot her when a passer-by intervened.[11]

In 1734, a gardener argued with his wife and killed her. He said he "would rather be hanged than live with such a woman."[12] But women were not always the victims. A wife hired four men to kill her husband so she could marry 'a poor deformed cobbler.'[13] Another man murdered his wife 'for fear she would interrupt his cohabitation with another woman.'[14]

In Gough's *The History of Myddle* appears an extraordinary account of some wives taking the law into their own hands. The 'young, wonton widow' Hodden married a quiet man but soon tired of him, so she joined with two other local women who also wanted to be rid of their husbands. They allegedly poisoned their husbands on the same night, but only Hodden's died. She fled, but was arrested in Wales, 'upon a hollyday, danceing in the toppe of an hill amongst a company of young people'.[15]

Under the law of coverture, the man and wife were treated as a single unit, but this made it impossible for them to sue each other for maintenance or access and/or custody of children. A wife could not give evidence in court or call defence witnesses if charged with adultery, so she was at risk of being falsely convicted by a malicious husband. But in the administrative chaos of the English Civil War, private deeds of separation came into use, which ensured the husband maintained his wife without accepting any debts she might incur. By the mid-eighteenth century, lawyers had become experienced at drawing up these deeds. They provided the wife with financial independence and protected her from being kidnapped or assaulted by her husband, and she was free to live with whom and where she wished. But it was unclear if this allowed the parties to remarry, or if it prevented the husband suing at a later date for criminal conversation.[16]

But such separations were often seen as encouraging adultery, which would allow the husband to obtain a legal divorce, leaving the wife with no money or possessions, and the prospect of never seeing her children again, as well as spending her life as a social pariah. Alternatively, it could be argued that such an agreement was proof of collusion, which would prevent the husband obtaining a divorce, so the action might solve nothing. Ultimately, the problem was that all these agreements could be — and sometimes were — challenged in law if the couple later fell out, especially if the husband wanted to remarry, which required a divorce. But this was only likely to be an issue when the husband owned property and was in need of a male heir.

Another factor driving wife selling was rising affluence from the mid-eighteenth century which led to a growing numbers of the 'middling sorts' who were unlikely to own property. Women were increasingly literate and more publicly active, but were still frustratingly inferior to men in the roles they could fill and of course their wages were low. As a result, many concentrated on their role as mothers, justifying their education as a means of instructing their children. The bond between a mother and child grew in importance at this time, as did her role in educating them, in part inspired by the writings of Rousseau and the concept of child-centred learning in the middle of the century. Couples increasingly made use of deeds which could be written to ensure the mother was granted custody of her children, especially if they were young.

Following prolonged chaos, particularly during and after the Civil War, when many churches closed or were converted to other purposes, religious marriage was often impossible, even for those who wished for it and could afford it. There were many different religious groups outside the auspices of the official church, so marriage came to encompass a wide range of practices, from a simple promise between the man and woman, to common-law relationships. Clandestine marriages were often made when the woman fell pregnant or the man was about to go to sea or to war, so needed to get hitched in a hurry. But the Test Act of 1704 made marriages outside the established church invalid. Thus, within their community, a couple could be married, but in the outside world, they were not. In most Nonconformist groups, the marriage was seen more as a legal contract, a concept widespread in other Protestant parts of Europe and the North American colonies.

Until the definition of a legal marriage was established in law under the 1757 Marriage Act, even those who were married in a church often had no way of proving it. Thus, many people were unsure if they were legally married, so it is no surprise that they were unsure how to become unmarried if things turned sour between them. In practice, it seems that if they shared a name, a house, and raised their children in a respectable manner, there were no objections from their community. The 1757 Marriage Act formally defined marriage and outlawed clandestine and other forms, though these remained legal in Scotland till 1856. This explains why so many couples eloped to Gretna Green and the less-known Coldstream and Berwick to tie the knot.

A more common alternative was to simply not to get married, which allowed the couple to separate at any time. This practice seems to have been widespread, especially among the poor, which makes parish records so incomplete for family historians, perhaps covering only half of the population. But unmarried women — then as now — struggled to find work to live on, and could not demand support from the father(s) of their children. Poor Law officers could not pursue fathers for the upkeep as paternity was virtually impossible to prove. If baptised, the children were listed in parish records as 'base born'. This meant that unless the mother immediately moved in with another man, her family would be left to the less-than-tender mercies of the poorhouse.

In the 1740s, a couple married in Gloucester but soon parted, and she was sold. Her new husband took her to Bath where they were married by 'Parson Crey, a lawless minister there'.[17]

Throughout this research can be found numerous attempts by people to try to do things correctly, and/or legally. Some couples tried to marry in a church, such as an instance from 1769; a wedding in Bruton was interrupted when the minister demanded the fee as the couple were exchanging rings. They were unable to pay, so the minister left. The press noted 'it is, however, imagined, as the lovers have not been to church since, they have determined to take each other's words for the remainder of the ceremony.'[18] No mention is made here of friends or relatives being present, who might have been able to contribute to the cost, so again, this was probably held outside their parish either to avoid embarrassment, or perhaps they thought they would get away without paying. .

Eliza Sharples was a famous free thinker and the common-law wife of radical journalist Richard Carlisle. She recognised wife selling's importance in divorce, but condemned it as being insulting to the woman and brutal. She claimed a much preferable option was merely to separate. She claimed that by participating in a brutal practice the women encouraged men to be brutes.[19]

Some writers claim that common-law marriage was the most common form of union in England, in which case, there would be no need for any form of 'unmarriage'. If a man abandoned his family, he would be pursued and punished by the overseers of the poor who would force them to support their families. But there was no official intervention if a woman absconded as she was not the breadwinner. This seems to have been fairly common practice, judging by the number of notices placed in eighteenth-century newspapers by husbands announcing that their wife had absconded, and warning the public he would not be responsible for any of her debts. These advertisements were similar to those announcing runaway apprentices and slaves.

Thus, the people involved in wife selling must have believed they had been legally hitched. But it is unclear how common this was historically. Family names starting with Fitz- referred to illegitimate heirs of royals and aristocrats. Following the plague's arrival in 1348, the Diocese of Exeter had a large shortfall of priests. Bishop Grandison obtained two faculties from the pope; one was 'for obtaining fifty men who were born out of wedlock'.[20] So it seems that in such dark days, illegitimacy was then both common and not a hindrance to advancement, even within the church.

The marriage contract made the husband financially responsible for his wife and any children they produced together. This is why so much emphasis was placed on the financial side of the selling. If the second marriage failed, or the purchaser predeceased his wife, the first husband did not want his wife to return, especially if that entailed any children that were not his. This financial break also allowed the man to embark on another marriage, though this is seldom mentioned and seems to have been of less significance. Farmer Thompson seems to have wanted a quiet life, and seems to have been delighted to obtain a dog to share it with. Many cases showed no sign of animosity; the marriage seems to have failed due to incompatibility. In an agreement from 1893 in Sheffield, a man stated his wife was 'free from me for ever, to do as she has a mind.'[21]

Records of some wife sales suggest — or state outright — that the woman had been unfaithful, and there were many cases where she had already left, which begs the question as to why the husband would pursue her. William Hodge was accused of frequently assaulting his wife and threatening to sell her, to which she was agreeable. She was sold to William Andrews, and both men were indicted at Plymouth.²² An army sergeant of Devonport Dock tracked his faithless wife to Liskeard in 1823 when they agreed to a wife sale.²³ Those involved in wife selling showed some diversity, as on The Pavement at York in 1827, the one-legged wife of one-eyed Mills was sold to Gallimore, with whom she had previously cohabited.²⁴ In 1837 John Allen tracked down his wife who had eloped to Whaley Bridge, and the matter was settled by her being sold at Wirksworth market.²⁵ In 1849, a wife eloped with a paramour when her husband was in the Hull Infirmary, taking much of his property. The husband tracked them down to arrange a sale.²⁶

Some cases state the new husband had been a lodger, suggesting he was not local, so had potentially the means to move elsewhere to start a new life. In Sheffield in 1796, one seller even gave the new couple a guinea to move to Manchester. This suggests the sale was not supported by his neighbours, or perhaps the husband just wanted to be free of his wife, to make a fresh start of his own.²⁷ There was also a sale in Sittingbourne of not only the wife, but also her five children horse, cart and all household furniture, which suggests either she had some strong legal claims to them, or that the husband was selling up and moving elsewhere, to start a new life. Or he may have been downsizing.²⁸

In some of these cases, the husband was violent and the woman had strayed, but this leaves us wondering which came first. Did the wife stray because of abuse, or was the husband 'disciplining' her for abandoning her vows and transferring her affections to another man? But there does seem to be a sense of 'closure' required here, at least in terms of finances. If the marriage had broken down to such an extent that a sale was even considered, most men would be glad to see the back of the wife. In the absence of wise friends or family, it is hard to imagine how a broken marriage could be repaired.

Tom Oxinden married fourteen-year-old Elizabeth for her wealth. But he soon eloped with another man's wife. He was later imprisoned for being a highwayman, yet Elizabeth still felt bound to him, either by law or by her own vows. She did not remarry till he died in jail.²⁹ This account is undated, but the highwayman suggests it was from the mid-eighteenth century. Given her husband's appalling record, it is possible she could have obtained some formal separation, at the very least to secure her assets. This is the sort of nightmare scenario that guardians of young heiresses feared, and which fuelled the famous flights to Gretna Green by young couples with parents or guardians in hot pursuit.

If people had the money to marry, they could probably find the funds to flee, especially before the founding of a national police force. The South Sea Bubble burst spectacularly in 1720 following the avalanche of other dubious speculations such as a scheme for importing Spanish jackasses to produce extra large mules and a gun which shot round bullets at Christians and square ones against infidels.[30] One young man who had left his Norfolk home in search of wealth in the capital saw his dreams destroyed by the crash. He wrote to his brother: 'the Sea is fittest for an undone man, and so I am for that.'[31] Many modern people seem intrigued by the bravery or stupidity of the huge number of British men who willingly went to sea despite the huge risks. For those without work or income, the option of staying at home meant a life of poverty and shame; they saw the sea not just as a chance to make a fortune, but also to redeem themselves. English men no longer fought duels over slighted honour, but their sense of male pride still drove their sense of duty to support themselves and their families. Flight was always an option for poor men. If they could get to a major port, they could always find work going to sea, beyond the reach of the overseers of the poor, and many of them did, possibly fleeing the responsibilities of unwanted families. This must have helped supply the manpower for Britain's merchant and naval fleets.

The Poor Laws began to break down as a result of increased mobility and urbanisation in the eighteenth century. People from the countryside moved to towns and cities but also within cities, especially the huge metropolis of London. Some may have moved in response to changes in employment, or fled rent or debt collectors. Even poll books, which record those with the rights of residence and earning enough to vote, show frequent changes of address.[32] Some women had children in different parishes, so establishing the place of settlement for a family became a matter of disputes between parishes. Some parishes issued certificates of settlement and refused to allow entry to anyone without them. Many wills provided for the building of almshouses, their upkeep and the education and apprenticing of poor children to try to help them rise above their poverty.

Given the almost constant skirmishes that Britain was involved in across the eighteenth century, there was a steady demand for men as soldiers and sailors, and in times of peace, there was money to be made from privateering, so going to sea was a common way out of a bad relationship. This could even be used by the wife to get rid of her unwanted husband, as the 'Delilah' of Bewcastle managed, after her husband failed to sell her locally, to persuade him husband to try at Newcastle, where he was arrested by the press gang in 1810.[33]

There were also cases of innocent bigamy, of the husband being away so long he was presumed dead so the wife remarried and even had children. In 1784 in Worcester the husband 'returned home after some years abroad', and another case in Sherborne the same year.[34] This was relatively common following after wars when soldiers and sailors returned after being assumed dead, especially in the aftermath of the American and Napoleonic Wars. This must have been a situation of long standing, particularly after the New World was discovered and ships journeys became much longer and often more dangerous. Selling the wife to the new husband, who was often by then the father of her children, allowed the situation to be settled amicably. Given Britain's long maritime heritage, these situations must have arisen frequently. The first husband often agreed to go away or sold his wife by private agreement. A woman could not be convicted for bigamy under such circumstances. There were also instances of men convicted and transported to the colonies who returned, and their wives were also not charged if they had taken another spouse.

Parson Holland of Somerset left no record of any wife sales, but he lived in the market town of Stowey, and his busy pastoral life suggests he would have known of and recorded them, though many of his books are lost. He mentioned a man in 1809 whom he refuses to dignify with a name, merely calling him 'The Botany Bay Man who lived at the Workhouse'. The man sought advice on his strange predicament. He was cohabiting with a woman who had borne him a child, but her husband was in Botany Bay. He wished to make an honest woman of her, but was told he could not, as her husband was still alive and was the man's brother. The parson refused to provide advice beyond advising him on the legal situation.[35]

The man demands our sympathy, as he seems decent and willing to work, and no mention is made by Holland of incapacity, so it is possible he was being shunned by local employers for his relationship or his criminal record, which was probably a minor offence. And yet outside England, marriage to a sister-in-law was not only legal, but sometimes expected as a means of maintaining a family. Henry VIII's first marriage had been to his late brother's wife, Catherine of Aragon. The man in the story mentions that other people have done the same, and with so many men being transported, this must have been a major problem. Terms were often for seven years, and many people believed that a separation of this period constituted a legal divorce. It must have either been supported by the couple's neighbours or done without their knowledge. If the couple had moved away, to where they were unknown or where clerics did not ask questions, the couple could have become respected members of the community instead of what appears to be pariahs. But moving cost money, and a returned criminal would not have had such ready funds. This is yet another instance of people trying to do the right thing but of circumstances making any resolution impossible.

8
RITUALS

Nearly the whole town had gone into the fields. The Casterbridge populace still retained the primitive habit of helping one another in time of need.
  Thomas Hardy

Many authors claim — or at least assume — that wife selling had its origins in some distant past, but there is no hard evidence to suggest this. Until recent times, the behaviour of common people did not feature in written records, but if it had, it would have been mostly lost or destroyed in the sacking of the monasteries or the Civil War. Most people lived in small, isolated communities, so it is hard to imagine how such a practice would have been necessary or become so widespread unless there was a single organisation to initiate it, suggesting it was begun by either the church or state.

Yet there are practices that seem to survive due to some innate need within us; they keep emerging in times of need and of stress, especially in relationship to death and grieving. Roadside shrines seem to have become commonplace since the death of Diana, Princess of Wales. The national outburst of grief seemed so un-English at the time, yet it seemed to open the door to something that had long lain buried and has since refused to go away. The huge sculpture The Angel of the North has become a focus for people to scatter ashes or leave tokens for departed loved ones. This is a secular artwork, yet it was made by the Catholic-educated Anthony Gormley, is based on his own body, and the pose echoes the Crucifixion. Is it the shape of the sculpture that matters, its place on a high point to allow views of the surrounding countryside, or is it a more general use of open space, a landmark for ritual practices?

Our ancestors lived lives that were to modern eyes unbearably harsh and exhausting, but the year was leavened with a wide range of Christian, pagan, astronomical, agricultural, legal and local events and celebrations. From the seventeenth century, when many had fallen into disuse or been outlawed, they became foci for curiosity; folklorists became interested in them and often overstated their importance and misunderstood their origins and purposes. Many rituals and practices became degraded, so their original purpose was lost which led to them being assumed to be of ancient origin. But much of the degradation and loss was the result of the suppression of many practices under the Tudors.

In the Netherlands peasant life was celebrated in the art of Bruegel and his peers. These images depicted the world of ordinary people after their independence from Spain, so were a celebration of nationhood. At this time, arts patronage was virtually non-existent in England, and religious art was extensively vandalised. There was no lack of art in these islands, but they were treated as plunder, created by the hated Church of Rome and so either destroyed or degraded by the public. Painters survived by producing pub and inn signs and when roads improved, painting coaches, the trade that Hogarth started in.

The successful completion of the harvest was central to the survival of our ancestors in grain-growing areas. They celebrated the harvest home to express joy and relief at the end of their back-breaking work and that they had averted famine. The final cartload of wheat was decorated for its journey to the farm, and a huge dinner was often laid on by the farmer or landlord. The only remnant of this huge event is the harvest service in parish churches, often associated with donations of food to the poor.

There was not a single calendar, but many, determined by professions and geography. Special days were allocated for the payment of rents and tithes, which often involved feasts and the distribution of charity. The royal courts and the legal profession had their own annual cycles, again, often linked with celebratory feasts. Many of these festivals were named after saints' days even after their suppression by Tudor Reformers. Elizabeth tried to remove many from the calendar, but some were too closely linked with civic functions, so they remained printed in calendars and diaries as black-letter days. The official celebratory dates were printed as red-letter days.[1]

Some rituals and superstitions survive into the modern age, or have been revived to boost tourism and bind local communities together. Yet in some areas, they were still evolving in the twentieth century, as several involved how to respond to an ambulance. One was

> 'when you see an ambulance, hold your collar until you see a four-footed animal. A less popular alternative is to lick your finger and put it on your head.'[2]

It is hard to make sense of these, as ambulances are so recent. Most likely, they were linked with impending death, so these strange practices may have been grafted onto earlier practices at the sight of a coffin being carried. Rituals are constantly evolving, as evidenced by the huge bonfire parade at Hastings which originated as a celebration of Protestantism, but has developed a life of its own, with some people attributing elements of ancient pagan rites to it, or perhaps it just draws out the primal fear in all of us of darkness, and the fascination with fire and danger.

When St Augustine came to evangelise the British, he was allegedly instructed to graft Christianity onto pagan roots, and many Christian places of worship show this practice as they have been found to be built on earlier shrines and temples. In the late eighteenth century, a strange account suggests how traditional practices were hijacked by modern events. Annual celebrations were held to replace the scented rushes used to carpet parish churches on 'Rush Sunday'. But in Middleton, the joyful procession was followed by a cart bearing an effigy of Tom Paine which the mob shot at and abused. The effigy was eventually executed on the Monday.[3] There is no logical connection between these two parades but a stranger may have assumed a link, and that guess may have become accepted as truth over time. What it mostly showed was the presence of two very different groups making use of a town's public space at the same time. If Rush Sunday celebrations died out and the Paine ritual continued, this would have made the link stronger but more incomprehensible. This may have relevance to the links between wife sales being held in beast markets. The sales may not have suggested parallels between women and beasts; they may just have been making use of the same public space.

Before the Reformation, communities supported a wide range of lively religious celebrations, especially at Christmas and Easter. In modern *artspeak*, churches were immersive environments where parishioners could see fine and applied art, inhale the scent of rushes and incense, and forget their normal lives. Churches provided respite from the stress of normal life and, especially for women, were a social space for them to take a break from their homes. Images and statues of saints were erected and maintained and lit with candles. This smacked of idolatry and was condemned in the Bible but practices served to draw communities together, and provided what is now termed *distraction* to help relieve mental illnesses such as depression and anxiety.

Confession encouraged people to discuss and evaluate their behaviour, and make amends for failings, so encouraged better behaviour towards others. Rogation ceremonies provided opportunities for people to walk and talk with their neighbours, especially with those they seldom saw; they confirmed their parish boundaries, and reconnected and made amends with friends, all of which was concluded with sharing of food and drink. When a person had a specific problem, they appealed to the appropriate saint to intercede on their behalf with God. They were especially important to women in childbirth, which was then a life-threatening, so terrifying as well as agonising event. In the absence of modern pain relief, prayer was their major source of respite

About half the images and pilgrimage sites that were banned were associated with childbirth, such as St Margaret of Antioch who had been swallowed by a dragon. Women often outlived their men, so churches also provided a quiet place to grieve and remember their lifelong partners. This makes Henry VIII's abolition of these rituals particularly cruel.

These rituals also encouraged mutual support, allowing women who had given birth to remain in bed to rest while friends and family carried out their housework and childcare which on recovery the new mother would carry out in her turn for others. When churches were closed or vandalised by the Reformation, these public spaces for women were lost, or shifted to civic spaces such as open streets, marketplaces and parish pumps. With the rise of new religious groups, these public spaces became sites for religious discussions, in particular where Nonconformists, especially Quakers, held forth their views that priests were not necessary to connect with God. When John Wesley was banned from preaching in Anglican churches, he joined the many other groups by preaching in open fields.

Carnival, or Carnevale is still celebrated in many Catholic countries, but England has no tradition of it. Religious festivals and celebrations were replaced by national events such as birth or ascension days of the Tudor and Stuart monarchs. Guy Fawkes' Day grew to special importance, having evolved from a celebration of the monarch being saved from death, a sign from God that the Protestant cause was just. In the immediate aftermath, processions were held across the country in celebration. In London, vast sums were spent by guilds on huge, rowdy events which echoed the pageants from Elizabethan and Jacobin times. The Whore of Babylon was burned in 1673, and in 1677, a cat-filled pope.[4] Smaller events were held across the former Royalist heartland of Salisbury, Taunton and Oxford. But they were rowdy and partisan rather than civic events.

Here, we can see the apparent origins of rough music, a form of mockery involving public processions to mock people accompanied by rowdy noise made by banging pots and pans etc., and the burning of effigies. They evolved and adapted to circumstances to condemn local people and infamous national figures. The language of these festivities could also be adapted to shame local events, such as in Bristol in 1768 when the area's unemployed weavers presented the city with a loom covered in black crepe to advertise their plight and to raise money from the benevolent, echoing traditional funeral processions.[5]

Various sources note the ritual of 'riding the stang', 'riding skimmington', of carrying effigies of people who had caused offence through a town, often ending with the burning in a public place to express public objections to moral infringements. There are early examples of forcing an adulterous couple to ride naked through the town, often with the man facing backwards, so the use of effigies was a degraded form of that, and reduced the risks of protestors being charged with assault or even murder. The practice probably emerged from the Civil War as military punishments made use of horses which were too expensive for the peasantry to own.

In 1689 when William of Orange's forces reached Newcastle, a statue of James II was removed from its horse, so losing its power over the animal, then dragged to the Tyne and thrown in. A source claims this draws parallels with the public humiliations known as 'riding the stang' in which a transgressor (generally military) publicly rode a wooden horse and was then dumped in a ditch.[6] This is similar to the incident described in The Mayor of Casterbridge, showing how widespread the practice was.

A History of Everyday Things in England presents a sketch from c.1340 showing two boys pulling another on a wheeled horse, playing at riding the quintain,[7] used to teach the basic skills of jousting, so this may be an earlier element. When jousting was replaced in warfare by guns, this training became redundant. Wooden horses were abandoned and made their way into the hands of the lower classes to use in mocking authority, as in the celebration of Carnevale in Europe. It probably appealed to the public as the wheeled horse allowed those being shamed to be seen above the crowd and to be paraded through the town for maximum exposure as it made the victim visible above the crowd. The Somerset Hobby Horse was probably of the same origin. It also echoes the use of the ducking stool which was not always used for immersing in water. It could be used as a warning to be leant against a woman's door, or it could be used to carry the woman round in public to avoid the dangers of dunking — or 'plouncing' — in winter. The use of a hobby horse for shaming seems to have been preceded in medieval times by public shaming of traders who used false measures at markets. They wore notices round their necks advertising their crimes, and were dragged on a sled to the pillory.[8]

There are even instances when the church was utilised to express public opinion. Bell-ringing was often part of religious festivals, a passing bell rung to notify the parish that a wealthy citizen was dying, urging them to pray for him. Bells were rung and cannons fired all night and day to celebrate a major victory over enemies or the birth of a royal child. In eighteenth-century Bath, the abbey bells were rung to announce the arrival of important persons, who were expected to pay for this service, so providing local jobs. In the nineteenth century bell ringing became of a competitive sport amongst young men. In the early twentieth century some parishioners on Dartmoor made use of bells for more personal, vindictive purposes. In 1850, bells were rung to celebrate the departure of an unpopular manservant. The account ended with: 'Church bells were not very ecclesiastical in those days.'[9] When the newspaper proprietor Latimer called the West Country Bishop a 'perverter of facts', he was charged with libel. The jury was told that if they acquitted him, this would make the bishop a liar. The bells rang in every Exeter church the day he was acquitted. This shows how traditional rituals — even those of the church — could be mimicked or hijacked by locals in order to make a statement or protest.

There were two recorded instances when wife sales involved bell-ringing, both coincidentally from 1787. In January, a farmer from Ipswich sold his wife to a neighbour for five guineas, so probably a case of adultery. The husband was so pleased at making such a good bargain, he gave his wife a guinea to buy a new gown, a variation on the practice of returning some of the price as 'luck money' when a cow was sold. He then went to Stowmarket and gave orders for the bells to be rung in celebration, so not a wedding peal, more one of joyful release.[10] In December, a man sold his wife at Nuneaton for three guineas; the couple embraced and wished each other well as they separated. The new husband 'gave the ringers a handsome treat to ring a celebratory peal, and they spent the rest of the day with the greatest joy possible'.[11]

The practice of wife selling acquired a range of rituals that varied in both space and time. At the very core of this behaviour was the belief that the sale had to be performed in public, in an open space, to ensure the transaction was made honestly. This seems to have been an integral part of trade until recent times, as in the 1740s when John Wood of Bath was building the new Exchange in Bristol, he proposed an enclosed, Egyptian-style hall for the traders, and mocked them for their ignorance in demanding the building remain open to the cold and rain

But it seems it had to be a particular open space, as the case when a woman was sold at Lansdown Fair in 1833s was seen as illegal, so the affair moved to Bath market instead. This seems a rather odd notion, as the difference between a fair and a market was even then often blurred, but it may suggest the fair was crowded, so the deal was held in a tent, where Henchard sold his wife in Hardy's *The Mayor of Casterbridge*. Other fairs, such as Swindon in 1775, Burton 1790, Barnet 1829, Bakewell 1838, and Horsham Colt Fair 1820, 1825 and 1844, are on record as successful venues for sales.

Leaving aside the sordid dealings carried out by overseers of the poor, sales seem to have been divided into roughly two groups: those

that were pre-arranged, and those that seem to have been spontaneous. In the former, the wife knew her husband-to-be, and was often already living with him. In several cases the first husband had to track down the errant couple, which raises questions as to why he was doing it then. Perhaps the original husband had tired of the single life and wished to be free to remarry. Or perhaps neighbours were causing him problems, and he hoped a sale would bring an end to this. In other instances, the sale was held some distance from all their homes, so it was an unlikely coincidence that the intended husband just happened to be there.

Some sales were spontaneous, driven by the couple falling out rather than the woman straying. There were cases of women objecting to the buyer, refusing to go with him, or several examples where friends or family intervened to stop the sale. The finest of these dates from 1850 when the wife of a boatman was offered for a 'Dutch auction' in Knott Mill. The bidding was slow, so the wife called out to a boatman in the crowd, telling him she would make 'a rare good Wife', so he bought her.[12]

There was also an insistence on her going to the highest bidder, which was common commercial practice at the time, and was seen as a guarantee of honest dealing. This echoes the grain riots from the mid-eighteenth century, which were supposed to be open to all, to ensure supplies to the poor, but the wares had often been already sold privately.

From the mid-eighteenth century, traffic — especially wheeled vehicles — increased, open spaces in towns were built upon, and cities became more crowded, so the requirement for openness became increasingly difficult and was replaced by private sales. This paralleled the shift of markets from open streets into sheltered crosses and market halls. Also reflecting common practice was an increasing use of paper contracts and stamped paper. Thompson claimed the sales became more furtive, probably the result of rising populations and the establishment of police forces which increased the risks of the sales being interrupted. This secretiveness may also have reflected the number of idle potential troublemakers in the streets, rising evangelicalism and the increasing emphasis being placed on women's rights, so such scenes were disapproved of by the public.

In 1852, a couple went to the Nottingham cattle market; they stopped for a drink and the woman kept the halter round her neck hidden by her shawl until they reached the sheep pens. She was put up for sale for two shillings and sixpence. A bid of two shillings was made, and the 'husband looked unutterable things at the bidder', but this was accepted as 'delays were considered dangerous'.[13] Buyer and seller were from the same street, and the former seems to have reneged on an earlier agreement for a higher price, so this was another pre-arranged sale.

But there were also examples of highly civilised events held inside venues, such as in Stamford as early as 1786. The sale was followed by a group of friends sharing a meal where the 'lady dined at the head of the table where great composure'.[14] This reads more like a wedding than a degrading performance by ignorant people. It seems that even at this early date, wife selling was solving a genuine demand from a range of people, and was grafted on to a number of existing commercial and even religious practices according to the needs of those involved.

By the late nineteenth century, wife selling was retreating to isolated communities such as the Potteries, Sheffield's steelworkers and some mining areas but the use of the halter had faded. Seeming to confirm this, a sale was stopped in 1845 in Geithorp, when the couple was given legal advice to try somewhere more isolated. No trace can be found of this place, which suggests it was a bustling town which has now been renamed, absorbed into an urban centre, or become a ghost town. This suggests knowledge of the ritual was still widespread but retreating before the advance of urbanisation.[15]

Medieval towns and cities often had several large stone crosses. Some formed the centre of markets which could spread along adjoining streets and had stepped bases where traders could display their wares. Others in churchyards were used in processions or for preaching before the Reformation. The high cross at a town's main crossroads was often mentioned as the site of wife sales, with one example from 1823 mentioning the 'higher' cross, opposite the market at Liskeard. Though suggestive of religion, they were major civic structures, with carved statues of the monarchs who had given the town its charters. They were landmarks where proclamations were made; they were repainted for important events such as royal visits and draped in black for mourning a monarch's death. Marriage banns were read there during the Commonwealth, which may have been the starting point for the ritual of wife selling. They were close to various 'engines of punishment', such as the stocks, pillory and whipping post, and were often the starting point for people being paraded round the streets to be shamed for fraud or lewd behaviour.

In 1799, a wife sale was held at Formby Cross, and appeared in their Catholic Register as a note recording the birth of a child to James Wright and Mary Johnson.[16] The woman was not given her husband's name, showing the Church of Rome did not acknowledge the legality of the sale. In the early nineteenth century Rachel Heap was sold to Samuel Lumb at Halifax Cross after her husband returned from the wars.[17] Other mentions of market crosses include 1801 at New Malton, 1807 at Knaresborough, 1815 at York, and 1852 at Selby Market Cross. In 1852, a man led his wife from Burton-on-Trent to Repton where he paraded her in a halter three times round the cross. The number three is often found in Christianity, echoing the Holy Trinity, and is often used in magic, so at this late date, attempts were still being made to establish the sale as an accepted practice. Many other sales were recorded at markets, and may also have made use of the cross, either as a landmark for potential purchasers or using its steps to display 'the goods'. But the increase in traffic and general decay led to the destruction or removal of many public crosses, while their original sites kept the name, so there may not have been a cross in a town that bore it in its name.

Another element of the sale was the use of the halter round the woman, and it seems this was the element which caused the most outrage, as it suggested the woman was treated as an animal. Sometimes it was specially purchased for the event, showing the participants were not farmers; in a few instances it was draped with ribbons, or even made of silk, with a lace shawl covering it.[18] In 1790 a woman was led to Thame market on a piece of string, and in Bradford, the bridle was replaced by a 'pink riband' in 1848. At Thetford in 1839 the woman was led by a handkerchief round her neck, and in 1828 in West Kent, it was around her waist. In 1839 at Witney, there was a further evolution of the ritual when 'the woman waving a blue handkerchief' was described as exhibiting 'a most bare-faced and disgusting effrontery'.[19] The shift from a handmade halter of straw to rope, kerchiefs and ribbons reflects the shift of the population from the land to towns and cities.

In most cases, the halter was around the woman's neck or waist. A few had both, with the latter being used to tether her to a market pen. The practice seems to have died out in parallel with the shift indoors. In Preston in 1870, after the woman had been 'knocked down' in a public house, a suggestion was made that a halter should be procured and the process completed in a pen in the market square, so it seems the market was still deemed important. But they instead settled for a few more drinks before departing.[20] The Bristol broadside cited in the Western Daily Press of 1933 claimed the ancient custom was for the halter to be round the woman's neck, but evolved to be round her middle. The shift may have reflected objections to such a shaming practice, or been to prevent the woman being accidentally strangled in the crush of the crowd.

This seems to be the ultimate in humiliation, comparing her with a dumb animal, but it probably served, together with the payment of relevant market tolls, to ensure the sale's legality. Probably the last use of the halter was at Hucknall Torkard, near Sheffield as recently as 1899, where 'a leading member of the Salvation Army' sold his wife to a friend for a shilling, and with the halter, she was led home.'[21] And yet links with animals may have been a matter of proximity, as several sales were held — or at least attempted — in corn markets. Some of the very earliest sales were based on payment per weight, and the woman had to be weighed. There are no suggestions that such examples mean that the women were being treated as grain. This was yet again adapting standard commercial practices to new circumstances.

There were several rituals associated with the halter; it was often used to lead her to and from the market, and in a few cases, in specific beast markets such as Smithfield and Canterbury, she could be actually be tied up in a pen, the toll for which was probably paid to ensure its legality. An edition of Punch from 1867 included a cartoon, the 'physiology of courtship'.[22] which depicted the French and German views of Smithfield sales. A young-upper class woman is tethered to a pen and courted by a gent while a cleric is selling his wife to an army officer. She stands uncomfortably in an animal pen, tethered by her wrist while pigs snooze nearby.

The husband generally held the halter during the sale and handed it over to the purchaser as part of the accepted contract or ritual, which echoed the practice of handing over a beast to complete a legal sale. In Sabine Baring-Gould's account, Henry Frise argued that his marriage was both legal and Christian as he had kept hold of the halter until they were inside his house and shut the door, so it seems the halter was held from the door of the woman's home to her new one.

More variations in the ritual occurred: accounts from Arundel record the woman being led by the husband a mile out of town before he placed the halter on her,[23] others took the wife through a single tollgate, or three tollgates or three villages where we see the incorporation of the number three again. Apparently this was to collect a toll ticket. They must have had some charge for miscellaneous goods or animal as at the markets. But the mention of a tollgate puts limits on the idea of selling being an ancient practice, as the first tollgates were not built until the 1730s and it was some time before they became widespread. A sale in a beast market involved the handover of the receipt for the market toll as proof of ownership; this may have been a confusion or evolution of the meaning of the term. This again shows the rituals were in a constant state of flux, and what was accepted as ancient or established practice may have been merely often repeated.

Halters were not new inventions, but their use cannot be taken to suggest sales were of ancient origin. It is possible there was a deeper meaning to the halter's presence in sales, as Menefee cites from what we now class as fairy tales for children, but at the time were widely shared amongst adults, helping to pass the long winter evenings. In a world where witches and curses were still feared, the ideas in these tales carried more weight than they do today. There is a story, *The Magician and His Pupil* in which the father sells his son in the market, but doesn't sell his halter: that was a symbol of ownership.[24] This suggests the halter may not have arisen from the sale of animals, but was more akin to the handing over of a woman by her father upon marriage.

In 1837, a husband tracked down his wife who had eloped with another man. The injured husband demanded three pounds for her clothes, which was agreed on condition they go together to Wirksworth market and delivered her 'according to the law'. So this is yet another case where participants claimed the sale was legal, and that there were set procedures to ensure this. The public handover was accompanied by a declaration in which James Allen, the husband, affirmed he was 'bereaved of my wife by James Taylor of Shottle',[25] and asked James if he would buy her. The man agreed; and the money was handed over in the presence of a local man.

All this sounds like normal commercial practice. The wedding ring was returned to Allen to acknowledge the undoing of the marriage, and he received three sovereigns, seemingly another ritual involving the number three. This demand for payment from the husband seems to be about compensation, but the goodwill at the end suggests it was at least in part a matter of closure for the injured party. Perhaps he had found another wife and wished to move on. Or he may have been subject to mockery by friends and neighbours, so wished for some form of formal settlement.

The staging of the sale is the most discussed part of the ritual, as it was the most controversial due to its alleged humiliation of the woman, but there was a complementary part of the process, that of 'unmarrying', which often involved the woman taking off her ring and handing it back, as above and in Suffolk in 1835. At Mansfield market in 1848, a husband demanded his ring back, but his wife swapped it for a penny brass ring. In an Alfreton pub in 1882, the woman 'took off her wedding-ring and from that time considered herself the property of the purchaser'.[26]

There were examples of speeches to encourage bidding, such as the famous cases of the Carlisle farmer who sold his wife for a dog, and the banter by Rough Moey which were pure street theatre. In several instances, promises were made publicly as part of the ritual of the handover, and even wedding-style feasts were shared, as at Stamford in 1786. There may also have been local variations, such the new husband stepping into his predecessor's shoes.[27]

The ritual often ended with a celebration, as one account stated that Farmer Thompson took his new dog and went on a three-day bender with the proceeds. A former husband at Thetford 1839 'danced and sang for being rid of a troublesome, noisy wife'. But for real style, the prize still goes to the farmer of Ipswich in 1787 who paid for the bells to be rung in celebration.

9
WOMEN AS VICTIMS

A woman's ne'er so ruined but she can Revenge herself on her Undoer, Man
Lord Rochester

Eighteenth-century England is often seen through the novels of Jane Austen in which few women worked for a living, so most were constantly in search of a rich husband. But the country was still predominantly agricultural and women often worked long, hard hours to save for their own dowries. Their choice of a marriage partner was often based on their ability to provide for themselves and their intended children. But working women left no diaries, and only emerge from the fog of time in parish registers and court proceedings. They were often thought to be illiterate, but many taught their children basic literacy, and their homes were often papered with ballad sheets. Women outnumbered men, so many women never married. They spent their lives as gleaners, dairymaids, gardeners, domestic servants, seamstresses and shop assistants, and helped out in family businesses; they were often well informed and socially active. Women often campaigned for good causes such as the abolition of the slave trade and for women's rights as well as raising funds for churches and charities.

The Industrial Revolution was only possible because it was preceded by agricultural improvements which made many labour-intensive jobs redundant, especially for women at planting and harvest times. This coincided with a shift from fair trading at markets to the commodification of essential supplies, especially grain and dairy foods.

A woman became legally invisible on her marriage. Such sacrifice was justified as being of benefit to the family unit and thus to the woman. This seems draconian, and was at odds with much greater legal independence in Scotland and Europe at the time where women could often keep their property and name after marriage. But coverture meant that a man became responsible for her protection, which suggests it was a practice born out of war. Coverture claimed to echo God protecting his followers, and David and Boaz protecting their families. This combination of Christianity and men grabbing land from women extinguished families where the woman had no brothers, suggesting it was of Roman or Norman origin, as a means for foreign soldiers to settle and acquire property from the conquered.

This notion lingers even now in the ban on a woman giving evidence against her husband in court; the couple are treated as a single person, this would amount to her giving evidence against herself, which is clearly nonsense. Married couples were sometimes described as being like a pair of oxen, yoked together through a life based on hard work, hardly a romantic notion, but necessary in a world of small, close-knit communities, and marriage was based on co-operation and hard work, and intended to last until death. Parson Holland of eighteenth-century Somerset and other observers of rural life saw how couples who had been together a long time often closely followed each other to their graves.[1]

The term 'paternalism' is often applied to the rulers of the past, but this suggests there was a two-way relationship. Parents cared for their children who respected, and when necessary, cared for them in return, hence the common image in churches of the cycle of life in which the Grim Reaper was often shown mowing the mature crops to make way for the new. There is also a sense of such relationships passing down through generations, further bonding families together.

In mediaeval times, the rulers were part of extended families, so the term was apt. But after the Wars of the Roses, peace reduced the need for close alliances to unite in battles; people built larger houses, so they were no longer living on top of each other, and tempers were less likely to fray. Young sons of allies were no longer invited into families to forge bonds and help keep the peace, so large households increasingly employed servants rather than relatives.

From the mid-eighteenth century, the enforcement of coverture became less common. Newspapers increasingly included ads from husbands announcing their wives had left them and they would not be responsible for any debts the wife incurred from a certain date. Not only were women demanding independence, these ads show that this was increasingly accepted, at least on a local level. By the mid-nineteenth century, the legal system was recognising this shift, as an article from 1848 listed a number of crimes for which women could be convicted in their own right, such as scolding, riot, receiving stolen goods, assault, fraud, and keeping a bawdy house without her husband's consent. And yet the article concluded: 'Still conviction may be uncertain'.[2] This shows an element of swings and roundabouts for women and the law, and that just because a law existed did not mean perpetrators were not always reported for it, or miscreants were always punished.

The Poet Laureate Robert Southey echoed the above when he wrote in 1807:

> 'A woman is more inclined to be mutinous; they stand less in fear of the law, partly through ignorance, partly because they presume upon the privilege of their sex, and therefore in all public tumults they are foremost in violence and ferocity.'[3]

Southey was referring to the high visibility of women in eighteenth and early-nineteenth-century food riots, which were generally attributed to crop failures, but they happened in autumn, i.e. during the harvest, which was a time of plenty. True famines occurred in the spring when reserves were running low, so these women were objecting to a shift from fair trading in grain to speculation and hoarding of essential foodstuffs, a shift from the guarantees of food supplies at fair prices for locals to the commodification of, and speculation in, essentials. Women were well aware that their communities were being exploited and they knew why. The poor brought in the harvests, they transported them to market; they manned the toll roads and the canals, the granaries and mills, so they knew more about supply and demand than the local justices, no matter how well meaning.[4]

The 1740s were a time of great agricultural collapse, now known as 'the hungry forties'. The economy was so depressed that no major country estates were built, so it also became the lost decade of architecture. A fight broke out between women and farmers at Newport Pagnell in 1740. The women claimed no food should leave the country when there was such a shortage of it at home. They 'swore they would lose their lives before they would part with it'.[5] The food riots seem to have peaked in 1766, especially in the West Country, when the free market took off and collections were made to subsidise the price of foodstuffs to stop the poor from rioting. But this was also when reading of the Riot Act, ordering the troops to fire on rioters, became increasingly common, so the bravery of the women came to the fore.

The West of England was often considered to be deeply traditional. It was nearest to the American and West Indian colonies, so its economic focus was maritime, and it provided some of the country's finest mariners, from Drake to Dampier, which furthered the loss of males for much of the seventeenth and eighteenth centuries. This created a huge demand for food to export to the colonies, and in wartime, to the armed services. This contributed to the high levels of disturbances during the middle of the century, especially during the Seven Years' War when food rioting became common, and at times threatened to spread beyond the region, teetering on the brink of a national crisis. The riots happened mostly at ports where food was exported. In Exeter in 1757, farmers agreed amongst themselves to put their wheat on sale at the market for fifteen shillings per bushel, but the locals heard of their plans and sent the women to demand it be sold at the fair price of six shillings, which they achieved, to the great benefit of the poor weavers and woolcombers. Farmers claimed they would stop using the market, but would sell via private agreement. The women threatened to take the grain from their ricks.[6]

Women were prominent in the riots, but as Southey claimed, there was no desire to prosecute them; nor was there any real attempt to hold their men responsible. In 1765, Tiverton was beset by rioting –– especially by women —against the corporation. An account described them

> 'dashing in upon the Mayor through the windows of an inn, pulling off his wig and threatening to kill him if he did not sign a paper'.[7]

Women were involved in food riots in England for two centuries, which shows their independence and their contempt for the authorities. These working women present a huge challenge to the conception that women were inferior or less valued than men. When sufficiently roused to outrage, they were often braver, more determined to achieve results and more likely to take risks than their men. Perhaps they were less likely to be employed outside the house, so lived less in fear of being discharged for their rebelliousness. Or perhaps as they were the ones attending market, whether to sell their wares or supply their family with necessities, they exchanged gossip and information so could unite in action with greater ease than the men. It is possible that the marketplace and parish pump where they gathered were greater sites of rebellion than the inns and pubs frequented by the men.

The fact that riots happened at all is due to the shift in land ownership at the time. Many people grew rich from urban businesses or overseas investments and spent their wealth on building country mansions in extensive estates. But few of them lived there, so they had little interest in their tenants, and they were not available to serve as justices or distribute charity when necessary. Many wealthy men owned entire parishes; some owned hundreds of them. To avoid paying poor rates, they could allow cottages to decay and knock them down, forcing the tenants into an adjoining parish. Once this 'social cleansing' was complete, a parish could be declared 'closed' and no rates collected. Thus the image of benign lords of the manor caring for tenants and helping them in need was increasingly replaced in the eighteenth and nineteenth centuries.[8] When speculation in food caused riots, collections were made by gentry in towns to subsidise the price of essentials. There was often no equivalent in the countryside.

When women rioted, they showed they were not always the delicate creatures in need of masculine protection, who were so popular in the romantic fiction of the late Georgians. They were often strong, well informed, well organised and not to be messed with. The authorities knew it, and they were afraid. They were very afraid.

This is an extraordinary account of the empowerment of women when the concept of affordable food for all was being replaced by the free market. Subsidies were paid to export corn, a legacy from Tudor times when the population was so low; there was a surplus of grain which provided a major source of national income. Elsewhere, there were accounts of women standing up to armed soldiers, or trying to seize the copy of the Riot Act before it could be read to unleash the soldiery.[9]

Perhaps the most dramatic account comes from Tiverton in 1765 when women were again prominent in riots. These women did not conform to the image of starving peasants; nor did they attempt to hide what they had done. They were described in the press as Amazonians and Grecians. Many accounts of wife sales described the women as being as meek as cows; but these rioting women were tigers. Or perhaps they were being ironic, as cows have been known to kill their owners in defence of their calves. They remind us that our ancestors were far more diverse, more capable of responding to circumstances and of solving their own problems than many histories suggest

Men not only failed to control their women under the laws of coverture, they took advantage of the low risk of prosecution in a riot against the export of grain at Poole, Dorset, in 1737. The men threatened that if the women were molested a mob would destroy the ships and cargoes.[10]

It is impossible to see these women as being inferior to any man. They were strong, intelligent and brave. Women must have supported their men in riots against tollgates and enclosures, but it was in food riots where they were most visible. Eighteenth century Bristol was notorious for its mobs, and became famous as the site of the biggest riot of the nineteenth century in England. John Latimer, in his *Annals of Bristol*, was clear on why this was so, from 1801 — again during wartime shortages — when the price of food rose beyond the wages of the poor:

> 'the flour of rice oats, barley, rye and peas was largely resorted to as a substitute; some housewives even attempted to make loaves from potatoes: while nettles were gathered and cooked in lieu of ordinary vegetables.
>
> When prices had attained their maximum, some of the poor, driven almost mad by the misery of their children, made one or two riotous attacks on the stall-keepers in the city markets, and soldiers had to be called in to prevent further outbreaks.'[11]

At a food riot at Tiverton in 1754, an officer volunteered to fire on the mob. The women grabbed him and confiscated his sword; he never got it back or lived down the shame of being unmanned by mere women.[12] So the women also knew and used the symbolism of emasculation and shame.

Such behaviour, in maintaining the status quo and local traditions is often described as conservative, suggesting that women were against progress, but they knew fair trading was of benefit to their communities and that change was dangerous. This was not just a clash between the women and farmers; it was also about local justice being threatened by distant powers. So-called progress was clearly detrimental, and they were against the speculators whose actions threatened widespread starvation.

No mention was ever made of the marital status of the women. It could be that single women were able to act independently. Anger and protest are often associated with young, single people with no responsibilities who have less to lose. There were always more women than men in the population, so it is possible this is another aspect to the angry, rebellious women.

This independence was of long standing, as the Swiss physician Thomas Platter's account of his visit to London in 1599 claimed that young women rode on horseback instead of in carriages, and had 'great liberty of action'. But he noted that

> 'the ducking stool, wooden cage and house of correction put some curb upon their pranks and machinations'.[13]

So even then, there were limits. It seems the loss of the moral control that had been exerted by the pre-Reformation church had led to women becoming rowdier as well as more independent, hence the perceived need for physical punishments to replace the religious practices of shaming.

The important point here is that in all these instances, the women appear to be recognisably modern. Their lives were light years away from the characters of Jane Austen. They tended to marry in their mid to late twenties, a year or two younger than their husbands, as most of them had to earn enough to set up house together. Most were from families either too poor or with too many daughters to provide them with dowries. Marital practices had changed from the sixteenth and seventeenth centuries when friends and families put immense pressure on young people to marry for money to ensure future security. It was believed that if a marriage failed, the community failed. But there seems to have been no requirement, especially among the upper classes, for a woman to be willing. Yet even by contemporary standards, there were abuses.

John Wilmot the Earl of Rochester was in need of a rich wife, so his mother tried to arrange a match with Elizabeth Malet, a wealthy heiress but was turned down. So he took matters into his own hands: in 1665 the young woman was kidnapped from a coach near Charing Cross and taken to a secret location. But before Wilmot could have his evil way with her, he was arrested. His defence was ignorance of the law.[14] It seems his only regret was that he was caught. This attempted kidnap and attempted rape in the centre of the capital is shocking. What made it worse was that a well-educated young man could dare to claim ignorance of the law. Such behaviour has always been wrong.

By the early eighteenth century, even in the highest levels of society, notions of romance and affection had become accepted as major considerations in marriage. In the late eighteenth century, a match was arranged between the families of the heir to the Duke of Leeds and Lady Villiers. They were sent away to the seaside, but when they failed to fall in love, the match was abandoned.[15] By European standards, the 'middling sorts' had also acquired extraordinary independence in their choice of partners.

For the lower classes, by the time they married, many had long since left home, either to become servants on farms or in great houses, or to towns and cities in search of higher wages and more exciting lives, so they often chose partners without the advice of older friends and families. It is also possible that they delayed marriage as long as possible to enjoy their freedom to the utmost. Despite the insistence that women were the weaker sex, some worked underground in the mines and in forges. Some female prize fighters were almost as popular as the men, such as 'Bruising Peg' who in 1768 fought an opponent at Spa Fields for the prize of a new shirt, and beat her adversary in a terrible manner.[16] Women ran foot races, though — unlike the men — they were not naked.

By the time they married, women knew their value. Agricultural servants were hired at annual fairs, where they stood in a line close to the boxes holding their clothing and meagre possessions. They negotiated their wages with employers so knew their value, and knew what was fair. At the Statute Fair at Aylesbury in 1825, ploughmen and carters were offered from eight to ten pounds a year, and less skilled labourers from six to eight. A good dairymaid earned ten pounds a year and other female servants about six.[17] Thus in the early nineteenth century, women's wages kept pace with those of the men in the countryside.

These wages seem pathetically low, but they included food and accommodation with the farmer's family. Farm workers had minimal outgoings, so these levels were better than they seem. The women were paid about the same as men, but as the agricultural revolution got under way, the large farm houses declined, workers had to find their own accommodation, and payment was increasingly made in cash rather than kind, so most workers became worse off. Wages generally fell behind the cost of living, but especially so for women, as the wages for able-bodied male servants who often worked with dangerous farm machinery, had risen to twelve to fifteen pounds per year whilst women's wages had stagnated at six to ten pounds.[18]

Men were worked to death on Suffolk farms in the nineteenth century, and despite their high levels of skill, were paid derisory wages. When the agricultural depression hit in the 1880s thousands of men —often the youngest and fittest — emigrated to new lives in the colonies. This depression was probably caused by the completion of long-distance railways in North America and the expansion of farming in Australia which allowed the mass importation of cheap grain. This also caused a shift in England from agrarian farming to livestock, which required fewer workers. Such conditions must have put a huge strain on marriages. This is claimed to be the reason for the men having little interest in improving themselves, or joining unions for their own defence, whilst their wives were drawn to join the Women's Institute for company and improvement. When a man came home exhausted — then as now — the woman's tongue, exercised only by baby talk, could open the floodgates to conversation. The man might complain of her talking too much, she might complain that he didn't listen.

Paying women low wages even now is defended on the assumption that women did not have careers as they would leave to start a family, so there was no point in an employer investing time in training them. To compensate for this lack of respect, attempts were made to present women as moral guardians of the home and family, even making them responsible for controlling men when they ran riot. In early North American settlements such as Chesapeake, 'bride boats' full of single women were sent in the hope of encouraging the men to settle down. In the early colony of New South Wales, they were seen as 'God's Police'. But this notion was seriously undermined in the early days of the East India Company in Madras. Heat and disease laid waste to the scores of young men who went there, and they took to heavy drinking and consorting with the locals. Bridal boats were sent out to calm them down, but most of the women also took to heavy drinking and consorting with the locals.

William Cobbett in his *Rural Rides* praised the work done by women in the home: carding, spinning and weaving woollen clothes for the family. This made use of local materials, cost the family nothing, and kept the women and children employed at home, which helped family cohesion and the education of the children as stories were told whilst they worked, enabling every family member to contribute to their survival. This was often neglected or underrated as it brought no money into the home; but it stopped money going out, and they could sell any surplus. The cotton cloth of the factories had to be paid for, and was less warm and water- and fire-resistant, so was less suited to British conditions.

There is a problem in reading modern women's history. The huge advances made by feminists in the 1970s are often taken to suggest that before that, women were always victims of male laws and male oppression as is so often portrayed. In part, this may have been based on the assumption that, as lifestyles improved over time, so did women's rights, therefore our ancestors must have been much worse off than modern women. But some decades ago, when E.P. Thompson was lecturing adults about the history of women's historical oppression, he was interrupted by one of his students, who with her peers felt insulted by his claims of female victimhood. She claimed: "We women knew out rights, you know. We knew what was our due"'.[19] He realised that women had always had their own social spaces, their own means of achieving respect and payment for their work.

His audience probably comprised at least some women who had been adults during the previous war when they filled the mud-encrusted boots of the absent men in farms and factories. When the men returned, women were angry at being made unemployed, at the loss of independence and income they had earned. The same was true during World War I, and in the English Civil War, when women of all classes defended their homes, town gates and families. This also applied to much of the eighteenth century when England was almost constantly at war with one or more of her continental neighbours. So throughout much of this period, many women were working alongside or replacing the men.

This is relevant in the area of marital relations, especially relating to wife sales. Despite the legal power men technically had over women, the laws were designed by, and for, rich men who needed to keep money and property in their families. They may have lived on Mars for all they knew or cared about ordinary people. Newspapers were littered with claims that wife sales were illegal or that they should be. Why was the situation never clarified? Why were so many cases dragged into courts and left to local justices to cause confusion, with long discussions on how to deal with each case as they saw fit?

Records show some wife sales were what the press claimed, i.e., brutal, ignorant, illegal acts. But for many women, being sold was liberating. If the husband was a brute, or if for whatever reason, the couple had never been compatible, the wife could be much better off. A wife sale was deemed legal only if the woman was willing, whereas many women through history were bullied, coerced or forced by poverty into unsuitable and sometimes abusive and violent marriages. Comments were often made about how meek the women seemed, which drew parallels with the cows whose stalls they were sometimes tied up in. But this does not mean they were being forced into the sale. If a husband really was a brute and demanded a sale, the wife would have had no choice. Once a relationship had reached this stage, it was beyond repair and could only get worse, possibly leading to violence or even murder. Wife selling was a solution to a problem, whereas the authorities' only advice was for them to go home and live peaceably together, which was no solution at all. They'd probably been trying that for years.

There were cases where the woman was clearly in favour of the sale, as in 1840 when a wife at Loughborough was so keen to be sold that she put the rope around her body herself.[20] She was bought by a sergeant of dragoons quartered in the town so must have been swept off her feet by a man in uniform. But there were also incidents where women were prosecuted for their roles in the sales, and some which suggest the women actually instigated it. The account of the 'Wife Selling Extraordinary' in Plymouth in 1822 claimed the woman had put a value on herself, and arranged for an ostler at the local inn to bid on her behalf when her intended partner failed to show. Many women — perhaps the majority — had already set up house with their new partner, forcing the husband to track them down to arrange the sale.[21] Many others were accused — directly or by implication — of being untrue. Where high prices were paid, especially if there was only a single bidder, the sale was probably held to avoid expensive legal action. There were also a few cases where both had strayed, all of which show the women to be far from victims, huffing and puffing from male editors notwithstanding. The editors were not there, so they didn't know.

The law of coverture, and society in general, did not just expect women to be submissive. Men were expected to be strong, manly and independent, to be master of their own home and business, so again was suited to violent or unstable times. When women misbehaved, the implication was that the man was weak, unmanly, a cuckold. George I was often mocked for being a cuckold, based on rumours of his wife's misbehaviour, but also due to the perceived lack of legitimacy to his claim to the English throne, doubling the assault on his manhood.

An extraordinary wife sale happened in 1775 when Jonathan Jowett, a farmer from near Rotherham agreed to sell his wife. He delivered her in a 'regular procession' and Jowett wore ram's horns with the words 'cornuted by William Taylor' painted on them in gold. A crowd of over a thousand spectators were claimed to have witnessed it.[22]

In earlier times, such performances could turn violent, as this shaming street theatre, or 'rough music' for a shrew, a scold or husband beater, as in Wiltshire in 1618. Hundreds of men, one of them suitably attired with horns, many of them armed, marched to a woman's house where they played a cacophony of music. The woman was dragged into the mud, beaten and threatened with the cucking stool at Calne.[23] This has echoes, though much abated, in Hardy's *The Mayor of Casterbridge*. Cuckoldry was not only about the woman straying, it was about male power.

It is hard to imagine anything more embarrassing or degrading than this bizarre incident. But the fact that the husband apparently volunteered for it suggests the problems with his marriage were so well known that he was pre-empting or joining in the public mockery of his neighbours. No date is provided for its origins, but near Kirby Muxloe is Cuckold's Haven. 'It is exactly midway between Hinckley and Leicester, so was equally available to the deserted husbands of either town.'[24] So it seems cuckoldry was a major problem. But as with wife selling, the numbers make no sense. If there was a surplus of women, why were the men being abandoned by them?

In 1753 in *The Manchester Mercury*, some additions to the recent Marriage Act were suggested, showing the language of rough music and mockery was still widely known, including:

'If a man marries a woman of ill fame, knowing her to be, he shall have a pair of horns painted on his door or if she be a known scold, a couple of Neat's [ox] tongues in the room of them.'[25]

The most reprinted account of a wife sale seems to have been that of Farmer Thompson at Carlisle, who gave a humorous speech describing his wife, as a serpent, his tormentor, a daily devil and much more, warning his audience to avoid her as a mad dog, cholera and an active volcano.[26]

In fairness, Thompson gave high praise for his wife's housekeeping ability, which in earlier times should have been enough for a successful marriage, but here again is a sense of a man active in the world with a woman frustrated at home. As was the case with many other husbands, the wife's behaviour was blamed for them parting. In 1819 'Moll' from Bilston was praised for her ability to cook, wash, bake and brew, as well as 'swear like a trooper an' fight like a game cock.'[27] How could any red-blooded man resist her? These and others find echoes in jokes about mothers-in-law, dating from the post-war housing shortage which prevented young couples from setting up households on their own.

There are a number of cases where 'willingness' was problematic, i.e. the wife was willing to be sold, but turned down the purchaser, so there was a conflict here between the woman and the concept of the open market sale, which in turn shows that women were not being treated as dumb beasts as the press often claimed because animals did not have a right to refuse to be sold. The wife of Waddilove, innkeeper of Grassington was sold to Mr Lupton in 1807; a guinea was paid as a deposit but when Linton returned with the remainder of the fee the following day, Mrs Waddilove was not willing. The deposit had already been spent on the previous night's celebrations, and Mr Lupton departed, 'perhaps to become a wiser man'.[28]

There is no description of 'Mattie' who was led to Wenlock market in the 1830s, but her behaviour summons up an image of a sturdy, hard-working countrywoman and a husband of lesser stature. When they arrived at the market place he lost his nerve but Mattie was adamant: 'Let be, your rogue. I wull be sold. I wants a change.'[29]

A Bristol broadside from 1822 entitled *A Modern Market Scene* [30] states that the woman knew she could not be disposed of by private contract, so she had some knowledge of the law. She agreed to a public auction, again challenging the image of women as passive victims. The case of the 'Modern Delilah" who lured her husband into the arms of a waiting press gang[31] has already been mentioned.

The incident headed 'Wife Selling Extraordinary' in Plymouth provides a window into the chaotic love life of a woman of independent means, but with no access to sound advice. A month after she married, she gave birth to a child, much to her husband's surprise. She moved in with another man, and had a second child. Her new paramour had agreed to bid for her, but when he failed to arrive, she got the ostler from a local inn to bid on her behalf.[32] The husband would have been within his rights to have thrown her out into the street or sued for divorce, but he seemed to have been more bewildered than angry at his wife's behaviour.

There were also instances where the marital problems became noisily apparent, with some dramatic street theatre. In Bristol in 1815, a mason called Cassell put his wife up for sale in St Thomas's Market; a bidder immediately appeared, and the three pounds was accepted. But it appeared that he was a proxy for the wife's favourite swain.[33] This raises the question of how many swains she had, and how she got away with such behaviour. The three then had a 'curious dialogue' which seems to have gone against the hot-tempered wife, as she then claimed the two children were not her husband's, which must have done little to calm the situation. The husband threatened to auction her in a public house the following night.

The famous case from about 1830 of 'Rough Moey' at Wednesbury in the Black Country involved a middle-aged man, his face scarred from smallpox and a gunpowder explosion, so not married for his looks, who had turned his attentions to another woman. When he came home drunk his young wife, 'as pretty as her situation in life allowed',[34] would unstrap his wooden leg and thrash him with it. She found herself a decent young man to be sold to, and who Moey suggested may have been her baby's father. She was hardly a victim, but the question here is why — as with other young wives — she married him in the first place. There was no mention of family or friends beyond her beau present at the sale, so was she an orphan, or an apprentice or servant out of work who had married him as an alternative to the poor house? Cobbett ranted against the huge costs of military pensions which were seen as accepted in contrast to the opposition to the costs of poor relief. Some took this further, claiming that a woman marrying a military pensioner was doing her national duty in accepting a secure income for life to produce children who could grow up to become soldiers. A woman who married a former soldier was set up for life. Moey's gunpowder injury and wooden leg suggest he was a war veteran, but for his young wife, this guarantee of security was not enough to make her endure his bad behaviour.

In 1849 a waterman named Ashton was in Hull Infirmary when his wife eloped with her lover and took many of the old man's belongings. On his release, the husband tracked the couple down. They agreed to a sale, and she was knocked down to her lover. Free at last, she 'Snapped her fingers in her husband's face, and exclaimed "there, good for naught, that's more than thee would fetch."'[35] This is one of the few examples where our sympathies tend to go against the woman. But the question here again is — as with so many other young women — why she married him in the first place. Was she in need of his steady income?

There is no doubt that the law was hard on women, but that did not mean those enforcing it were without compassion, understanding, and even humour. At Smithfield market in 1841 Mary Ann Barratt, a seventeen-year-old who had been unhappily married for a whole four months, but who had objected to being sold, was taken before the magistrates. The alderman joked that, 'if husbands and wives were allowed to separate, Smithfield would be too small!' He then explained to the frightened young woman,

> 'how the sale was illegal and advised her to avoid her purchaser in case her husband could abandon her on the grounds of adultery. He

then urged her and her friends to get him arrested 'for this scandalous outrage'.³⁶

It is hard to see any happy outcome for this, though Mary Ann at least had a girl friend brave enough to speak up for her in court, and they left together.

Finally, here is an example which is not a wife sale, but was described as shocking at the time, and shows how hard ordinary people struggled to survive. It involved a "memorandum of separation'.. between William Capas and Emily Hickson of Birmingham. They agreed to live together and support each other for the rest of their lives. The woman admitted signing the document and said she believed a lawyer was paid one pound and fifteen shillings to draw it up. Capas was fined two shillings and sixpence, and the bench commented in strong terms on the document. The account does not make clear what the full story was here, but this document, with its apparent legality, is an extraordinary example of a young couple entering into a mutually supportive relationship and living together, but with no mention of intimacy. This was, in effect, a sexless marriage, which, in the absence of a welfare state, and the fact that the law was so heavily biased against the woman, seems perfectly sensible, and utterly revolutionary. The fact that it was seen as shocking is further evidence of how out of touch the laws were in terms of dealing with the realities of life for ordinary people, especially women.³⁷

Much has been written in this chapter about how women could be stronger and more independent than they seemed. But men could also be gentle and empathic, even silly at times. Today's men are commended for their humanity, for their ability to express their emotions rather than bottling everything up which is often linked to their high rate of suicides. They are expected to share the housework and any father who refuses to change nappies is rightly condemned.

But even in the late seventeenth century, occasional glimmers of light into the hearts and minds of men can be found. A cleric wrote to his best friend on his wedding day. He should have been with the wedding party, but it seems he was so excited, he had to commit his extraordinary thoughts and feelings to paper, even though they would not be read for some time. If this was written now, he would have been setting the internet alight with his excitement. He writes of how he has been transformed from 'an Insipid, Uninspiring Batchelour into a Loving Passionate Husband,' and 'I am going to lose my Maidenhead'. He had been warned by older men of the dangers he was about to face overnight, but 'I hope she will be mercifull, and not suffer a young beginner to dye in the Experiment.'[38]

10

SCOLDING WOMEN

Slamming their doors, stamping their high heels, banging their irons and saucepans, - the eternal flaming racket of the female
   John Osborne[1]

When a reason was given for selling a wife, the commonest seems to have been that she had strayed, which was the only grounds for divorce until modern times. But running a close second were claims that 'she was not warranted quiet', 'could swear like a trooper and fight like a game cock'. Or from Gloucester in 1838 when the man praised his wife for being a good housewife, but "her got such a tongue, and kips on nagging from monnin' to midnight. I can't have a moment's piece for her tongue."[2] Another complained 'she had a tongue in her mouth'; well, where else would it be? But women speaking out, or speaking in anger seems to have been a problem for some time. To these cases we can probably add a number where the husband claimed they did not get along, which could become unbearable within weeks or months of the marriage.

Farmer Thompson of Carlisle provided one of the most famous wife sales, largely due to his humorous speech. It was full of wry humour, and respect for his wife, whom he praised as being a good housekeeper, and yet the sale was unusual as there seems not to have been anyone else involved. He was driven to separate as he could no longer stand his wife's behaviour. Maybe he was just too old to adapt to married life, but this conflict has been an enduring trope that has endured into the modern age. 'Henpecked husbands' were long a standard in comedy, as were claims of the woman wearing the trousers and even the post-war mother-in-law jokes

Women had traditionally worked beside their husbands in the family businesses, with childcare provided by servants or older children. But in the course of the eighteenth century, these positions were changed, with women withdrawing to the domestic world. To provide them with a sense of value, their role as mothers was upgraded, as teachers of moral behaviour as well as literacy and numeracy. Comments were made in the press of how wagons taking farm produce to market returned full of books for the young ladies. But there were still too few men to go round, so young ladies were encouraged to be quiet and demure in order to attract a husband, which in itself suggests the opposite caused problems.

They were also expected to be productive, with middle and upper-class women often being depicted with their embroidery, and lower classes plaiting straw or sewing and repairing family clothes. For centuries the defining skill of a single woman was spinning, hence they were known as spinsters. Caroline Herschel grew up in northern Germany where the practice of sitting quietly, (*stillsitzen*) was encouraged for women while they remained visibly active. From *stillsitzen* derives the German word *Sittsamkeit* – 'demureness or modesty'.[3] She applied these skills to her astronomy; she sat patiently gazing at the heavens through many cold damp nights to make more discoveries than her more famous brother. The much-underrated skills in design and precision shown in embroidery also helped female astronomers and artists; women were banned from life drawing, but several became famous for their illustrations of nature, such as Sarah Lee who produced a book on English fish, and Elizabeth Blackwell the botanical illustrator.

The link with women and science was encouraged in the

daughter of Lord Byron, who was educated in mathematics in the hope of preventing her following her father into madness. The result was that the woman later known as Ada Lovelace became a pioneer in computers and programming. But this enforced passivity was often held responsible for scolding as women's outbursts were blamed on them sitting still for too long, causing their energies to build up without any outlet. Lack of exercise is today widely linked with depression; working indoors causes vitamin D deficiency which has the same effect, hence the female population probably had higher risks of mental illness than the men whose lives were more often based outdoors.

William Cobbett's early nineteenth-century travel journal *Rural Rides* praised the work done by women in the home. They carded, spun, wove and stitched woollen clothes for the family, as opposed to the cotton of the factories, which had to be paid for, and were less warm and did not repel water or fire. The women's work made use of local materials, cost the family nothing, and kept the women and children employed at home, so helped value all members of the family unit. Its importance was often neglected or underrated as it seldom actually brought money home, but it stopped it going out which is the other side of the same coin. The huge cotton mills of the Industrial Revolution did not just suck in the population from the countryside; the cloth they made undermined the value of homespun, so caused more hardship for those already struggling to survive. Cobbett wrote of the ideal situation where wives and daughters spun or sewed, men and boys ploughed fields and industries were scattered across the region, so a mixed economy was the most successful for ordinary people.[4]

Cobbett also described how, until the eighteenth century, most farms were based around large houses where family and servants lived and ate together; it was like an extended family wherein women developed specialist skills and a social environment where they could chat and sing as they worked in the kitchen, the laundry, the brewery and the dairy. But these large farms went into decline from the late eighteenth century, largely due to the numerous enclosure acts. Nuclear-family units became the norm, and women were increasingly isolated except when helping with the harvest. More of their days were spent with their children than with their friends, their conversations on more of an infantile level. They also had to be constantly watching of their children in houses with dangers from boiling kettles, open fires and candles, toppling crockery, and falling down stairs or into coal-holes. The window tax led to houses becoming darker and more poorly ventilated, so the family health deteriorated. More and more young people moved to towns and cities in search of better wages and more interesting lives, so the countryside was increasingly populated by older people.

This is where the story becomes recognisably modern. Men worked outside the home, often with colleagues, so could talk and joke, eat and rest together; when they came home, they were often too tired for conversation. At the ironworks in Middlesbrough, men worked exhausting shifts which were constantly changing through night and day, which meant their sleep was poor in quantity and quality. They often came home and collapsed into exhausted slumber. An explosion happened at the top of one of the smelters and a man fell in. Another close by 'nearly lost his head' and stepped forward to follow him. Another dazed man was grabbed before he was lost.[5]

For many women unable to work for various reasons, their chances of socialising with peers and friends were at church or the market if either were in reach. In good weather, they might chat to neighbours in the street, but before modern household appliances, housework was heavy and time-consuming. In a place like Middlesbrough, the air was filthy, so washing and dusting were endless. A woman's tongue — exercised largely by baby talk all day — was often in need of conversation when her husband came home. The man might complain of her talking too much, she might complain that he didn't listen. The playwright and politician R.B. Sheridan claimed that men were passionate creatures, though not necessarily prone to scolding. But women were less exposed to stressful situations so coped with them less well than men.[6]

We are all apes, and apes can be noisy, demonstrative creatures. But we are the top of the evolutionary scale. We are *homo erectus*; we walk upright. We have opposable thumbs, so can make and use tools. But most important of all, we speak. Perhaps we should rename ourselves *homo loquans*, because without speech there would be no means of recording information, so no science, no arts, no history. Speech is something that needs to be practised to improve our skills, but it also needs to be exercised, just as a dog or a bear kept in a cage can turn vicious, which is probably why women have long been criticised — and sometimes punished — for being scolds.

Men were reported for scolding, but it seems cases of females scolding, and punishments increased from about 1560 to become a veritable epidemic. One source blames the epidemic on a 'crisis in gender relations' and that there seemed to be a rising sense that women were a threat to the patriarchal power.[7] Women brawled with their neighbours, at home, in the street and even in church. From late medieval times, scolding was generally punished with a small fine, but from about 1550 the range of punishments increased, from the pillory, being paraded round the parish on a tumbrill, and various forms of stools, even a trebuchet, which sounds like an early ducking stool.[8]

Urbanisation was also blamed for the rise in scolding, with more people living in close proximity to each other, with no sound insulation so combined with less access to the countryside, this was a factor. But the Reformation seems to have played a role. There were fewer religious festivals where women could relax and celebrate with neighbours. There was less involvement for women as they no longer prayed to saints, decorated the church and used it as a social space to meet their neighbours. The rise in scolding paralleled the rise in witchcraft accusations which also fits, as when the monasteries closed, priests were given pensions and often married, whereas the women were thrown out onto the streets where they were poor and isolated, so often treated as vagrants or worse. Many probably made use of their knowledge of herbalism and medicine which they had practised as nuns, but if their treatments failed or if there were some unfortunate outcome, they had nobody to defend them in court. In the early seventeenth century punishments for scolding varied widely, but in Westminster, a woman was ducked. When she was charged again, she was dragged across the Thames by a boat, which seems to echo punishments for witches.[9]

Scolding was not just cited as a source of marital breakdown. Unlike wife selling, it had long been an indictable offence. Some women were accused of keeping a neighbourhood awake by shouting and screaming. This behaviour is now recognisable as a form of mental illness. A source claimed that one woman not only annoyed her family and neighbours, she cast 'a general stigma upon the whole sex'.[10] A suggestion was made that such vixens should be transported to the colonies or taxed to try to reform them. Scolds were even held responsible for the large number of bachelors, many of whom were allegedly afraid of marriage for fear that a wife might turn into a scold from whom they would never be freed.[11]

Local parishes were forced to build and maintain engines of punishment, i.e. stocks, pillories, whipping posts and ducking stools for the disciplining and shaming of miscreants. Ducking stools were initially used on market fraudsters, when bakers and brewers sold underweight goods, but this punishment was later commuted to fines. Suggestions have been made that this was sexist, but fraud is an economic crime, so a fine was more appropriate. Late medieval punishments for scolds and market fraudsters had been for them to be dragged round the parish on a sledge to publicise their shame, so was inflicted by the churches who mostly owned the markets, the major open space, so probably where a lot of scolding happened.

Ducking was also earlier used to punish fornicators, adulterers and papists —those who committed moral crimes — to wash away their sins, and seems to have had parallels with baptism in which sins were washed away. Again, this seems to have been used by religious rather than civic authorities. In the early English colony of Jamestown, the Dale Code was introduced, based on rules devised by a Dutch prince to control his troops in battle. 'Intemperate railings' against the authorities became a capital offence, on the same level as murder and sodomy. Blasphemy and failure to attend church were likewise punished with the utmost severity.[12] Thus the severity of punishment reflected the wider state of society at the time. Ducking stools were expensive to build and maintain. After immersion in water, they probably didn't dry out, so rotted. Small parishes seldom used them, and in some cases preferred to pay fines for their absence.[13]

Being tied to a chair on a moveable arm and immersed in water became firmly associated with rowdy women. When a bridge was being proposed across the Firth of Forth in 1775, an article suggested boats should attend to rescue anyone who might fall into the water.

> 'But one of those viragos commonly called scold-wives are expected there, as the boats will not take such up, at least until well ducked.'[14]

Thus, being a scold meant a woman ceased to be recognised as human. But being driven to such extreme behaviour, the woman had probably already stopped caring.

This immersion in a cold and probably filthy pond seems like overkill for a woman being a bit rowdy, but for a woman to be reported to the authorities, her behaviour must have been ongoing and she must have alienated her friends, family and neighbours for them to have made such accusations, though there were a few instances where the charges formed part of ongoing disputes. They were generally given several warnings to behave before being punished. Keeping their neighbourhood awake all night requires stamina, so they were rarely noted as old; they tended to be associated with women of a certain age, sometimes — but not always — associated with drink.

In 1736, a man tried to hang himself on Chelsea Common; when cut down, he claimed he had been driven to such a dreadful act by his wife being a scold.[15] In 1721, a woman became so agitated when scolding her servant that she died.[16] In 1726, a woman was convicted of being a common scold and disturber of the peace; she was sentenced to two months' hard labour in the house of correction.[17] Yet in 1732, 'the Tyger of Westminster' was put on trial for being a common scold. When she was found not guilty, in part at least on technical grounds, it was 'to the great satisfaction of many of the best Housewives of the parish who apprehended that if Prosecution of this Nature was too much encouraged it might infringe their English liberty.'[18] Was this liberty to scold or was it to do with what she was saying? Yet again, this story this item is hard to comprehend at this distance

Allan Fea claimed

> 'in Georgian times this mode of cooling down a virago's wrath was not so prevalent, though still resorted to, and even in the early part of the last [i.e. nineteenth] century the 'stool', professional or improvised, was resorted to as a last resource in obstinate cases.'[19]

The decline in scolding seems to have paralleled other improvements for women. Witchcraft ceased to be a crime in 1736, and the lack of men left plenty of room for women to be educated and to become successful and famous in a wide range of fields. In Bath, one third of their blue plaques commemorating residences of the famous are for Georgian women. But there were huge regional variations, probably reflecting women's access to employment in and outside the home, the closeness of communities etc.

In Suffolk in 1840 the press claimed the cucking stool had been seldom used in almost two hundred years and most people had forgotten it existed.[20] In York in 1854 they claimed to have discontinued its use a hundred years previously 'but now we live in more gallant times when anyone can express their loquacity with impunity.'[21] An early twentieth-century source suggests it may need to be revived as a result of the 'rapid strides of women's emancipation'.[22] This sounds like a man who had his dinner at the club or in the dog.

Ducking was the most spectacular of punishments as it often attracted noisy crowds, and the woman was often reported as screaming as she was ducked, so the penalty had a strong element of street theatre. The legal system often inflicted minor punishments for first-time offenders, escalating if the person failed to learn from it and reform. Ducking was generally claimed not to be a life-threatening, but many poor women had only one set of clothes, so risked colds or fatal pneumonia, especially if the punishment was administered in the middle of winter.

The assumption seems to have been that the water was clean, and some are noted as being in rivers, especially on the south bank of London's Thames. But this was so polluted that the Houses of Parliament were emptied in the mid-century, the result of 'the great stink' in 1857. Some ponds were used to wash animals or to receive waste which could also make the woman ill. Allan Fea provides an inappropriately light-hearted description from a century ago with a picture of a surviving ducking stool in Warwick:

'The labour of trundling the lady-scold to a handy pond or river was by no means arduous, but rather a labour of love, if the husband assisted to see that the lowered chair in which his spouse was strapped was raised again with promptitude.'[23]

There seems to have been a widespread assumption that ducking was meant to punish not to kill, and one source claims there were almost no accounts of death, but some of injury.[24] Yet this same book features an image on its cover of a woman in a ducking stool who drowned at Ratcliffe Highway in East London,[25] so she must have been ducked in the Thames, probably near some filthy outflow. Tudor and Stuart legal commentators stated that

'scolds are to be ducked over head and ears into the water in a ducking stool.'[26]

It may not have been the intention to severely harm or kill the scold, but the ducker probably had little experience, the water may have been surging, and the woman may have been struggling or hysterical. There is also an account of a ducking at high tide in Southampton in the late fifteenth century, used 'at full sea'.[27] If the arm of the machine was rotten, it could break and the woman would have no way of extricating herself from the chair so would likely drown. Ducking was a terrifyingly inexact science.

It seems incomprehensible that the term 'labour of love' could be applied to such torture, but it shows the husband could limit the extent of his wife's punishment, though he could not protect her from punishment by being held responsible for her crime under the law of coverture. But the account continues:

> 'By means of ropes attached to the farther end of the balance the dipping could be carried out to meet the requirement of the case, the limit of time being when bubbles cease to rise.'[28]

Just pause for a moment and read that again.

Now tell yourself that ducking was not meant to kill a woman. No original source is provided, so this may have been a misinterpretation. But in the context of the above, maybe not.

There was another — terrifying — form of punishment, or torture known as the scold's bridle or brank. But it seems to have been seldom used, and it is unclear under what conditions. It was found in the North and West, some were foreign-built, of wood and leather rather than the more recognised one of metal which was similar to the medieval torture implement the iron maiden. It may have originated in Scotland and spread when they joined the union.[29] It was a metal frame secured over the woman's head with a metal tongue forced into her mouth. She would be paraded round the marketplace on market day, then tied up like a beast for several hours to be thoroughly shamed. Several bridles have also been found in the former slave colonies of the West Indies.

As with so many other engines of punishment this seems to have a military origin. In the absence of purpose-built jails, prisoners were often kept in cellars or dungeons, but if an army was on the move, such an object would have controlled the prisoner, especially if they were a small group trying to evade capture. If a brank was worn and the person's hands tied, it would have been very difficult to escape, or to call out for help if they passed a settlement.

The bridle is generally assumed to have been merely to silence a woman's tongue, but if the woman resisted, she could break her teeth or even her jaw. In the absence of modern dental surgery, such injuries could be fatal either by causing infections or by preventing her from eating solid food. Fea provides us with yet another unapologetically non-feminist take on this:

> 'In the seventeenth century the brank, or scold's bridle, was introduced to lighten the labours of the stool, and in this there was no fear of its victim lashing her oppressors with her tongue during operations, for fastened to the metal framework which enclosed the head was an iron plate, which, fitting over the tongue, enforced a rest.'[30]

A Dr Plott wrote in his History of Staffordshire that the brank was preferable to the ducking stool which endangered the health of the victim and also allowed them to be noisy between each dip, which apparently defeated the purpose of the punishment. He praised the effectiveness of the brank as it restrained the tongue and was not removed until the victim had been shamed into silence.[31] The change of punishment seems to have reflected advances in medicine, shifting from the ancient concept of cooling a person whose temperament was overheated. The ducking was a form of rowdy street theatre in which crowds often encouraged the punishment and were delighted by the woman's distress. The Westminster stool was in Green Park, an area known for public entertainments and was apparently still in use into the 1760s, so was one of the last.[32]

The fact that women were punished at all is significant, because single women were under the control of their fathers or male relatives. When a woman married, she became legally invisible under the law of coverture; all her property and possessions became the property of her husband, and she lost the legal and commercial independence of a widow or single woman. But when women became widows they gained far more control over their lives and could often act on behalf of themselves and their families. In medieval times, when men went abroad on business, pilgrimage or war, their wives had full powers to run their family and businesses. Defoe claimed that the best skill a woman could learn was how to run her husband's business, as if he died, the alternative would be the poorhouse for her and her children.

The Packingtons were a powerful family in Buckinghamshire and in 1572, the widow of Thomas 'issued a writ in her own name as "Lord and owner of the town of Aylesbury"' appointing burgesses for the constituency.'[33] Thus, in the absence of a male head of the family, a woman held as much power as a man. But she was only filling his shoes to ensure the continuation of the family. This did not represent female independence or liberation in the modern sense, but the image of couples being yoked together as a pair of oxen meant that if one stumbled, the other had to bear the extra load.

Examples of scolding can be found in the press; they seem to cover a similar time frame to wife sales but are less frequent, though they are incredibly variable, and often printed in great detail, as examples of curious and at times comical behaviour.

In 1726, Rosamond Cole of Clerkenwell was convicted as a common scold and common disturber of her neighbourhood, and was sent to the house of correction for two months' hard labour.[34] In 1736 a woman in Newcastle was put on trial for being a common disturber of the peace. Forty witnesses were examined over five hours, so her behaviour had harmed a lot of people. She was declared guilty and fined twenty pounds.[35] In Edinburgh, a woman was reported by her neighbours, both male and female, for being a 'notorious scold and an outrageous invader of their rights, privileges and immunities.' Mention was made of the 'atrociousness of her crimes and her most impudent behaviour'. She was sentenced to live on bread and water for six months in the house of correction. But when the sentence was read to her, she showed why she had been arrested, when she 'said she would have a chop and a fresh Tip and go where she would; then snatching up a large brush that lay on the table, let it full drive among them.'[36]

As with wife selling, the complaints of scolding by women are said to be of ancient origin, but it seems to have been linked with the Reformation as some of the earliest uses of the brank were to punish female Quakers who caused offence by preaching at town crosses; they were punished by being paraded round the same structure, as a mockery of their faith as well as shaming them. But it also raises questions as to whether the epidemic of scolding was a result of the Reformation, whether the large, unified parish communities allowed more involvement and social activity for women. Then, as now, women tend to be more involved in religious practices than men. It may not be a matter entirely of them having stronger faith, but having the time, and the need for social space which their husbands find in their work.

A final aspect of this subject is that the age of women was not recorded, though if they were young, this would probably have been noted. Perhaps the need for demureness in order to find a spouse kept their rowdiness in check, or maybe they just hadn't lived long enough for their anger to build up such a head of steam. Given recent research into the symptoms often suffered by women at the menopause, such as hot flushes, insomnia, poor concentration and irritability, this raises questions as to whether scolding was primarily a problem for mature women. The punishment of ducking, of cooling off the woman, seems to suggest she was overheated, which may be a response to hot flushes and/or her hot temper. Could this represent a segue from a genuine attempt at medical intervention to a form of torture, as the original reasoning was lost, perhaps yet again as a result of the amount of knowledge lost at the Reformation? The enforced lack of mobility expected of some women would have exacerbated the symptoms, as exercise is now seen as beneficial in relieving the worst of the effects of menopause.

11

A WIFE'S WORTH

Wives are young men's mistresses, companions for middle age, and old men's nurses.
Francis Bacon

Our bodies have changed little since wife selling was widespread, but our perceptions of them are worlds apart. A life expectancy for our ancestors of thirty-five years is often cited, suggesting most of them shuffled into their graves at an age when most of us are getting into our stride. But this thirty-five is an average, heavily loaded at the lower end by the high infant mortality, the result of their poor diet, hygiene and occasional epidemics. This meant that if a person survived childhood, and avoided major accidents, they were generally robust enough to reach the biblical life expectancy of seventy or more. Some people — especially in the countryside — were reported as having lived extraordinarily long and active lives. The village of Tibshelf in Derbyshire, with one hundred houses in 1797, was claimed to be home to seventy to eighty people over sixty years old, with four nearly centenarians.[1] Two years later a ninety-four-year-old veteran of Newmarket attended the muster for volunteers to defend his country from the French, carrying a javelin and signed his name without spectacles.[2] A woman in Abbey Ladercost, Cumberland was reported in 1794 as being an extraordinary one-hundred-and-sixty-four years old, with a daughter of one-hundred-and-three. In the same parish were six women over ninety-nine years old.[3]

Our modern press — with its focus on deaths and disasters — tends to give us a false impression that modern life is dangerous when for most of us it is anything but. In Georgian and Victorian times, the main cause of death for women was childbirth, often due to uncontrolled blood loss, poor hygiene and medical ignorance. Queen Anne was almost constantly pregnant yet none of her children survived into adulthood. John Loveday of Caversham (born 1711) wrote of his fears for his wife's health every time she went into labour. She and her three sisters all died within twelve years: three from childbearing, the other from tuberculosis.[4] So even for the gentry, life was often cut short. But in Tudor times, most women only had about five children and the maternal fatality rate was only one per cent per birth.[5]

Dangers for men were far more varied; people who worked with animals — which was a large group — risked being trampled or gored. Until the 1920s every police station in England had a shotgun in case of farm animals running amok or being mortally injured and so in need of despatch. In the absence of health and safety regulations, dangerous industries included mining, construction, metal foundries, glassmaking, and lime burning. Gunpowder manufacture was an inexact science, and explosions were common. Fireworks were often made at home beside open fires, and used for blasting in mines and quarries, but also for export, so added to the already high risks of fires in warehouses and especially on board wooden ships.

The many wars in the long eighteenth century killed many men; others were taken hostage, were stranded or settled abroad, so women formed a significant majority of the British population. Today, intimate relations between the sexes are seen as recreational as much as procreational. While people then struggled to produce children, the focus in modern times is often on preventing them. Women now have the choice to have children, and if so, when. So it can be hard for us to see it as a seriously life-threatening activity for women via childbirth or to both sexes with the spread of syphilis and other mysterious venereal diseases.

The press often carried reports of the dangers of everyday life: open fires, candles and lamps could set alight clothes, hair and furnishings, so children had to be constantly watched. Setting foot outside your home in towns had risks: falling roof tiles or flowerpots, slipping in unswept streets which were full of human, animal and food waste, toppling into open cellars, being run down by car men, coaches and barrows. On market days there was the increased risk of butchers' animals escaping. Medical problems that would be minor today, such as broken limbs, appendicitis and rotten teeth, could prove fatal, and the lack of pain relief made many people's lives a prolonged misery. This probably contributed to the surprisingly high levels of suicide in the eighteenth century, despite this condemning the person to be buried at a crossroads and denied resurrection in the afterlife.

Dickens exposed the horrors of child labour in the mid-nineteenth century, but for most of human history, people lived on the land, and everyone had to contribute to the family economy. Children helped by scaring birds off the crops, minding sheep, feeding animals and clearing rocks and weeds from fields. Milton recommended that poor children began some form of suitable work from the age of three. This was not abuse, but common sense before compulsory education for children. We are horrified by the practice of Victorian boys working as chimney sweeps, but it was common for children as young as seven to be apprenticed, to relieve the family of the costs of their food and clothing, and for them to learn a trade. Once qualified, they saved up to start families of their own and the cycle began again.

Most people lived in close contact with animals until recent times. They saw them as friends, but there was no sentimentality when they were eaten. Today, we compare people with animals as a form of insult, but for much of human history, humans and animals lived under the same roof for warmth, so were mutually dependent upon each other. People who worked as shepherds, cowherds or drovers spent more time in the company of animals than humans; some gave them names, knew their personalities, grew fond of them, but they knew the animals only existed to serve people, as stated in *Genesis*. Literature is full of animal metaphors, sometimes of people who changed into animals and vice versa. They were stories of real creatures, with independence and spirit, capable of teaching lessons in life, not the farm animals bred for placid behaviour and sycophantic pets of today. Agricultural servants were often hired at the same annual fairs where beasts were auctioned, but there was no shame attached to this. Some wives who were sold had already sold themselves in this way, or had seen it happen, so being sold by a husband did not carry the burden of shame that modern writers ascribe to the process.

But animals were not always worth emulating, as they acted on their instincts, untouched by Christian morality or social mores, so this name-calling was more effective as an insult to the upper classes. When the Duke of Norfolk — a man expected to set standards of behaviour for lesser citizens — flaunted his mistress at the Norwich Assizes, the couple were compared with cattle as they showed no moral sensibility, propriety or manners. It is in this sense that wife selling was often complained of. By stepping outside the realms of church and state, a sale was seen as offensive, a threat to the established order.

The Waltham Black Act passed by Robert Walpole in 1723 drastically changed the concept of the value of human and animal lives. Theft of horses and cattle had long been a capital crime; the animals cost money to raise, and much effort could also have been expended in training horses. But deer and other game were seen as wild creatures that cost nothing to breed or maintain. By making poaching a capital offence, the new law equated the life of wild animals with those of humans, degrading common people. This equation was subsequently expanded to many other misdemeanours, such as damaging ornamental plants, appearing in public with a blackened face and even impersonating an Egyptian, which is completely incomprehensible, unless it involved fortune telling so involved either fraud or dabbling in magic. The Black Act was a tool introduced to prevent poaching in Waltham Forest but was adapted and applied by the authorities to a wide range of antisocial activities which were not covered elsewhere. In 1802 in Thetford, a woman was executed for setting fire to a pile of fodder which she had probably made herself, and was valued at two guineas so this was the value put on her.[6]

In the age of piracy, mariners and travellers were sometimes taken hostage and great efforts were made to redeem them; sometimes appeals were made to the monarch for financial and/or diplomatic assistance. The value of victims reflected their status and their family's ability to pay, at least as the pirates perceived it. At the top end of the scale, in 1646, Charles I surrendered to the Scots who handed him to the English parliament for four hundred thousand pounds. So it was not unknown for humans to put a price on individual lives.

Again, we are dealing with a wide range of cases over time and place, the status/income of those involved, and in wife sales, the perception of the woman's value, as some were described as young and pretty while others were noted for their domestic skills and ability to work hard, or even to fight.

'Luck money' was noted in several cases as being returned by the seller, so could be seen as reducing the perceived value of the woman, but giving such a refund to ensure her good health reinforced the element of goodwill in the exchange, an aspect of trade that was highly valued until Thatcher abolished it. It also suggests that a woman parted on good terms with her husband, which in turn suggested she had a good nature and character so would make a good wife. It also helped reduce the risk of disputes or negotiations in the future.

It is hard to establish patterns of how wives were valued for sale and this is further complicated by other costs such as the type of halter. If made of straw, it probably cost nothing to make. Some halters were new, which suggests those involved did not work with animals and had no further use for them, so its cost had to be allowed for. Some purchasers later sold the halter but one found no buyers, possibly a sign of disapproval at the sale. In the famous 'Smithfield Bargain' sale from 1815, the woman wore a silk halter covered by a rich lace veil, which must have been the woman's own. Several women wore handkerchiefs, one of which was waved in celebration, but these were not part of the value of the woman per se, though they probably enhanced her value.

Some cases noted the market toll was paid, and recorded in the market book, which was the responsibility of the seller. There is also a mention of the wife being taken through a tollgate to obtain a receipt as proof, which again would be borne by the seller. Some had agreements drawn, sometimes by attorneys, which were probably paid for by both parties; in one instance a man went into a stamp office to obtain special paper for the agreement.

When parish overseers sold wives, the process involved removing a woman and any potential children from their parish, so they would have required legal advice. Many parishes included a gent with some legal experience who — like everyone else on the council — would have provided his services gratis. When parishes sold wives, their overseers of the poor had to pay for the remarriage, often by licence which provided both speed and privacy, and also an incentive for the poor to agree to it, such as a dinner to celebrate the couple's newfound 'happiness'. In 1741, an unnamed London parish relinquished its responsibilities when a 'miserable blind youth ... who plays on the violin in Moorfields'[7] was given forty shillings to marry a poor woman, and the parish paid for a quick, cheap Fleet Marriage, the practice of which was outlawed by the 1745 Act which established the legal definition of marriage. This seems a huge sum to pay, but it meant that all costs and liability for the woman and her children would be shifted to Moorfields, so it would have been seen as a worthwhile investment, as long as the family stayed put, which was never certain.

Precedents for parish sales date from 1615 when the Corporation of London, in an attempt to rid itself of the hordes of street children, made an agreement with the Virginia Company to ship some of them to the plantations as 'apprentices' which seemed to provide a future for them.[8] John Donne praised the venture to provide work for the children and clean the city streets.[9] The children were taken without the permission of their parents, and on arrival were sold for tobacco. They were never given any training, but most were worked to death and never saw their homeland again. Their average lifespan there was a pathetic two years. Male settlers were encouraged by ships full of women — 'bridal boats' — and the offer of more land if hey married.[10] Objections were raised to such practices, but they were continued by people known as 'spirits', hence the term 'spirited away'. When a spirit was prosecuted in 1680 for kidnapping a young woman she was confessed and was fined thirteen shillings; if she had stolen a horse she would have hanged.[11] The sale of England's poor in this way shows how the value of women and children was not fixed. Most of those sent to the colonies were seen as having less than no value; they were potential criminals, so were expected to cost the state money. But by sending them to the New World where labour was in short supply, they acquired some value, even though —like many of the slaves that followed them — they were soon worked to death, so were expendable.

In 1814 in a messy and highly dubious case, Henry Cook of Surrey, was arrested as the father of an illegitimate child by the officers from another parish and forcibly married. But the couple never lived together and six months later the woman and newborn child continued to be a burden on the parish. With Cook's consent, she was sold to John Earl, but he abandoned the woman with her many children when he discovered the marriage was not valid. She and her children ended up on the parish after all. The forced marriage was said to be 'in accordance with the old system',[12] but it is unclear what this was. It suggests this selling of females was a widespread practice by overseers of the poor and masters of workhouses. It shows yet again that poor women were valued at less than zero until their children were old enough to become apprenticed and hopefully able to support themselves at the end of their training. The overseers paid for the sale, the marriage and even a wedding dinner to save themselves the long-term costs of supporting the woman, so they must have been able to justify the expense.

It is hard to establish how common such sales were, but Parson Holland of Stowey in Somerset described a 'parish wedding' from September 1802 as 'strange work', claiming to dislike forced matches. He questioned the young couple and was convinced that they were willing so the marriage was completed.[13] This is an oddity as the tradition was to marry in the wife's parish, though Holland seemed unconcerned about the liability to his own parish if the marriage failed.

The draconian Elizabethan Poor Laws continued with few amendments until the mid-nineteenth century. Responsibility for the poor lay with their legal place of settlement. But problems arose when a couple were not from the same parish as often happened when they met in a large city, especially London. If a woman from Cornwall, for example, married a man from Newcastle, that city became her place of settlement and future home should her husband die or abandon her. She and any children would be forcibly transported to this place of settlement. Yet even on arrival the parish could deny them support. The transportation could be incredibly cruel if the woman was pregnant. Some gave birth during transit, and even died. Parson Holland wrote in 1810:

"A worthless girl in the Poorhouse is in a sad state, she has begun to be in Labour."[14] She was full of disease and it seemed the baby was already dead. The parish was legally obliged to provide accommodation and medical aid, but she seems to have been unmarried, so received no sympathy from the cleric or anyone else. Despite this, she gave birth to a healthy child. The care may have been from the local surgeon who may not have been of high standard as Holland wryly mentioned in 1800: 'Met Mr Forbes the surgeon going to kill a few patients.'[15]

※

The press claimed that wife sellers were the poor and ignorant, but the poor had no money for a church wedding, so were unlikely to become married via a sale. Yet many tried to do the right thing. In 1769, a young couple were being married in Bruton, Somerset; when the rings were about to be exchanged, the minister asked for the fee. But they were unable to pay, so the minister walked off. The newspaper claimed the lovers had not been near the church since, so had probably decided to accept each other's vows for the rest of the service.[16]

Couples married by the parish probably continued to be under it control, so would not have had the freedom to change partners unless again forced to by the overseers. Accommodation in the poorhouse was meant to be segregated by gender, and complaints were made of the cruelty of separating elderly couples who had been together most of their lives. Where segregation was enforced, there was little point in being married. And the poor being poor, they were unlikely to have any spare money to buy a wife. So it comes as no surprise that the poor — though by far the largest social group — were rarely mentioned in records of wife selling.

In 1837, George Hutchinson sold his wife at Walsall market. The new couple had been living together for three years, so this was clearly not an open sale for half a guinea. Hutchinson had led his wife in a halter through a turnpike gate, the only one on record to have done so, adding to his cost, but also providing evidence of the ritual, which helped validate the sale and free him of responsibility for her.

At the top end of the market are some serious financial transactions; in each case there is a statement or implication that the woman had been unfaithful, so the high price can be seen as a means of avoiding a case of criminal conversation. In coal-mining and iron-smelting regions where most of the work was for men, the population had expanded very fast, creating a desperate shortage of accommodation, so many families took in lodgers for extra income; in some areas this happened in a third of homes. The downside of this was the obvious intrusion into their privacy. But the presence of a stranger — often a young man — may have aggravated existing problems between the couple, leading the wife to share her problems with, and be drawn to, the lodger. The large crowds at sales may have been hostile as the adultery occurred in the husband's home so undermining trust so there was a sense of personal betrayal involved.

Showing a bizarre choice of date, on Valentine's Day 1774, a man took his wife to Hull market but they attracted such a large crowd, the sale had to be deferred till later in the afternoon. She was later bought for twenty guineas by a man who had been their lodger for four or five years.[17] The value here was again based on her adultery.

In 1805, a good-looking woman was put on sale at Smithfield at an asking price of fifty pounds, but attracted little interest. She was probably overpriced as she was not warranted 'quiet and free from vice',[18] so failed to sell, but was eventually knocked down for two guineas, still a large amount for such allegedly damaged goods. Again, the huge price suggested a case of criminal conversation, but no particular buyer was named, so it seems the husband had failed to do his market research. Or it could be that he needed some money, perhaps to move away from the area and start a new life.

In May 1872, a man in Exeter was attracted to the wife of a friend, who claimed she had 'too much dash' for her husband, and an offer of fifty pounds for her was accepted.[19] This incredibly high price suggests the wife was an adulterer, or that 'dash' made her prime quality. Perhaps she was well presented and had independent means, so was a worthwhile investment.

The case which most challenges the accusations of sales being the realm of the poor and the ignorant was from July 1815, when at Smithfield Market: 'a beautifully dressed young woman arrived in a coach, exposed to view of the purchaser, with silk halter round her shoulders which were covered in a rich white lace veil.'[20] It was claimed that all three were persons of property. She was put up for eighty guineas but they settled for fifty and a horse. Unlike with most sales, Smithfield beast market was an appropriate venue for this one, as the purchaser was said to be a celebrated London horse dealer, and the seller a cattle grazier who would have been known there. This shows that the practice was well enough established in the lower classes to have become acceptable by their so-called betters. The high price confirms what the newspaper claimed 'The intention of these disgusting bargains is to deprive the husband of any right of prosecution for damages.' Unusually, this legal claim was correct. The seller, by receiving money, was colluding in his wife's adultery, so any claim for compensation would have failed. Hence the couple had — perhaps unwittingly — entered into a state of legal limbo, unable to divorce or remarry. Like many young couples embarking on marriage, they were living for the moment, convinced that they had a rosy future together.

Another prestige sale happened on The Pavement in York in 1831, when the wife of John Bealby was sold to countryman Flegg for a 'nominal price' of sixty guineas.[21] In the absence of other bidders, this must have been prearranged, so yet another alternative to paying criminal conversation charges. A sale at Lansdown Fair near Bath was for what seems to be the standard rate, of half a crown, but the woman was described as 'dashingly attired' and her halter was of silk,[22] only the second sighting of such an elite accessory.

In 1822, a sale — claimed to be the last in the city — was held in Paradise Square, Sheffield. The woman was sold for five shillings, a silver watch and gold chain, and described as being 'nothing loth to the transfer'.[23] There is no suggestion that the purchaser knew the woman, and his lack of ready cash suggests it was not pre-planned.

A sale which drew the closest parallels between women and beasts was in 1764 at Parham Fair, Norfolk, when the wife was exchanged for a bullock. This was probably due to the buyer not having lot of cash on him. The seller later sold the bullock for six guineas. As in so many cases, there are too many details missing to be able to decipher this account fully.[24]

At the bottom of the wife market are examples which show how short of cash people were. In 1772 there was a sale at Derby Market-place for a mere eighteen pence, but writings were drawn and witnesses present, so being poor did not mean skimping on legal details.[25] Another bargain was struck at Knaresborough in 1807 when the price was sixpence plus a quid of tobacco.[26] In 1829, a wife was sold in Bristol for a donkey, and in 1839, for a tub of swedes.[27]

But these may have echoed the situation described by Baring-Gould when a query was raised as to the legality of a cash sale without an auctioneer's licence. There were also problems with both the amount and quality of cash in circulation, so the exchange of goods may have reflected this, especially in country areas where knowledge of legal currency would have been limited.

At Boston in 1817, a wife was sold for a mere three farthings, but this also included her 'paraphernalia', a shoulder of mutton, basket etc.[28] But perhaps the saddest case was from 1836 in Cornwall where a woman was sold to a pair of tinkers for four pence. The husband had to pay a penny for the market toll, i.e., the rate for a pig.[29] This might suggest something of a bargain basement ménage-à-trois, but was more likely to be a way of the men getting their food cooked and clothes washed while they were on the road.

But low prices did not necessarily mean poor-quality merchandise, as shown by sale in Mansfield market in 1848 when the woman sold for a shilling and sixpence including the halter, which was resold and raised threepence. When the husband asked for the return of the wedding ring, his (ex) wife cleverly swapped it for a penny brass one, so she sold for a mere fifteen pence,[30] which may have meant her husband made a loss on the transaction. With such sound business sense, she was likely a good investment for her new partner.

In a few cases, the husband made some form of calculation as to the wife's value in terms of what he had spent. At the 'Dutch Auction' at Knott Mill near Manchester in 1850 a boatman put his wife up for sale, and the first bid was for fifteen shillings but he protested that the wedding ring had cost ten shillings, and the marriage fee five shillings so he demanded a sovereign minimum.[31] This suggests that the sale also imparted a 'state of marriedeness', as the buyer, having paid the costs of the marriage helped confirm the validity of the sale as a marriage contract. It is also noteworthy here that the marriage fees were paid solely by the husband, even though, in most marriages, the woman was still expected to provide some form of dowry.

When Rough Moey sold his wife at Wednesbury, he objected to a low bid of eighteen pence with "Why, you'd ha' to pay the parson seven and six for marryin' yer!"[32] So here also the sale was seen as a cheap form of marriage, as opposed to the usual claims that it was primarily a cheap form of divorce, though it is not clear whether a legal marriage had taken place.

Other costs are only hinted at, as in the Black Country sale, where Rough Moey made use of a fiddler and a couple of minders to keep the curious crowd under control; they must have been paid, in cash or — more likely — in alcohol to help celebrate the event. Most sales seem to have involved alcohol, in part or whole payment or in celebrations of the event, often spending all the money raised. When Farmer Thompson of Carlisle sold his wife for fifty shillings and a Newfoundland dog, it was reported that he 'spent on treating all the money he received for his wife — another singular verification of an old proverb about the fate of ill earned money'.[33] But this may be missing the truth. Thompson was celebrating his freedom. As with many sellers the value of his wife had nothing to do with his need for money, but the sale was a means of ensuring she went to a good home and to ensure the agreement would be binding. It seems likely here and in several other cases that the husbands would have been willing to pay to be rid of their troublesome spouses.

There were other reasons for the involvement of alcohol, the most obvious being that the sales were either in open spaces with nearby hostelries, or actually inside them, and celebrations of the deed were common. There may have been a lack of ready cash, so the publican or innkeeper may have offered drinks on credit to those involved. Or the drinks may even have been donated by the publicans in anticipation of the increased trade the celebrations would bring. There are several accounts of publicans selling or buying wives themselves.

The choice of drink was often mentioned, and varied. Some were a crown or half-crown bowl of punch, suitable for celebratory sharing. Ale had a short shelf life and was at the bottom of the market. Single women or widows were often noted as being the proprietors of alehouses, often as part of their own house, so they could be tiny. As brewing techniques improved, and hops were grown and used as a preservative, brewing shifted from women's work to that of men, so yet another source of income for poor women was lost. This is shown by the mention of celebratory drinks such as beer and porter, which suggests they were in licensed drinking establishments.

Sharing drinks was a tradition of long standing, along with shaking hands, to seal agreements, so getting hammered after the event could be seen as part of the legal conditions. It was this sharing of drink, or as it was sometimes described, 'going on a spree' that at times made the sale appear on the written record when the wedding party could become drunk and disorderly, as in 1834 in the Gorbals when a modest looking young beau and a carter' were fined ten shillings and six pence each for over-indulging.[34]

There were also a few, highly unusual cases where the woman paid for herself. An enterprising young woman from Oxfordshire went to London where she sold her long blonde hair to raise fifty pounds which her fiancé demanded.[35] She had no family or friends to help provide her dowry so she raised the money herself. Is this a value of her, of her husband to be, or the value of the marriage itself? This seems like a mercenary young man to demand such a payment, but he may have had hopes of starting a business, or obtaining a home for them, so it would have been of benefit to them both. Alternatively, if he had saved up some of his own money, this may have been to ensure she was seriously committed to the union.

In 1844 an unhappily married man discovered his wife was 'finding solace in the affections of a neighbour', so they made an agreement for her to be sold for what seems to be the standard rate of half a guinea, which was paid for by the wife. This shows the woman had her own income, and had not lost it on her marriage under the law of coverture, but also that the husband was not in great need of her money. The new husband claimed it was the best bargain he ever made.[36]

The account titled *Wife Selling Extraordinary* from Plymouth in 1822 claimed that the woman had priced herself, but it seems she had merely put an upper limit on what she could afford to pay when her lover failed to arrive. Again, she was of independent means, and was free to spend as she pleased. Even so, she was forced to accept payment in instalments, i.e. twenty pounds, with three pounds deposit and the remainder by Christmas.[37]

The pricing of a woman may appear to have been a degrading act, but in 1865 a man on trial (presumably for selling his wife) was asked if he was worth twenty pounds. He triggered much laughter in the court with: 'No, I aren't, but my wife and children are'.[38]

12

CHILDREN

If you bungle raising your children I don't think whatever else you do will matter much.
   Theordore C. Sorenson Kennedy

The Victorian family, with a brood of children gathered round the Christmas tree is a potent image. But beyond this were many women who were exhausted by the endless cycle of childbearing without pain relief, and child rearing, only to endure further agony when their children often predeceased them. Many also struggled with poverty, malnutrition and poor hygiene. Though Dickens was a highly successful author, he decided he could not afford any more children after their fifth arrived, yet his exhausted wife produced five more. When Effie Grey married John Ruskin, the relationship was not consummated, and he was condemned for denying her children. His behaviour was described as cruel, and condemned more than if he had assaulted her or been unfaithful. Bearing children was seen as both a woman's duty and her destiny, and barren women were seen as tragic figures — lonely, marginalised and unfulfilled —or extreme cases, as witches, scolds, vagabonds or shrews.

When London mystic Anna Trapnel went to Cornwall in 1654, she was arrested on suspicion of being a witch, a vagrant and probably a whore. But she defended herself in court by stating she had inherited money which allowed her to live independently, that she had provided money and sold her jewellery for the army and to support public life, but was not called a vagabond then.[1]

This concept of a woman being defined primarily as a baby-maker was the main reason for the various accounts of parish authorities selling them. Even those without children were seen as potential sources of hungry mouths which local taxpayers were unwilling to support. Before the Reformation, religious houses had been a pool of non-breeding adults, so when they were closed by Henry VIII, there was a population explosion, especially among the poor. It became necessary for the state to deal with them, resulting in a series of Poor Laws from 1601. Women were especially hard done by, as most priests were paid pensions, whereas the nuns — by then mostly elderly — were turned into the streets to fend for themselves as best they could. The priests were apparently expected to set up home, so needed finance, whereas the nuns were expected to find a man to marry and support them. Some may have become wise women, putting to good use the medical skills they probably learnt. But if their medicine was ineffective, or if the patient accidentally or incidentally died, they risked being accused of witchcraft.

The bedrock of the new laws was that people were to be cared for by the parish in which they were deemed to have 'settlement'. This was determined by place of birth, but could be purchased in order to trade in a town, acquired by completing an apprenticeship or by marriage to the daughter of a freeman, a system which also allowed freeholders to vote in elections. But as with coverture law, a woman lost her single rights, i.e. her place of settlement, at marriage. This meant that if a woman was widowed or abandoned, she could only obtain help from the parish of her late husband which she might never have visited, so claiming it would involve her being transported far from friends and family. The 1601 Act established the system of poor relief in England and Wales; it divided the poor into three groups. The impotent poor who were too sick or disabled to work were placed in the almshouse or poorhouse. The able-bodied were generally seen by the authorities as being lazy, so were sent to the work house or house of industry. Those who were seen as being idle or vagrants were sent to the house of correction. Most parishes were too small to need or afford all three, so they provided one general-purpose house.

Across Western Europe, urban life in the seventeenth century was a seemingly endless drudgery for masters and servants. There were no schools for children, and little play either, with John Locke claiming in 1697 that the children of the poor should be working part of the day from the age of three. The European practice of lifelong work abused and enslaved people just as much as the better-known conditions in Victorian England.²

For centuries, the age of marriage was determined by the couple's ability to save enough money to set up home together, often when the man was freed at the end of his apprenticeship. Women often went into service at an early age, which meant that men and women tended to marry in their late twenties. But the decline of the apprenticeship system in the late eighteenth century, and the rise of new industries, allowed men to earn adult wages earlier, which in turn led to a fall in the age of marriage. Women married and produced their first children at a younger age when they were stronger, so the babies were more likely to survive, and families tended to become larger. The very nature of towns and cities also had a positive effect on birth rates, as there were more places and opportunities for young people to meet, so again, this was likely to lower the age of marriage. Counteracting this were the many young servants who, by the nature of their employment, were unable to marry, but such jobs had a high turnover and for many women were a means of saving for their dowry.³

The poet John Clare and radical journalist William Cobbett decried the loss of access to nature and open spaces from the late eighteenth century, and the traditions of country festivals which added colour to their lives. Much of this was attributed to changes which began in the seventeenth century and accelerated in the eighteenth and nineteenth, of enclosure acts which denied people access to what had traditionally been communal grazing, foraging and wood for building and firewood. This caused soaring levels of rural poverty and homelessness by the late eighteenth century. But unlike in industrial cities, in the country, children were able to contribute to the family income by scaring birds, removing weeds and rocks from fields, feeding animals, and working as shepherds and cowherds.

Some poor families were heavily reliant on their family cow, but without access to communal pasture, children walked their animals along the edges of roads and fields in search of grass, as Wordsworth described in a country walk:

> *'a hunger bitten Girl,*
> *Who crept along, fitting her languid gait*
> *Unto a Heifer's motion, by a cord*
> *Tied to her arm, and picking thus from the lane*
> *Its sustenance, while the girl with pallid hands,*
> *Was busy knitting in a heartless mood.'*[4]

There was no urban equivalent of the various forms of rural labour for children, so they were mostly seen a liability until they were old enough to work. They had to be constantly watched for fear of getting too close to a fire, tipping furniture over, or falling down stairs. An account from 1835 tells of a four-year-old girl who was burnt to death when her parents left her to play with another in a cellar; it ends with: 'The frequency of such accidents ought to put parents on guard not to leave children alone in apartments.'[5] But there was no childcare, so this was the situation until —or if — they reached the age of seven or so, when they would be apprenticed, so providing extra income.

A similar shift in North America may be the reason for an item from 1871:

> 'A widow with half a score of children, forty years ago, if we may

believe Dr Franklin, was an object for the fortune hunters of America. It is not so now. The demand for widows, and for every sort of ready made family is beginning to be over.'[6]

Perhaps the most surprising aspect of wife sales was the extreme rarity of children. This may be due to the articles in the press being too short; the children may have been elsewhere, or they were simply not seen by the reporter within the crowds. But most sales were at markets some distance from the woman's home; and the wife often left with her purchaser, echoing the practice of farm servants who attended hiring fairs with all their worldly goods. Thus, if the wives had children, they should have been mentioned as being part of the negotiations. It is hard to imagine the press pontificating about the evils of wife selling not using the presence of children as ammunition to further condemn those involved.

When children were involved in the sales, the younger ones often stayed with the mother. In this the wife sale was an improvement on the legal system where a woman lost custody of, and generally all contact with, her children, so this may have been part of its appeal. This is also why so many women stayed with their husbands, despite uncomfortable and even violent domestic conditions. But the younger children may have — as some accounts suggest — gone to the correct father, so the domestic situation seems to have been non-traditional for years before the situation was resolved by the sale.

Some of the sales were after marriages of short duration, as in Rochdale in 1856, where the marriage was six months old, but the couple had only lived together for seven weeks.[7] A case was brought before the magistrates following a sale at Smithfield in 1841 when the wife had been married unhappily for four months. In such cases, it is possible things went wrong before the marriage was properly consummated.

Of the few wife sales that mentioned children, the earliest seems to be from 1777, when a gardener from Witham in Essex sold his wife with child, a fowl and eleven pigs to a neighbouring bricklayer. The animals were probably thrown in as the woman was the one who fed them, suggesting, as in many cases, the original husband did not have another woman in his sights. Two years later, in an event that seems to have been unique in the record but was probably anything but, a Yorkshire blacksmith sold his pregnant wife to his workman. The newspapers claimed he had 'sold the child to the right father' so another case of the wife straying — but not far — from the nest.[8] In higher-class circles, this would have been a classic case for criminal conversation proceedings, but here the trio managed their own affairs without the huge cost and time of a trial, so the child seems to have been born into a welcoming home.

In 1815 a sale at Maidstone was for one pound, including one child, leaving the woman's other four behind.[9] This suggests again that the youngest belonged to the buyer. A woman was sold at Horsham market in 1825 for two pound five shillings, which included one of her three children.[10] All of these were aimed at consigning children to their genetic rather than legal fathers.

Rough Moey sold his young wife with a baby, which the old reprobate claimed in 1830 may or may not have been his, and in 1885, in Wrexham a 'Lilliputian collier' tried to sell his wife with 'sucking babe' after he came home drunk and they fell out over his wages.[11]

A sale in Tuxford market in 1805 was for five shillings for a wife and child. The press account suggested the seller had no idea he was still liable for their support.[12] In 1811 a woman was sold in Sittingbourne for ten pounds with five children, a horse and cart and all the household furniture.[13] In 1802 at Chapel-en-le-Frith, a wife was sold for eleven shillings with her child and 'furniture of room'. Both of these suggest the couple were effectively living separately in the family home. The husband claimed these extras 'would set me up as a beggar',[14] yet it must have been worth it to be free of her. The inclusion of the furniture suggests the husband was leaving the area, perhaps to avoid shame, or to start a new life, perhaps abroad. Or the items may have been part of the woman's dowry, so he felt he had no claim to them. Yet again, this is a better deal for the wife than a divorce would have provided.

In Lincoln in 1813, a woman was sold for two guineas which included her infant child, and what appears to have been a wedding feast, similar to those provided by overseers of the poor, with a leg of mutton and plum pudding. But the seller also included a bed and bedding, so it seems that, yet again, the buyer needed some extra incentive.[15]

A famous case featured a 'Yankee' who purchased a wife and her two children in Wolverhampton in 1865.[16] Most men were unwilling to take on the children of another, due to problems of inheritance and the children being unable to adapt to a new home. But if the children were seen as sources of income, it made sound economic sense to obtain a ready-made family, without the danger to the mother and other problems of childbearing and raising. Infant mortality was high, but if the child survived their early years, they were probably robust enough to see old bones, so buying children could be seen as a better investment than a man making his own.

In 1870, a wife was sold in Bury. She had eight children; the four in receipt of wages went with her, to provide future income for her purchaser, and relieve her husband of any responsibility for childcare.[17] But this sale was more complicated than most, as three bids were made, suggesting it was an open sale, but her buyer was a man who lived opposite and whose wife had recently died, so there was opposition to him not spending enough time in mourning. Neighbours burnt the wife and then her buyer in effigy.

From Halifax about 1805 comes a tale of a returned soldier. His wife, Rachel Heap, had assumed him dead in the wars so married Samuel Lumb in 1802 and had three children by him.[18] There were many similar instances, described in detail elsewhere.

In 1857, Ann Arthur of Roche, Cornwall, was charged with bigamy having remarried with the consent of her husband, believing the arrangement was legal. This case is unusual as most seem to have accepted the sale as including a legal remarriage, so this is the only account of a woman remarrying in a church. As with so many cases, she was trying to do the right thing, to prevent any future children being stigmatised as illegitimate.[19] This case is hard to read as it is unclear whether the sons were from her first or second marriage.

Baring-Gould wrote of a nasty incident of a man of North Bovey 'some time before 1868', who walked into Chagford to sell his wife via a private agreement, for a quart of beer. It was so private he seems not to have mentioned it to his wife, so when he returned home, the woman repudiated the agreement and took her children to Exeter, probably to her family.[20] She only returned for her husband's funeral. Was this a moment of drunken madness? Or was it the result of long-simmering domestic problems with this proving the final straw for the wife?

Another strange case is from Devon in 1870, where a 'bachelor in easy circumstances' in Dittisham, took a fancy to a neighbour's wife and agreed a sale for fifty pounds, which included her baby. But the couple vanished without paying. This was a case of fraud, but it is unclear whether the woman was complicit in it.[21]

The lack of children in wife sales could have been caused by low fertility, from poor hygiene, via infections and sterility. There was also — especially in the eighteenth century — widespread use of heavy metals — famously lead — in medicines, makeup and distilling, especially of rum. But there was also a huge difference between the size of families in North America and those in England, with the former producing huge families where those in England sometimes struggled to produce a single child who reached adulthood, especially in towns and cities. Queen Anne, who had a luxurious life with access to the best quality medical care and was constantly pregnant, failed to produce an adult heir, so it was not just a problem of the underfed poor. In Henry Reed Stiles' book *Bundling*, he described the practice of couples sharing a bed before marriage:

> 'To this sagacious custom… do I chiefly attribute the unparalleled increase of the Yankee tribe; for it is a certain fact, well authenticated by court records and parish registers, that wherever the practice of bundling prevailed, there was an amazing number of sturdy brats annually born unto the state, without the license of the law, or benefit of clergy. Neither did the irregularity of their birth operate in the least to their disparagement. On the contrary, they grew up long-sided, raw-bred, hardy race of whoreson whalers, wood-cutters, fishermen and pedlars; and strapping corn-fed wenches, who by their united efforts tended marvelously towards

populating those notable tracts of Nantucket, Piscataway, and Cape Cod.'[22]

These colonists were extremely well fed, and sturdy from so much fresh air and exercise, as opposed to the increasingly unhealthy, half-starved, Britons. In the Canton family of Maryland, three sisters moved to England and made spectacular marriages: Marianne to the Duke of Wellington's elder brother, Louisa became the Duchess of Leeds and a friend of the queen, while Bess was a successful speculator on the stockmarket. Their sisters back home had large families, but they did not.[23]

What seems to have motivated the sisters' move to England was to escape boredom, to exercise their minds and meet interesting people. It seems they and their husbands preferred not to have children, but to have active social lives. This is part of the reason why so many young people flocked to the towns and cities from the early eighteenth century, in search of higher wages, and access to the many social opportunities and entertainments which were also a means of meeting partners.

Did those involved in wife selling make a deliberate choice not to have children? If so, and in the absence of reliable, safe contraception, this means they were not consummating their marriages. This, in turn, means that their marriages — like that of the Ruskins — were technically void, so could have been annulled instead of ended through a sale. But this would still have involved the wife having to prove herself a virgin, which she may not have been; perhaps the couple had tried consummation but, well, the magic never happened, so voiding the marriage before the 1857 Act would still have involved costly litigation and embarrassment for them both.

Another possibility comes from the modern rise in middle-aged couples choosing to divorce. These are mostly the baby boomers, the so-called 'Golden Generation', so perhaps they have higher expectations of life. But it could be the result of 'empty nest syndrome' when the couples' marriages went stale much earlier, but they stayed together for the sake of their children.

13

FRIENDS AND FAMILY

Serve God duly; love one another; preserve your victuals; beware of fire, and keep good company
   Sir John Hawkins, 1565[1]

The making of traditional marriages involved extensive input from family and friends in the hope of ensuring the young couple were compatible and that they would be blessed with a long, fruitful and happy partnership. But this was not always necessary.

In *The History of Myddle,* Richard Gough described one of his ancestors who married against the advice of elders. They met and fell in love at school, and when they decided to marry, 'they could not make passing thirty yeares betweene them', but they had a happy marriage with many children.[2]

But by the eighteenth century, young people were becoming more independent, local community ties were weaker and many people were moving to towns and cities in search of work and better lives. But this meant there were fewer sources of advice and support when marriages developed problems. Many wife sales took place in new industrial and mining towns of the Midlands and the North, which were often compared with North America's Wild West. They often developed too fast for churches and local government to keep pace, so what social space existed tended to be at work or in pubs and inns. In mining and iron-smelting areas, there was little work for women, so they tended to marry young and, unless they took in lodgers, were unlikely to have much contact with men who could lure them away from their spouses. The lodgers provided adult company when the husband was absent, and there were many instances where they became wife purchasers. But the lodgers probably worked for the same company as the husband, so such an unacceptable relationship often got them fired or punished by their neighbours.

Among the upper classes, where considerable money and property was at risk, parents continued to force their children into partnerships. In 1793 the famous arranged marriage of Elizabeth Pierrepont became a scandal when her husband sued her partner for criminal conversation. Her barrister Thomas Erskine defended her by claiming she had been forced into marriage despite being in love with a noble young man, Mr Howard. He used highly shocking, highly emotional language with Elizabeth 'stretched upon this bridal bed as upon a rack' and described the marriage as 'the legal prostitution of parental choice in the teeth of affection.'[3]

Though this refers to an aristocratic family, it shows the level of control that parents could have over the choice of life partners. It also shows that by the end of the eighteenth century, the law was catching up with reality and acknowledging the importance of young people's right to choose their own partners, and of the emotional cruelty of refusing this. The citing of the rack was of particular relevance to a country emerging from long-term chaos to take the lead in the European Enlightenment, rejecting its violent and ignorant past, and embracing the rising opposition to the African slave trade.

The English were unique in sending so many of their children to be educated and trained by strangers, but the habit was probably a degraded form of the medieval practice of aristocratic households including the children of their allies. This helped forge alliances and diversify the young people's education, and they could be used as bargaining chips or even hostages if the families became enemies. In the eighteenth century, many families could not afford to support their children. Young girls went into service at the age of sixteen, and boys were sent into apprenticeships from the age of seven, though increasingly this was at fourteen or so. Domestic service was often available in the nearby manor house, which could employ vast numbers, sometimes a veritable army of domestic and other types of servants.

From about 1700, the rich became increasingly mobile, visiting friends' estates, London and the various spas. In their absence, their country residence was closed up and only a skeleton staff retained. Temporary servants were employed at the various spas and resorts. This caused many servants to have unstable work histories, and when out of work, they survived on their savings, took lesser-paid work or returned home to their families. It is this instability that led to claims that many female servants were forced to become prostitutes, a reputation that in turn lowered the status of domestic servants. An anonymous tract of 1749 described how many young women were attracted to the capital by the promise of better wages in domestic service, but when this dried up, they were forced into the bawdy houses: 'so that, in effect, they neither make good whores, good wives, or good servants'.[4] Where the 'season' was in the winter, such as at Bath, this provided a form of proto-industrial employment, allowing servants to work on farms, especially on the harvest. But the nearby Hotwells had a summer season, so some servants were able to follow the work between the two sites. This social mobility of the rich converted the former jobs for life of their servants into a wide range of 'zero-hours contract' posts, with all the stress and insecurity that modern workers suffer.

This early work experience gave many young people an unprecedented level of independence which they also showed in their choice of partners. Their parents were too poor to provide dowries and were far away and often dead before their children married, which tended to be in their late twenties. Single people met in their places of work, at fairs, festivals and dances, all of which were unchaperoned. Knowledge of the risks of pregnancy seems to have varied, and was probably higher in the countryside where the young saw animals in action from an early age. If a girl became pregnant outside of marriage, the overseers of the poor could force the man to marry her. But there were also many cases of servants disposing of newborn babies, and they were often charged with infanticide, which a capital crime.

Such social and cultural changes seem to be reflected in the rarity of mentions of family members being present at wife sales. They may have been too far away, unable to take time out of work, stayed away due to the shame of the event, or been present but not recorded in the limited space of newspaper reports. When they are noted, this suggests they supported the sale and were probably there as witnesses to the contract and to ensure the wife was treated fairly. If the sale was held at a crowded site, male friends and relatives perhaps attended to protect her from the mob should it turn against them.

Agricultural servants were hired at the annual fairs, and in the case of specialist workers this could result in families becoming spread over large distances. Caleb Bowcombe was a Wiltshire shepherd described by W.H. Hudson in *A Shepherd's Life*. He often grieved at being separated from his favourite brother, yet neither wrote to the other, preferring occasional meetings at the annual sheep fair near Wilton. After years with no news from him, Caleb travelled by train and on foot to the fair. He waited at the sheep pens, then went round the site before at last questioning some shepherds who told him his brother had died two years before.[5]

Agricultural wages were famously low, and many young people found life in the countryside unbearably dull and restricted. They flocked to the new industrial towns in search of better wages, but this cut them off from their friends and family, and it was these towns that reported many of the wife sales.

Birmingham in the mid-eighteenth century was incredibly socially and economically diverse, operating on multiple levels, bringing a wide range of people into contact with each other to form relationships which could include marriage. It was a major commercial and industrial centre where men and women worked in anything from shops to smithies. Birmingham was also the entry point to the agricultural hinterland of the Midlands and to the industrial areas later known as the Black Country and the Potteries.[6] The city and its surrounding region developed a reputation for the high numbers of wife sales, with one of the earliest being in 1773 when the agreement was witnessed and entered into a market toll book at Edgbaston near Birmingham.[7]

Many Welsh people seem to think that wife selling was widespread in their history, with some even naming suburbs where it continues to this day, though this sounds more like swinging, a far more modern practice. Very few records support this claim, but few Welsh newspapers survive from before the mid-nineteenth century. Merthyr Tydfil was reputedly famous for wife sales. It exploded from a small, poor parish in the mid-eighteenth century to become by 1801 the largest town in Wales with men fleeing poverty in the surrounding countryside. But it was a one industry town, with little to do between shifts but drink. A nervous local magistrate described it as 'naturally turbulent'; and an assizes judge on circuit in 1790 recommended the 'soothing influence of matrimony.[8] There were few jobs for young women, so it did not attract them young in search of a husband. The men were from small, close-knit communities so mostly married women they had grown up with who followed them as the town became more established. Yet the mechanics there were described as developing a wide range of skills and many could write, which made them more advanced than their European counterparts, as noted by a French visitor in 1754,[9] which suggests they would be likewise innovative in dealing with any marital problems.

The links between town and country, between industry and agriculture were not always clear-cut. There were a range of industries that sprang up to support the poor, whose main work was helping with the harvest. Where these proto-industries, such as weaving and pin-making existed, migration from the countryside could be slowed. In 1747, a delivery of nails to London from Wortley, near Sheffield was delayed as 'the Naylers have been busy in the Harvest'.[10]

❇

When the Church of England was founded at the Reformation, many festivals and holidays which allowed people to meet their future spouses were downgraded or abolished. But this abolition did not erase the need for such rituals. Marriages and funerals provided welcome opportunities to celebrate, so were expected to be public events, with liberal supplies of alcohol. In iron towns such as Middlesbrough, a funeral provided a rare opportunity for a family to welcome people into their home, so they often spent extravagantly on it. This was part of the reason the Victorians were so fond of elaborate funerals. They were to commemorate the dead by a display of largesse and a rare chance for communities — especially the stay-at-home women — to socialise and celebrate, and forget their mundane lives.

Marriages were expected to be public events, so it makes sense that unmarrying and wife sales would also involve friends and family. In Birmingham in 1823, a violent ex-soldier named John Homer was alleged to have treated his wife brutally and to have finally sold her against her will in a halter in the market. But the purchaser was her own brother, who for three shillings was 'buying her out' of the marriage, or 'redeeming' her'.[11] This seems an odd practice as the woman generally brought a dowry — which she had often earned herself — into the relationship, so in effect the husband was paid for marrying and for un-marrying her, which seems unfair. But the husband had little time to enjoy his new independence. So certain was he that the deal was legal, he remarried in a church but was convicted of bigamy and transported for seven years.

A *Dutch auction* was held in Knott Mill in 1850 by boatman Peter Cawley, as mentioned earlier The woman's brother was present, suggesting he thought the sale was legal, and was probably there to protect his sister and her rights.[12]

Only one father is on record for intervening in a sale when Jackson from Bullocksmithy put his wife up for sale in the marketplace at Stockport in October 1831. The wife's father paid the asking price of two shillings and sixpence, who received a shilling and sixpence in return 'for luck', so the family was probably rescuing her from a failed, rather than abusive marriage or one in which the woman had strayed. The 'luck' means there was no ill will, so the couple probably just drifted apart.[13]

The most cited examples of family intervention came from mothers, but they were still rare. Perhaps they were widows so had control of their own finances and were free to attend the event. There were three such examples, from Birmingham in August 1823, Halifax in 1833, and from the Derbyshire area in 1835, all of which were probably redeeming the wife from a failed marriage. In the muddled attempt at a sale in Bristol when J Nash attempted to sell his wife, but the buyer reneged, then resold her, but she refused him, unless forced by a Magistrate to accept him, so she 'made off with her mother'.[14] In 1827 Robert Burns sold his wife to her mother at Longton Fair for five shillings.[15]

There is also a rather confusing case from c.1868 recorded by Sabine Baring-Gould of a man who sold his wife for a quart of beer, but when he returned home with her purchaser, she took her children to Exeter — presumably where she came from — for the protection of her family. This is unusual as it seems the wife was sold in absentia, and without her consent, so it seems it could not be considered legal on any level.[16] The purchaser may not have known her at all, which seems a strange arrangement. As with many cases, there seems to have been alcohol involved.

An incident from oral history from Shepton Mallet in Somerset was a rare example of what so many claimed — an act of brutality — which dates from about 1848. It was claimed that the husband married her to get hold of the woman's house, and then tried to sell her off. But 'neighbours brought her in' and took her back to her parents' home'.[17] This is also a rare instance of a crowd — probably friends and neighbours — intervening to protect the wife. It is also unusual in happening so close to their home: most sales were at a distance to avoid embarrassment and possible interruptions. But it also raises questions as to how the woman could own a house if her parents were still alive, especially as there is no suggestion that she was wealthy.

In St Austell in 1857, Anne Arthur was remarried with the consent of her husband, so this was not strictly a wife sale. She was put on trial for bigamy and her bond was posted by her sons.[18] It is unusual in that it was the woman was charged rather than her husband, a downside for her of the passage of the passage of the first divorce Act passed that year. Her behaviour was no longer the responsibility of her husband, and she was prosecuted in her own right. It seems to have been one of the last sales before the passage of the 1857 Act and her solicitor commented that he hoped the new act would avoid the need for such sales in future.

The most intriguing of this batch is from January 1835 near Manchester, when a wife was sold to her brother-in-law in the presence of a crowd of hundreds.[19] This was cited as a family intervention, but they had been cohabiting, which may have been innocent, with her acting as his housekeeper or just for company. But it potentially puts wife selling and family intervention into a whole new light. The marriage of a man to his late wife's sister was still defined as incest, echoing the grounds used by Henry VIII's first marriage, to his late brother's widow, Catherine of Aragon, centuries before.

In 1789, a carpenter at Petworth did penance with his late wife's sister at their parish church for marrying each other.[20] This seems rather strange as there should have been objections raised to this at the ceremony, unless it was in private. Even so, local gossip should have raised questions.

This also opens up a whole new field of possibilities, as to whether wife selling — despite the many claims to legality — could have been a cover for illegal marriages. An authority claimed: 'A handful of men sought secrecy since they were incestuously marrying their deceased wife's sister or a niece'.[21] Such a union could not have been tolerated in their home parish, so again this suggests the couple were away from home and from people who knew and probably disapproved of their arrangements.

In the above case, the couple were sacked by their employer out of disgust, which shows that in the absence of civic intervention, the participants were still at risk of punishment. But it is unclear whether this disgust was the result of the sale or of the incest.

This form of incest was considered to be so shocking that it was accepted as grounds for the first divorce brought by a woman in England in 1801. Mrs Addison's husband had been having relations with her married sister, so he was also cuckolding another man. Her husband was deemed to be of such poor character that she was granted custody of her children, which was another legal first.[22] There was another shocking betrayal in the case of a criminal conversation case in 1815 when Lord Roseberry sued his brother-in-law Sir Henry Mildmay for fifteen thousand pounds. To avoid paying damages and going to prison, the couple fled and were married in Stuttgart after her divorce but due to the English law on incest, they could never return.[23] Being sent into exile was once a common form of punishment for people deemed to be an ongoing threat to society. In this instance the couple effectively punished themselves.

14

MISSING MEN

The sea is fittest for an undone man, and so I am for it.
James Windham

If wife selling was a contract, then it defied one of the basic tenets of commerce, that of supply and demand, as throughout this period, men were outnumbered by women. Men were involved in dangerous industries such as construction, fishing and mining; they fell out of trees, onto sharp objects, and into rivers, especially after a night out with the lads. They blew themselves up making fireworks, poisoned themselves with bad booze and were trampled by farm animals which had yet to be bred into submission. There are many accounts of young men setting off to seek their fortunes abroad, and writers are often intrigued by their apparent bravery, but for many people, life in Britain was unbearable. Some fled when they lost their businesses, and this was popular after the disaster of the South Sea and other bubbles of the early eighteenth century. Suicide rates were surprisingly high, and became infamous as 'the English Disease', especially in the wake of Thomas Chatterton's famous, though now disputed, self-murder. Many men just seem to have become fed up with their lives and left their homes, families and communities. Some may have expected to return with a fortune to help out those who they left behind, but were never heard of again.

Across the long eighteenth century, Britain was almost constantly at war with one or more of her European neighbours. When soldiers and sailors went abroad, this put a huge strain on their families as wages were generally paid on their return. In the absence of savings, this plunged their families into poverty. This problem was recognised by Captain Coram, a ship's captain in London, who established the Foundling Hospital to care for the children of mariners. But they were not orphans in the normal sense, as children were left by their mothers, who left a token: a scrap of fabric, or some small item, which would allow them to be reunited when things improved. But very few returned. The mothers may have died in a poorhouse, or found work, probably into service, or they remarried and started new families with men unwilling to adopt another man's children. The foundlings were fed, clothed, educated and put into apprenticeships, so were better off than many.

There was a major outbreak of wife selling after 1815 when many soldiers returned to find their wives had remarried. Some of these men had been away for years, fighting battles, as prisoners of war, or stranded and unable to pay their passage home. Remarriage became the only alternative to the workhouse for most women. Many women had started new families which further complicated the situation.

Some couples resolved this by going to the market with the woman in a halter where she was sold by her first husband for a few pennies, leaving him believing he was then free to remarry. This must have been common, as 'in the manufacturing districts in 1815 and 1816 hardly a market day passed without such sales, month after month'.[1] The authorities failed to intervene as such arrangements provided the simplest solution. If they had become involved, there would have been an expensive prosecution of the wife for bigamy, but given her dire circumstances, she could have expected to be shown leniency, especially as the authorities would have had to deal with the problem of who was to support the children. This silence from the authorities helped confirm the belief that such transactions were legal. There seems to be no evidence of the community objecting to these sales, which may have encouraged people to believe they were legal.

It is at this time that French officers, as prisoners of war at liberty on their oaths as gentlemen, were able to witness these sales and their accounts were read on the continent, which is how so many Europeans believed that English wife selling was commonplace. But they failed to understand their context, and that during and in the aftermath of wars, unusual behaviour could appear to be normal.

Accounts of sales being triggered by men returning include a husband who returned to Worcester in 1784 after 'some years abroad'[2] which may have been from North America: either serving in the forces, or from earlier transportation. The following year provided a record from Liverpool of a returned sailor.[3]

Following the French Wars were another few, with 'a soldier returned after ten years', in 1815.[4] A soldier returned to Halifax and sold his wife to the father of her three children. But this was apparently not seen as legal, or not for long, as the new couple had to wait till the first husband died twenty-five years later before they could marry.[5] E.P. Thompson claims such arrangements were not common, but he is relying on press and other accounts. The husband had probably missed his family while he was risking his life abroad, and longed to return. To find he no longer had a family must have been heartbreaking for him and his family. He had made the ultimate sacrifice for his country only to have to make another sacrifice for his wife and her new family. Communities understood this, and the sale was probably a very painful, private matter, so never made it into the press.

There was a long tradition of young women falling for, and sometimes being seduced by, men in uniform, and many couples married in haste on the eve of his departure for battle. This ensured that if the woman became pregnant, she was not shamed as a fallen woman, and would be entitled to a pension if her husband was killed. Such practice was tacitly encouraged in wartime as it ensured the production of the next generation of cannon fodder for the nation.

But women who travelled with their soldier husbands could exacerbate these problems, as in 1800 an expedition arrived at Malta, and all women not needed as nurses were sent home. But on their way home, the women fell in love with an Irish regiment, and when they were informed their original partners had died, they all remarried their new Irish beaus. But the disaster reported to them had never happened, and when the two regiments met, only one of the original husbands took his wife back, and was widely mocked for it.[6]

But there seems to have been a reversal of this practice by the time of the Crimean War, when *The Birmingham Journal* reported in 1859 that the divorce courts were busy, claiming it was mostly military men freeing themselves.[7]

William Cobbett wrote extensively of the unhappy state of Britain in his *Rural Rides*, including complaining of the high cost of pensions for war widows. He claimed any single woman would be a fool not to marry a military man to ensure an income for life for her and her children. So these mass divorces seem to be at odds with this view, especially as these divorces happened just after the Matrimonial Causes Act of 1857 which permitted divorce. But it was still only granted on the grounds of the wife being proven to be an adulterer. The Act was not a major reform, more a tidying up of the system which allowed the process to be handled in a single court rather than the usual three, in London. So *The Birmingham Journal's* article is utterly incomprehensible unless these divorces were being ordered by the government to save money on these pensions, shifting the cost of supporting war widows and their children onto local poor rates.

The infamously draconian British laws from the early eighteenth century made many petty crimes into capital offences. But these sentences were often commuted to transportation for seven or fourteen years to the colonies. North America was close enough to allow some to return, so they may have found their wives had remarried. But at the outbreak of the War of Independence, convicts were sent to the other side of the world to found the future nation of Australia, a much longer, more expensive return trip which few managed. Unlike servicemen, they may not have been accepted back into their communities, as a result of their convictions, and many men may have found life in the New World preferable to Britain's rain and poverty.

Transportation to the colonies seems to have seeped into the concepts of local law, as several instances of wife sales claimed that an absence of seven years made the original marriage void, leaving the remaining partner free to remarry. But this practice seems to be part of an older tradition, as the number seven is often significant in Christian stories. There is a story linked to an ancient wayside cross at Thryburgh in Yorkshire. Leonard de Reresby is claimed to have been fighting in the Holy Land and imprisoned by the Saracens. His wife waited for news of him, but after seven years had abandoned hope and planned to remarry. One version of the legend is that the pious de Reresby prayed for his release and he was

> 'miraculously delivered and insensibly conveyed with shackles and gyves upon his limbs, and laid upon the East Hill in Thryburgh Field as the bells tolled for his wife's second marriage.'[8]

As the author continues, it is hard to imagine any sense of joy in the wedding party confronted by a

> 'dirty fettered prisoner whom they found lying in the field on their way to church'.

But the concept of seven years as a unit for punishment and remarriage seems to have been of long standing.

Not surprisingly, returning transportees rarely feature in wife sales. The only instance found is a passing mention of a husband who returned to Devon from transportation in 1838.[9] Parson Holland of Somerset mentioned a 'Botany Bay man' who was living in the local poorhouse in 1809 who asked for marital advice, as mentioned earlier.

In January 1848, the press reported a spectacular mass desertion of fifty-four men in the area of Shoreditch in London, 'leaving no fewer than 217 individuals a burthen to those parishes'.[10] This was reprinted in Scientific American, a decade later. Before the spread of modern communications, it was incredibly easy for a man to vanish. The colonies were full of such men, as were the armed services and merchant fleets.

But how could such a large group vanish without someone noticing they were making preparations? In earlier times, men were sometimes taken by the press gang; this would have been very public and widely known, but as they were not mariners, their impressment would have been challenged. The American author who cited this should have recognised the significance of this date; it was at the start of the American gold rushes, though they were not announced for another month and produced the famous 'forty-niners'.

California had already been promoted for English settlement, so there were probably plenty of rumours doing the rounds. The missing men were mechanics, who were not likely to have followed so many Britons in fleeing poverty. Uprooting from home, friends and family was a huge step to take, and potentially a permanent or fatal one. If a man ever returned, he risked being prosecuted for abandoning his family. These men would have been in high demand anywhere in the New World, including the gold fields. So this was no normal abandonment, but was a large, organised, well-informed group heading off to seek their fortunes. Their families and workmates must have known of their plans and supported them. They may have intended to send for their families when they settled. But leaving their families to the not-so-tender mercies of the poor officers seems an act of cruelty, though they probably justified this as a means to them becoming wealthy.

There are a couple of incidents which show a comical, well-meaning side to wife sales in the late nineteenth century. In 1875, a man from Belper in Derbyshire fled his debtors for America. To satisfy his creditors, all his goods were put up for sale, but his wife demanded part of the money; when this was refused, she demanded to be included in the sale as part of her husband's assets. The newspaper wryly noted: 'There was no sale of "Lot 29"'.[11]

And finally, in 1888 an unemployed man in Sheffield left his wife to seek work in Australia. But on the way out, he met a young woman and they formed an attachment. But when she found he was already spoken for, she suggested his wife might wish to sell him. Apparently in jest, he suggested she write and ask. His first wife agreed, asking a hundred pounds for all her rights, but she eventually settled for twenty. The payment was made and the new couple were married in Australia.[12]

This raises all sorts of questions. If the man was unemployed, how did he find the cost of the journey? The National Agricultural Workers Union was established to assist country workers who were struggling to survive on their low wages. It was founded in 1872 by lay preacher Joseph Arch, and the certificate of membership shows images of accident, sickness or burial. The fourth image is, surprisingly, that of a family boarding a ship, as the organisation also helped families emigrate to the New World.[13] There was a great abandonment of villages from 1881 when seven hundred thousand agricultural labourers and their families were helped to move to the colonies.[14] This was probably due to the huge influx of cheap grain from the USA, Canada and Australia, which undermined local production, so much land was converted to pasture which required less manpower.

15

MOBS AND CROWDS

I want to take you all to Romford!
Karl Hyde, Underworld

The belief that a wife sale had to be held in an open market allowed the husband to find a buyer or, if the sale was pre-arranged, to give the impression of doing so. They were held after the usual sales, when people were spending their money in pubs, and enjoying some rare leisure time before the long walk or ride home. But this also risked attracting the attention and condemnation of the public and the authorities. Rowdy young men could also cause trouble, the reason given for banning many fairs from the mid nineteenth century. This is reflected by the majority of arrests related to wife sales being for disturbing the peace, causing public nuisance, etc. This is often the reason for their many mentions in the press.

Britain's increasing population and the congestion in cities led to a loss of many open spaces that were suited to wife sales, but the nature of employment also had an effect. Factories enforced standards on their workforces who were seen as more hard-working and more law-abiding than domestic or farm workers. Industries created standardised working hours, while in major ports or established urban centres much of the labour was casual. Such fixed hours limited the number of people loitering in the streets or attending markets to witness the sales. But when factory workers had time off, they gathered in much bigger crowds, especially on Sundays and holidays. This increased the risk of civic intervention and arrests for public disturbances, so sales were often driven indoors or further afield.

This regularisation of work meant that sales became restricted to the accepted time off for the workforce, which often included the sellers, so this also added to the degree of organisation required. The couple could no longer merely turn up at the market or street and expect a crowd to gather.

The crowds themselves may have acted differently. Where the industry mostly employed men, the women married young, so tended to be more conservative in their attitude towards marriage, and more likely to object to wife selling. Many factory owners were Nonconformists who encouraged literacy, and the development and improvement of the machinery they worked on. Such problem-solving at work may have encouraged workers to reject the idea that an unhappy marriage was something to be endured, so they may have been more likely to take action such as separation or wife selling. But where employers were conservative in their beliefs and/or evangelists, they may have been more likely to intervene if they saw the sale as a breach of their own moral codes. This was a far cry from mentions of country people who welcomed it as free entertainment.

The open marketplace was traditionally a site of contracts being sealed with a handshake, of fair dealings in the presence of witnesses, so a location where the process could be seen as being legal. Crowds were often reported as being large, with one instance where the woman could not be seen above it. The lack of details makes it difficult to predict the behaviour of crowds as their responses depended on the story presented to them.

If the husband had mistreated his wife, the new couple were cheered on their way. But if the husband was seen as a victim of his wife's betrayal, as in many cases where she became involved with their lodger, if the husband was respected by the community and perhaps seen as marrying beneath himself, or if the woman was seen to be lacking in shame, the new couple were often hissed at or pelted with mud or snow. If the woman was pretty, or had been abused or betrayed by her husband, the crowd's anger was turned on him. There was a case where an old man's betrayal of his young wife resulted in him and his new wife being burnt in effigy on the village green,[1] which shows the survival of traditional community protests in small communities well into the nineteenth century. Another couple were burnt in effigy outside their own home in what was seen as a particularly shameful affair: the mother of twelve children moved in with a neighbour.[2] What made it more shameful was that her new husband's wife had recently died, so the couple were perceived as insulting the dead as well, a matter not treated lightly at the height of the Victorian age. The dead wife was probably friend and neighbour to many in the area, so this sale was a personal insult to the community. But the crowd's response was not always negative There were instances where the crowd thought the sale was valid and protected the parties from arrest; one such case was witnessed by a French officer at Ashbourne Derbyshire during the French Wars.[3]

There were also oddities, such as making bids 'for a joke' by a chimney sweep at Cheltenham in 1830 or of nobody bidding at all as in Bristol in 1823 and Great Torrington market in 1810. These may have been due to lack of money or need, but could also have expressed moral condemnation. Yet another factor here may have been the individual police officers or justices of the peace; if they were unpopular, the mob may have been acting against them rather than defending the sale per se. In many cases the response of the mob hints at matters that fail to reach the printed records, which makes them more intriguing. Even if the sales happened without any record of crowd intervention, there was also the risk of later, possibly ongoing problems, such as the man who sold his wife in 1865 to a rich Yankee and remained in his largely empty family home, 'subject to not a little annoyance by his neighbours'.[4] Another source claimed the husband was taunted by boys in the street with cries of 'who sold his wife'. How many of those involved in wife sales were snubbed in the street, ignored in shops and pubs, their businesses boycotted? There were many ways that neighbours could make life difficult for those involved in sales which have not found their way into press records. This could have made lives lonely and unbearable; they may have turned to alcohol or some form of self-harm, or been driven to move out of the area.

The eighteenth century was a time of widespread civil disturbances, with riots against tollgates, corn hoarding and export, and the press gang, all of which could result in bloodshed and capital convictions for those involved. These caused considerable concern for local authorities; in the absence of professional police forces, they had to rely on local gentry, who often served as justices of the peace, but they were unpaid, and at times were unavailable, so as civil unrest rose, the means to control it struggled — and sometimes failed — to keep pace. If the disturbances were prolonged, they could take the drastic step of calling in the militia, but this took time to arrange, and many were unwilling to use force against their neighbours out of loyalty or in fear of retaliation.

Two sales which took place away from markets were at Haverside near Manchester in 1835, where the participants were discharged by their employer in disgust, and in 1858 in front of a beershop near Bradford, where the factory owner kept the intended purchaser at work and threatened to sack those involved,[5] which shows the ability and willingness of employers in the industrial areas to keep the peace in the absence of legal authorities.

In the introduction to Richard Gough's *The History of Myddle* is a description of Shropshire as comprising large areas of common land and woods into the late seventeenth century. Near Myddle, a squatters' colony settled and became part of the local community. Many were poor, with one family living in a cave and another in a hollow oak, but as they became established, with hard work, they thrived.[6]

This squatter community — these edge-dwellers — probably

never married legally. Many lived in forests, and on land reclaimed from marshes, outside the parish system, so they are missing from church registers. Their relationships were based on social acceptance rather than the rule of law. These men were fit, resourceful and brave; they provided much of the manpower for the army and navy as a means of personal advancement. They also provided labour for the factories, but as with most working people at the time, unless they drew attention to themselves by exceptional skills or law breaking, they failed to appear on the records. If they sold their wives — especially via private agreements rather than in public spaces — there is no way to trace them.

The term 'mob' often appears in eighteenth-century literature, and in Bristol it was sometimes raised to suppress soldiers rioting when bored waiting to go abroad. They were often hired to bully opponents in elections, and occasionally rioted, especially against the actions of the press gang. By the late sixteenth and early seventeenth centuries in England, there were many large groups of men who had no hope of ever becoming masters, and established their own businesses, so they were highly mobile and largely beyond the law. They were inventive and independent but often poor so they sought better lives in factories and the armed forces. Many were squatters, dockworkers, or itinerant labourers who were unconcerned with religion or politics, but who could be mobilised for public action by anyone with funds. This is yet another effect of the closure of the monasteries which had managed to limit the size of the population and could often control their behaviour. The mob became a useful tool when they were bribed to cause chaos for political opponents during election time. 'It could be used by Presbyterians against the Army in 1647, by royalists in 1660, by church and king men under Anne.'[7]

The risks were exacerbated by the growing populations of towns and cities, the move from packhorse to wheeled vehicles for goods transport, and the need to build on central open spaces, so these open spaces shrank as the people using them continued to grow. The mob became so feared in Manchester that, from 1760, the authorities moved their markets from the centre of the city.[8] Fear of the mob grew dramatically during the French Wars, when public gatherings were increasingly seen by authorities as dangerous, so punishment for wife selling shifted from being a moral issue to one of public order, threatening life and property.

Wife sellers thus became confronted with a conflict between the need for open sale to ensure legality versus the fear of arrest, as shown by a case in 1845 when a sale was stopped by police in Banbury Market Place. The participants sought legal advice, and were told to go further away [9] But by this time, many marketplaces had been abandoned as improved transport allowed selling to be more centralised, in the many market halls that had been built, so the remaining open spaces were no longer policed by market authorities. In Nottingham in 1852, the wife was sold on the open market, but at less than the asking price as delays were considered dangerous'.[10] The sellers managed to evade the mob at Callington in 1846 when the husband, afraid of a ducking, sent a friend dressed in female clothes as a decoy for the mob whilst the real sale took place unmolested.[11]

A sale in Bilston, Staffordshire in May 1819 used guards to clear a path to an inn where the post-sale celebrations were held, but Menefee suggests this may be a reworking of an account of another sale.[12] These private security arrangements seem to have been a rarity; though friends may have been invited and not recorded. Several sales mention relatives, so there may have been friends and family nearby in case of trouble. Sellers seem sometimes to have acted like guerrilla units: involving only the minimum of people, who appeared suddenly, achieved their goal and vanished before trouble could arise.

The most interesting case, due to the immense amount of detail, is that of 'Rough Moey' and his wife, where the crowd was attracted out of curiosity. Moey was escorted by four men with truncheons, perhaps in anticipation of trouble, or, as with the fiddler, was a part of the street theatre. When his wife appeared, the crowd exchanged banter with the auctioneer and master of ceremonies, Moey. His wife held up well, but then something in her snapped; she handed her baby to her future husband and burst into tears. The fun was over; the crowd and her beau turned on Moey, urging him to get it over with.

Similar changes of allegiances can be seen in a broadside from Edinburgh in 1828. The wife was allegedly sold for her drunkenness and adultery, though it seems she retained her good looks. The crowded streets meant that the auctioneer was mounted on a horse, but at first was unable to be heard above the crowd, probably due to the novelty of the event. Several characters competed to outbid each other, starting with a Highland drover and a Killarney pig jobber who was of course drunk, A brogue maker who was a friend of the wife then attacked the auctioneer. The crowd — initially claimed to be several thousand but now a mere seven hundred — became outraged at the sale and hurled rocks. Police were claimed to have restored order, but why were there no arrests? Bidding recommenced, with a Jack tar finally being outbid by a widowed farmer, with whom the wife rode away. Plenty of detail was provided here, as with the Rough Moey account, but the broadsheet account is so scattered with stock characters as to raise doubts about its veracity.

An account that has a strong sense of reality comes from Herefordshire where the husband objected to the low bids, claimed his wife was worth more and was told by the crowd to 'keep her master, keep her for her good looks'.[13]

Crowds often turned on husbands who mistreated their wives. In Cheltenham in 1830 a husband had to flee for fear of being treated with the pump,[14] a punishment often used in the absence of the ducking stool to punish scolding women, but also a quick, readily available form of punishment which suited crowds as it was hard to blame a single person for its use or abuse. Another messy sale was in 1829 at Barnet Fair. The couple were pelted with mud, and the wife was left behind. This was probably made worse by the fact that the woman refused the first sale, so was put up again, leaving time for a large crowd to gather and express their disapproval.[15] At a sale in Pontefract in 1803, the couple were also pelted with snow and mud.[16] At Hertford market in 1834, the magistrates were in session, so the town clerk and constables attended, but the husband escaped. The couple were warned they faced jail if they continued. They were abused by the crowd, and the woman became ill from her injuries.[17]

Rough music was described by Hardy to shame the Mayor of Casterbridge, but it was a stealthy affair, hiding from the constable. Mobs often demonstrated against acts of adultery, but especially when it was flagrant, when it was seen as a threat to other marriages, even to the institution itself. This was the case when a couple eloped when both were already married. Many communities accepted illegitimate children as they were innocent. But there was often outrage when adultery was between a wife and a lodger, as they were seen as betraying the trust of the master of the house. This was even worse when attempts were made for the ménage-à-trois to continue under the same roof, as in Tonbridge in 1828 when the trio were charged with rebellion and sent to prison.[18] In Flora Thompson's novel *Lark Rise to Candleford*, a labourer's wife's lover shared their home, and the family were subject to rough music before being expelled from the parish.

In some cases, the woman was singled out for the anger of the mob, and some were called 'hussy' or 'slut', words which strangely have no male equivalents. One such woman was claimed to have mistreated her first husband and another waved a kerchief. There were instances where the mob's behaviour is incomprehensible, so they clearly knew more than was reported in the paper.

A man bought a wife at Chipping Norton market about 1855, but was subjected to three nights of rough music with horns, trumpets, tin whistles and beating on cans with sticks. Then the mob burnt him in effigy at his door.[19]

Opposition from neighbours is implied in many cases by accounts of the couple having already moved away, so the husband had to track them down to arrange the sale. Their removal may have been an attempt to avoid either of them being the objects of community backlash. In Sheffield 1796, a man sold his wife for a mere six pence but then paid a guinea for a coach to take the new couple to Manchester.[20]

16

BEYOND SMITHFIELD

The English lord marries for love, and is rather inclined where money is.
Nancy Mitford

The Normans established markets to ensure reliable food supplies; they were generally about seven miles apart: within walking distance of everyone, but not too close to compete with each other. Many were established by local churches as acts of charity, and by the Knights Templar in the parish of Temple in South Bristol. Some were set up by wealthy landowners who benefited from the extra income and the convenience of having fresh food at the gates of their estates such as at Wilton in Wiltshire.

Some flourished, especially those where beast markets were held for the animals to be fattened up after their long journeys for local consumption over the ensuing year. Other markets failed, often due to depopulation of the region when local industries died out or when enclosures drove locals from their homes. By 1600 there were about eight hundred market towns, but improved transport, especially the construction of turnpike roads from the early eighteenth century allowed farmers to use huge, wide-wheeled wagons. The arrival of the railways sent many markets and their towns into terminal decline.

London was by far the most populous city in Britain throughout this period, but though some wife sales were recorded there, the numbers were not in proportion to its vast size. Virtually the only venue mentioned was Smithfield Market, a site with its own rules and regulations, beyond the reach of the civic authorities. This raises questions as to whether it attracted sales, or whether they were held elsewhere but were never recorded.

But London cannot be taken as being representative of the rest of the country. By international standards, it is unusual in being not just the centre of the court and of parliament, but also of commerce and trade, of fashion and the arts, so it was much larger than its nearest provincial rivals. It acted — then, as now — as a magnet for anyone in Britain who dreamed of getting ahead in the world. The downside was that it had far more problems as a working city: providing food and removing vast quantities of human and animal waste, housing, and controlling crime and disease.

Its crowded streets meant it had no equivalents of provincial street markets; to this day, London's big markets are wholesale, so people relied on street vendors and home deliveries before the age of modern shops. In the provinces, markets and open spaces in towns and cities were the centre of communities, places for all members of the town and its hinterland to meet, socialise and exchange news. Many markets have occupied the same place for centuries, a few were much older. Local businesses made extra revenue on market days, so where a market has declined or ceased, so has the area where it was held. Before the Reformation, they were often owned and run by churches which are now empty while many markets are experiencing a revival.

The most famous or infamous site for wife selling was London's Smithfield beast market. But accounts of these accounts were mostly from French officers, prisoners of war whose movements were restricted, so they carry an inherent geographical bias. They were probably present when wife selling was at its peak, which further skews the record. This link with beasts suggested the women were being treated as cattle, especially when pens and halters were also involved.

Smithfield was a centre for highly specialised trades such as drovers, shepherds and graziers who came from as far away as Scotland and Wales, while the butchers and innkeepers were local. Large sums of money changed hands, on various terms, which also encouraged wife selling. So it was more than a public space; it was also a major site of exchange, where practices from far afield could be introduced to or spread from the metropolis. There was also a degree of freedom for those who attended as they were beyond the remit of the city and of Westminster. There were very few sales within London itself, despite its reputation for the practice, so wife selling cannot be described as a local practice.

Market spaces varied immensely. Where animals were sold in the centre of town, such as in Boston, Nottingham, Wisbech or Devizes, the space was huge, so could be used for open-air banquets, fairs or balloon launches. Many have been converted into civic squares: acres of concrete, potted plants, fountains and statues of forgotten worthies. In 1852, a wife sale was recorded in the sheep pens of Nottingham beast market.

Elsewhere, the market outgrew its original site at the central crossroads, and spread into adjoining streets. Some towns had specialist markets such as Yorkshire's cloth markets; Ipswich and many others had grain markets. Salisbury had designated streets for different trades, and some towns remember these with names such as Butchers' Row and The Haymarket. At the other extreme, some places had markets without marketplaces; the most famous probably being London's Eastcheap and Cheapside, but also Exeter, Worcester, Colchester, Chester, Chichester, Bath and Bristol. A wide range of people attended, from poor country folk selling their wares to the local squire, parson and innkeeper. A 1739 account from Brackley suggests a surprising diversity, with

'Mr Arnold the one-eyed butcher, Master Gill of Brackley (who gathers mushrooms and has but one leg) and a soldier man and a woman with him who showed us the alligator'.[1]

Fairs are often confused with markets, but the former tended to be large, diverse affairs, with some such as Stourbridge near Cambridge which — like St Bartholomew's, which adjoined Smithfield Market — specialised in wool, and attracted traders from great distances, sometimes even from abroad. They were generally annual events where merchants purchased stock for the following year. Vast sums of money were exchanged which attracted pickpockets and highway robbers. Pirates plundered ships coming to England from Wales and Ireland. Entertainments were provided from early times as an added attraction which extended the fair's duration by several more days. Many became so large they had to move to the outskirts of town. Goldsmiths — the forerunners of bankers — often attended, which allowed loans to be paid. When the national coinage became worn out as at the end of the seventeenth century, vast amounts of old coins were exchanged for new. At local fairs, doctors provided refreshments for patients when they paid their bills.

Being outside the restrictions of the civic authorities, fairs held an extra attraction for wife sellers wary of being arrested. In 1833, a wife was sold at Lansdown Fair near Bath, but the sale was not considered legal as it was not in a public place, so they moved to the crowded market in town and were arrested. Lansdown was a mixed fair so it may not have been strongly linked with animals, which may have caused problems. More likely, as in the sale in Hardy's *The Mayor of Casterbridge*, it may have been held in a tent, and deemed not public enough. As towns and cities grew, the open spaces declined, so the element of openness became more difficult to maintain.

The link between wife sales and animals may have been stronger at fairs, as some of them specialised in certain animals, such as Horsham Colt Fair, which was the site for sales in 1790, 1825 and 1844. Also noted were Burton Fair (1790), Longtown (1827), Barnet (1829) and Bakewell (1838), but there were probably more where the records have not been searched.

Most sales do not specify that a market was involved, though this was often implied by it taking place in a central open space. There were few other mentions of beast markets, such as Canterbury in 1820 where the seller attempted to employ a salesman, but when this was refused, he paid the market toll himself and put his wife in a pen to be sold.[2] This is generally cited as an example of the woman being treated as a beast, but it seems to have been more a means of allowing the sale to happen and to have it accepted as legal. There were also sales at cattle markets at Gloucestershire (1838), Nottingham (1852), and Oxford (1859) and three sales from St Thomas's Market, Bristol, in 1815, 1823, and the last of which was one of the first sales in the new beast market at Temple Meads in 1830.[3]

There is also a problem in assuming that open spaces — even if named as markets — were not solely used for commerce. Our ancestors held celebrations and played sports, many of which have since either died out or moved indoors. Some wife sales mention a market cross or high cross, a central landmark for making public announcements, which featured steps for the display of wares, including wives. High crosses were at the town's central crossroads where they were often joined by other civic furniture, or 'engines of punishment' such as the town stocks, pillory and whipping post, with the ducking stool at a nearby water source. The gathering of people for fairs or markets often coincided with the holding of courts. This maximised the crowds to witness and express their opinions upon miscreants, especially of those convicted of market fraud or pickpockets, as market rubbish was at hand to throw at offenders. This is reflected in the several instances when wife sales were interrupted and taken before the magistrates or justices of the peace.

Crosses were sites of proclamations: of wars, ascensions, births and deaths of monarchs, and military victories. They were painted and gilded when royal visitors arrived, or draped in black crepe when they died. Town criers made announcements there of civic matters, auctions and sales, warnings to lawbreakers and of new laws passed or old ones amended or rescinded. They were the sites of celebratory bonfires and burning tar barrels, especially for

Gunpowder Plot celebrations which could damage the ancient structure. Early Quakers preached there, and scolds punished with the bridle or brank, were paraded in public before being tethered nearby. The Blacks — a group of masked poachers from Windsor Forest — protested at the draconian poaching laws in 1723 by dumping a dead deer in the market place. High crosses were also noted as the site of several wife sales.

During the Commonwealth, when some churches were closed or converted to other uses, marriage banns were posted on the cross instead of in the church porch. The Mayor of Bridgewater in 1774 posted a letter complaining about a satire on his son-in-law which had allegedly been attached to the cross. He called the author 'a impudent raskel and Durty Scoundrel' and advised him to mind his own business.[4] In 1783 during protests over corn shortages, a notice was fixed on Carlisle market cross demanding that two men stop starving local people by exporting corn to France to collect the export bounty, then threatening 'by the Lord God Almighty we will give you Bounty at the Expence of your Lives you Damned Rogues.'[5]

Streets were used for performances by travelling players who set up stalls, or for mystery plays which were performed on mobile stages wheeled about the town. Trades and guilds held annual processions and feasts, and theatrical protests against unfair taxation were held, such as at Ledbury, Gloucestershire, in response to the introduction of a tax on cider in 1763. The procession made up of the various trades people involved in cider production as well as the poor made its way through the main streets. A drum beat the dead march and church bells were muffled throughout the day as the mock funeral expressed the widespread expectation of financial ruin.[6] Elections were popular local events, and in Norwich in 1679, the victors were carried in chairs in a candlelit procession after much celebratory drinking and feasting. By then it was too late for the exhausted crowds to stagger home, so 'people slept in the markett place and laye like flocks of sheep in and about the crosse.[7]

The behaviour of crowds attracted to wife sales varied widely. They could show sympathy, and turn against the authorities, echoing the situation when Dorothy Waugh, a militant Quaker had tried to preach at Carlisle market cross around 1656. The mayor condemned her to wear the scold's bridle and to be mocked, but locals were appalled by such violence; people wept and the torture implement 'became the crown of a martyr'.[8]

England's famously damp weather has always been a problem for open markets, churning up mud in the streets, soaking people and damaging the produce. From the early seventeenth century when the population in most areas was rising, improvements were made to crosses. The shaft was used as an upright support for a covered space such as the cheese cross at Cheddar. Some churches had arcades along the walls which they rented out for market stalls to bring in extra revenue. Where the markets were run by the civil authorities, they built arcades for markets with space above for civic use such as the storage of unsold goods, market or town administration, a school or even a theatre or assembly rooms. As incomes rose for many from the mid-eighteenth century, complaints were made about mud and filth in the streets. This was often cited as deterring middle-class women from shopping in the streets, and by improvers to encourage the building of market halls. This absence of middle classes tarrying in the streets reduced the status of the open marketplace, and led to a decline in people likely to report events such as wife sales in the press.

There were also problems with the increasing traffic being forced to a standstill on market days, so larger towns and cities moved their markets indoors. Bristol's narrow streets became such a problem in the early eighteenth century that the city's high cross was removed in 1733, but it was also condemned as an unwanted relic of popery. A decade later, the city built a large corn exchange with markets behind it, but they had to ban the sale of goods on the streets to force traders to pay to be protected from the elements. There are no records of wife sales in the old street markets, which makes sense as they were overlooked by the council house, so would easily have been stopped by the authorities. But south of the river was a poorer area, so sales may have been held at Temple and St Thomas's Market. When the latter was rebuilt, several sales occurred which suggests it was a local tradition which has left no record.

Though Smithfield was known for wife selling, press accounts are less common than expected; being recorded in 1797, 1801, 1803, 1805, 1815, 1828, 1832, 1838 and 1841, so they seem to have been mostly during the French Wars. But two of the most atypical examples were also found there. In 1841 the seventeen-year-old wife was arrested after the sale and given legal advice by the local justice, and in 1815 'a beautifully dressed young woman' wearing a silk halter covered with a lace veil arrived in a coach. She was sold by a cattle grazier to a famous horse dealer, so they were not strangers to the market. The high price of fifty guineas and the single bidder show it was not an open sale. So Smithfield catered for people across a wide range of incomes.

Other specialist markets where sales were held include Cheltenham Corn Market in 1830 when a wife was rescued by the crowd from her brutal husband who tried to force her to be sold. There were also sales at Retford Corn Market (1856) and Bradford Butter Market (1837). This suggests the link with animals was not crucial; nobody has ever suggested that sales in specialist markets meant that the women were being treated as lumps of butter or bags of corn. Though some of the earliest sales priced the woman by weight, which suggests grain markets were used before those for beasts.

It is hard to make sense of a sale recorded on Dartmoor in the 1890s. A farmer was seen standing by the side of a road beside his wife with a halter round her neck dressed only in a shift. She was priced at ten shillings. Was there no market nearby, or was the farmer lazy? Did the wife's lack of clothing mean she had run up debts which had made her husband wish to be rid of her?[9]

The marketplace, fairgrounds or streets therefore need to be seen in the context of wider notions of public space. When couples had arguments in their homes, they were often overheard by neighbours and sometimes the arguments spilled out into the road where friends and neighbours intervened. Town criers were employed by civic authorities to announce major events, including summons to town meetings, so people were accustomed to listening for cries, and were often able to leave whatever they were doing to respond. In towns and large cities there often seem to have been young lads hanging about; in one sale they climbed on a town cross to get a better view but this interfered with the sale. Being too small for adult work, lads were often underemployed; even after education became compulsory till the age of thirteen, many were unable to find work until physically mature at sixteen. In the interim, they spent much of their time on the streets, available to run errands or get into trouble. An account from south Bristol in 1844 compared local children to a swarm of locusts, buzzing like flies: 'settled upon horse and dog cart, curricle and wagon as each rumbled by'.[10]

As markets became crowded, several announcements were made for wife sales at landmarks so they could be found. Sales were held at the Preston Obelisk in 1817, the Bolton Obelisk and the Gas Pillar at Manchester, both in 1835. Market crosses were named at Halifax (c1805), York (1815), Selby (1852 and 1862), and Repton (1852). In 1865 at Grantham, 'the honoured structure was taken possession by a multitude of exciteds',[11] whose noise attracted the police. The couple dared not proceed.

In the eighteenth and nineteenth centuries, improved transport allowed some markets to expand at the expense of their neighbours. Some evolved to cater for specialist goods, such as cheese at Cheddar, while others died out. When developers built new squares, especially in London's West End, they often included a small market to make homes more desirable with supplies of fresh food on their doorsteps. But such small, middle- and upper-class sites were not noted for any sales. New towns may never have had markets, so increasing numbers of potential wife sellers lacked access to a suitable open space.

In 1817, a sale was held on the quay at Dartmouth. In the Dutch auction, described as being on Tonmarton Street, Knott Mill, both the buyer and seller were boatmen, so it may have run beside or near a canal. Spa towns, inspired by the success of Bath Spa, built paved areas for promenading, so became popular open spaces, which could have been venues for wife sales, though the only suggestion of this comes from 1827 on York Pavement. 'One eyed Mills and his one legged wife'[12] who was sold to a man with whom she had been cohabiting do not sound like the usual genteel spa visitors. In 1831, a countryman bought a wife there for sixty guineas and led her away amidst a cheering crowd.[13] In London, there was a sale on Broadway, Westminster, in 1809 where a woman was sold for two guineas to 'one of her gallants'[14] so this was another example of the practice being adopted by more affluent people. At the other end of the social scale, and of the city, a 'wretched looking fellow' sold 'a respectably dressed woman, aged about thirty' outside a pub in Whitechapel about 1833. This was condemned as yet another pre-arranged event.[15]

The sale by Thompson in Carlisle in 1832, made famous by his humorous speech, makes no mention of the venue. The use of a chair for the woman to stand on suggests they were outside a public house which supplied the furniture, so the auctioneer and the 'goods' could be seen above the crowd. The even more famous sale by 'Rough Moey' at Wednesbury in the Black Country was on an open street, but seller and wife both stood on upturned tubs, and beer was supplied by a nearby hostelry. There is a brief record of a sale at St Peter's Square in Nottingham (1855) which seems to be the only mention of an urban square, possibly a former market place, and in Bradford (1858), a large crowd witnessed a 'woman adorned with ribbons and halter' sold on a public street, suggesting there was no suitable open space within reach. Another sale was held outside a beershop at Little Horton, Bradford (1858). The site may have been chosen to allow them to retreat indoors in case of trouble. The woman had already been sold, but some detail had been omitted, so they employed an auctioneer on horseback, suggesting a large crowd had gathered.

Finally, a sale that would have worked as a storyline in a soap opera: a neighbourhood: in the village of Husband's Bosworth, Market Harborough in 1859, when the town crier announced that John Berry's wife was for sale. The novelty drew a large crowd into the street. 'There was a great deal of chaff' and many bids. The wife was jeered by the public, and she 'tried but failed to come to better terms with her better half and live peaceably and quietly for the future,' echoing advice given to couples by the authorities. It seemed he was determined to dispose of her for another, but when the police arrived, the husband was terrified and the sale was called off, at least for the time being. This case seems unlikely to have had a happy ending. But it is also unusual as it was the husband who was seeking a new wife while the reverse was far more common.[16]

In 1764 a carpenter in Southwark had discussed his unhappy domestic situation with a workmate, claiming there were only two solutions, for him to murder his wife or to sell her.[17]

This was the reality for untold numbers of our ancestors. In the furthest corners of the empire, the Danish-born adventurer, playwright, and convict who had fought both for and against the British, Jorgen Jorgenson ended his days in Hobart Town, but even he was incapable of finding marital peace and happiness.

"In Tasmania he embarked on the greatest adventure even of his adventurous life. He was married to a stout, elderly lady who, it was recorded, would frequently chase [him] through the streets of Hobart with any weapon on which she could lay her hand, from a rolling pin to a broom handle.'[18]

17

EXTRAORDINARY CASES

People who say it cannot be done should not interrupt those who are doing it.
George B. Shaw

Wife selling caused considerable outrage, bemusement and amusement in its wide variety of forms, and claims could be made that every sale was extraordinary inasmuch as it happened at all. Some have echoes of early Christianity, others suggest pagan roots, and some seem to have been agreed over a few jars in a local hostelry. There was also a huge range of expectations from marriage itself, from the young men who accepted each other's fiancées to couples who split up after only a few months together. All of which makes it impossible to define what constituted an ordinary wife sale; but the following sales do stand out.

When John Allen tracked down his wife in 1837 and agreed to her sale at Wirksworth, the contract was verbal, and he claimed to have been 'bereaved' of his wife by James Taylor, a term usually associated with physical death, so it imparts a real sense of the loss of his wife: the empty house, the silence that greeted him when he returned home. His demand for payment for her clothes seems at first petty, but at a time when most people had only a set of work clothes and another for Sunday best, clothes were handmade, so they were expensive and long lasting. But his anger seems to have been dissipated by the ritual of the sale. In modern parlance, it seems he obtained closure.[1]

In Rotherham in 1775, Farmer Johnathan Jowett's extraordinary procession wearing cuckold's horns may well be the most bizarre sale, and seems to have drawn the biggest crowd, at least outside the capital. It shows that the language of ritual was still widely known and practised. This happened at a time when the Enlightenment was well under way, so such behaviour should have been relegated to the dustbin of history. Or perhaps this was another act of closure long before the term was coined The term 'cuckold' has largely fallen out of use in parallel with the importance of the contract of marriage itself, with so many couples preferring to cohabitate. Yet in an episode of *Hill Street Blues*, a cuckolded police officer saw a box of stolen goods on his desk which included a horned Viking helmet. He put on the helmet and ranted about his friends mocking him. As with the farmer, and Parson Holland's scoundrel Davies, he was defusing the mockery, but in this instance he was mistaken. Sometimes a Viking helmet is just a Viking helmet.

A very odd and confusing case comes from the diary of a vicar in Hadley, Suffolk from before 1840,[2] claiming an agriculturalist named John Frost had given his wife one hundred pounds to make her more desirable for sale at market. He then married his housekeeper, but continued to support his first wife in the poorhouse after her purchaser's death. What are we to make of this? The legal husband was liable for his wife's support, so she should not have been accepted as a pauper by the local parish. It seems they accepted her second marriage as valid, which allowed her to be housed as a widow. It seems the reason for the sale was Frost's desire to be rid of his wife, so perhaps he had fallen for his housekeeper, a common enough event. But his continued support for her means he still felt responsible. What makes this case so odd though is that the vicar notes that Frost was at times mad — whatever that meant at the time. Also, the couple did not go to church, though Frost's second marriage was in the parish register. Was his second marriage in another parish where he failed to mention it, or was his first marriage a cohabitation? This is utterly bewildering.

Claims were made that from the middle of the nineteenth century, sales became more furtive. This was probably caused by the establishment of police forces, and the rising risk of the authorities intervening, such as in this example from 1852 titled 'Wonders Will Never Cease', which occurred at Nottingham's beast market. A couple with two friends went into a pub to steel their nerves. The wife was described as attractive, and was the only one who could write, so seems to qualify as a member of the 'middling sorts'. With a shawl covering her new halter, she went with the others to the sheep pens. The husband grasped the halter and announced his wife was for sale for two shillings and six pence, but was met with silence. A navvy offered a shilling, but the husband 'glared unutterable things at the bidder... declaring that the bidder knew her value better than that!' But the bid was accepted as 'delays were considered dangerous' and they withdrew to a pub to draw up the agreement. The woman was the only one who could write. This was clearly an arranged sale to deal with the wife's adultery, and may be the cheapest of such sales, so the purchaser had taken advantage of the dangers to get a bargain.³

There were ways of avoiding mob intervention, as in a clever tactic from 1772. The sale was such a novelty that a huge crowd had gathered at Hull market, so it had to be called off. A decoy couple appeared later in the afternoon which allowed the sale to proceed uninterrupted elsewhere.⁴

It seems that by the mid-nineteenth century, sales were moving up the social scale. In 1852 the landlord of a pub at Oakington sold his wife to a respectable widowed farmer for ten pounds, which suggests a case of adultery. But the sale seems not to have been prearranged as the buyer did not have the ready cash. More likely the woman was healthy and a good worker. He provided a deposit to seal the deal and the husband handed over her ring, making her 'unmarried'. The buyer returned next day with the remainder, agreeing to lead her home by halter the next morning by the halter, completing the sale and the remarriage, thus the account was unusual in reporting the duality of the custom. By naming of the venue the article emphasised the belief of the participants that there was no sense of illegality or shame associated with the act.[5] This rather contradicts the notion that the sales had become shameful, as a publican was a man of stature in his local community.

A sale from 1764 in Southwark suggests how wife sales were initiated; as in so many instances, alcohol was involved. A carpenter moaned to his single colleague that the only way to free himself from his wife was by murdering her, but his colleague suggested he sell her instead. The husband claimed 'no one would be such a fool as to buy mine', but to his surprise, his companion made him an offer. His wife seemed happy in her new relationship, but he either became lonely in his empty home or felt guilty, so he repeatedly visited his wife, demanding her return, but she claimed 'A sale is a sale, not a joke'.[6]

A sale in Midsomer Norton by private contract for six guineas in 1766 is also an oddity as the buyer was a gentleman, and there is no indication as to why he bought the woman and her youngest child. This price was high enough to be based on adultery, but the woman was not consulted. The husband was violent, and this case appeared in records as he failed to honour the agreement, and demanding more money and threatening to murder the couple. He was imprisoned, and the wife later had to appeal to the magistrates for protection from him.[7] Was the purchaser a single gent interested in benevolent causes who was in need of a housekeeper?

In 1865 appears the most expensive sale on record, of a Wolverhampton wife sold to a rich 'Yankee' or sailor who agreed to buy the woman and her children for one hundred and fifty pounds. The woman lost her nerve, but an extra fifty convinced her to agree to the sale. However, only five was paid, so the husband, having seen them off on the train, telegraphed to have them detained, another example of a non-legal activity making use of the legal system. When the payment was sorted out, the father kissed his children and bade them all a good trip to London.[8] But an earlier account claimed the new family were going to Leeds, and the seller — a coal dealer — was left to rattle around in his deserted home 'with not a little annoyance by his neighbours'. No mention of rough music is made, which doesn't exclude it, but there was a multitude of ways for neighbours to express their disapproval, not least by boycotting his business. Local boys were reported as hooting at him 'who sold his wife'.

This case is strange on so many levels, not least as to how did a 'Yankee' meet a married woman in deepest Wolverhampton? This was after the Californian gold rushes, which must have been a real magnet for many coal miners. The family home was described as being in 'California' which suggests that many had left, and perhaps returned, with or without fortunes. It thus seems likely that the buyer was a local man who had previously known the wife. Were they former sweethearts? Had the man promised to return for her with a fortune, but she tired of waiting and settled for the coal dealer? If so, this was a sale that echoed the return of soldiers and transported convicts. A woman cannot wait for ever.

The most widely reported case was that of Thompson of Carlisle. His amusing speech, comparing his wife to cholera, Mount Etna etc. was balanced by praise for her housekeeping. It has been suggested that his speech was invented, but he seems to have been a countryman of some stature, probably fond of dining with friends, so was likely capable of composing such a speech. His acceptance of a Newfoundland dog in part exchange for his wife drew claims that his wife was compared with it, but barter was still common practice, and a good dog was of immense value to him for security, hunting and even for pulling a dog cart. People seldom travelled with large sums of cash, due to the risk of robbery. This case is unusual in that it seems the couple had no major falling out, they just realised they were ill-suited and the man preferred a quiet life. No children were mentioned, which suggests this was a marriage based on companionship rather than intimacy.

The most complete account comes from the Black Country wife sale of Rough Moey which was a glorious piece of street theatre. It was introduced by a fiddler; there were men with truncheons to keep the peace, and Moey and his wife stood on upturned tubs. Locals were drawn to the noise, and at first, the old man's humorous banter drew them into supporting the sale, as the young wife seemed to be enjoying the show. But suddenly it all changed. The wife handed her baby to her future husband and broke down in tears; the audience turned on her husband and ordered him to get on with what had suddenly ceased to be a joke.

This case is also unique in having included the opinions of the crowd, making it more like modern journalism. It is probably also the longest piece on the subject. In 1933 The Lichfield Mercury printed an article on the town's history, claiming wife selling had been common in the Black Country and Staffordshire though there were no records of it in Lichfield. It names the author of this account as William Robert Hackwood, 'the unsung hero' of Wedgwood's Etruria factory, who was probably the designer of the seal promoting the abolition of the slave trade. But this begs the question: why was he there? Was he just passing, or had he heard of the incident in advance? Was the subject of particular interest to him and his friends? This suggests the middling sorts taking an active interest in the practice, and a possible link with the local 'improvers' such as the *Lunar Men*.[9]

A Thetford broadside of 1839 described another piece of street theatre giving the crowd insights as to the cause of their separation. The husband danced and sang to be rid of his troublesome wife, which amused the crowd. But the wife turned on him, accusing him of being a useless old dog, with no need for a young wife, and the women in the crowd began clapping their hands at him. He claimed she ate too much; she called him a miser. The husband endured this abuse and walked off singing.

A broadside from Bristol in 1815 descended into a bad soap opera. The couple attracted a large crowd, and a man appeared to ask terms. A bid was accepted, but it appeared he was a proxy for the woman's favourite swain, so the deal fell through. No mention was made of how many swains she had. She lost her temper and claimed the children were not those of her husband, so he announced he would sell her privately. This washing their laundry in public has a toe-curling veracity.

An incident from Kennington, near Oxford, in 1786 is curious in respect of the above, as a man bought a wife, for six shillings, but in the afternoon made a present of her to a friend. Did he really change his mind so quickly, or was he acting as proxy for the wife's lover, so was it another case of deception or fraud?[10]

A broadside which survives in Manchester's John Rylands Library relates something that allegedly happened at Edinburgh's Grassmarket. It was described as a 'full and particular account' of a sale on 16 July 1828. This is specific, suggesting a real incident, but the wife was alleged to have been a drunkard and adulteress, so hardly a desirable purchase. A parade of pantomime characters start the bidding, with a Highland drover, a stout tinker, Killarney pig jobbers and a Newry brogue maker, but the crowd became violent and police intervened. A sailor opened the bidding again, but the wife rode off with a widowed farmer. It is hard to know what to make of this. Menefee claims the event was not mentioned in local papers, though there could be many reasons for this, including a desire to discourage both sales and rioting, but the characters and their behaviour seem to have stepped from a comic opera. It was printed in Newcastle, possibly because nobody in Edinburgh would touch it for fear of attracting complaints. It may have been written to demonstrate the ignorance of the Scots and Irish, so propaganda for the more civilised English. Allegedly.

There were many people at this time who have left no trace in parish records, who worked within small communities that operated on their own lines. The railway navvies were often accused of immorality, but they had incredibly tough, unstable, lives and those who wrote about them were often evangelists, so less sympathetic to their reality. This case of canal workers — another close community, — shines a rare light on the workers on the canals, and how chaotic their lives could be. This is a rare citing from the Cheshire or Liverpool Assizes of 1864.

The most convoluted and confusing account concerned Hannah Green, who was charged with bigamy for marrying twice while her husband was still alive. A friend claimed Hannah had been sold in a halter at Brummagen Fair nine years earlier, but in court, it was unclear if she had been legally married. The judge claimed that wife selling had formerly been common, but he thought it had died out and that ignorant people should be warned against it. Despite this, the jury found her not guilty, probably because they couldn't make sense of her love life.[11]

In 1775, a shoemaker of Wootton Bassett agreed to sell his wife to a cattle dealer at Swindon Fair for fifty pounds, but there are no details to explain why the price was so high. The man returned the next day with a group of friends, all wearing white cockades as for a wedding, but the sellers had fled.[12] This is yet another case which raises so many questions. How did he know the woman? Why was she so valuable? How could he assemble a wedding party at such short notice? Did he pay the full amount, and if so, did he pursue the couple for fraud?

In 1823 William Hodge put his wife up for sale after repeatedly threatening to do so. She was agreeable, but William Andrews 'anticipated the transaction of the sale by abducting her'. This is another action which is incomprehensible. Hodge was indicted for the attempted auction. For purchasing her, Andrews was sent to prison as a warning to others.[13] This suggests the sale was prearranged, but that wife selling was new to the area so the authorities punished them as a warning to deter any others who might copy them.

There are suggestions some sales were triggered by a husband's drunkenness and/or violence, but there are a few instances where one's sympathy is with the husband. The case of a wife robbing her elderly husband whilst he was in Hull Infirmary is one of them. This descended into soap opera with accusations flying of him being mean and her being wasteful. But an attempted sale in Boston in 1864 was a tragedy. The husband was a publican who seems to have been at his wit's end as his wife was a hardened alcoholic. She stole from him for her habit, and was clearly failing to fulfil her role as his helpmeet.

He tried to sell her for a pittance but this caused such outrage, the authorities intervened. He was so desperate, he offered to pay for her to be kept in the poorhouse, but he was legally bound by his marriage vows to support her, 'in sickness and in health'. He was fined for her misbehaviour and forced to take her home. Mercifully, she died a few days later after a final bender.[14]

Perhaps the most extraordinary sales were those of husbands. They were legally responsible for their wives, so these examples show that some women believed they could carry out contracts, and that they were financially independent. It also shows a level of humour and goodwill by the couple which is often lacking elsewhere. In 1774, the town crier of Leeds announced the sale of the unnamed husband of Joanna Cruttley. He was said to be a good carpenter and devoted husband, so sold for a very reasonable five shillings and a gallon of gin.[15]

The same source claimed a woman named Price had announced the sale of her husband in Manchester, at the end of the eighteenth century. The man good-humouredly listed his accomplishments, including flute playing and bootmaking, presumably not at the same time. The bidding rose, and he was sold for a guinea, a pair of fowls and a new dress.[16] There was also a record of a woman selling her husband in a halter — apparently the only such case — at Dewsbury market in 1815 for a mere sixpence.

An account from 1888 described how an unemployed man from Sheffield left his wife to go to Australia but on the way out formed an attachment with a young woman. When he told her he was married, she suggested a sale, so he jokingly suggested she write to his wife who asked for a hundred pounds but settled for twenty.[17] This is strange as the man was unemployed, so how did he get the funds to emigrate? And how did his wife survive in his absence? Many parishes paid for families to emigrate, but he left his wife behind, and she seemed not to be in any great need of funds, so this is very confusing.

The sale which seems to make the strongest case against the notion that wife selling was brutish dates from Thirsk Cross in 1855. The couple married when she was nineteen and he was sixty-four and had been happily married for ten years. She was sold for two shillings and sixpence to a shoemaker. They separated because the husband was becoming infirm and was unwilling to become a burden on his young wife. This seems to have been a really sad parting, with the husband preparing for death whilst setting his young wife free to start a new life.[18]

18

ON SHAME

I have lost my reputation. I have lost the immortal part of myself and what remains is beastial.
   Othello

The terms 'shameful', and to a lesser extent, 'disgraceful' and 'disgusting' are frequently found in accounts of wife selling. To readers then — as now — they seem apt, as leading a woman in a halter to an animal pen to be sold to the highest bidder is clearly marking her as an inferior creature or a commodity. It suggested women were being treated as animals, slaves, or both. As the French often noted, this coincided with women demanding better education, to own their own property, to divorce and to vote, so these sales were at the very least an anachronism. Also frequently noted was the meekness of the women, who seldom showed any sense of shame or anger as they endured being put on display to endure the bidding. This passivity further confused commentators. There were examples such as when a woman gaily waved a handkerchief, or insulted her former husband, so there was a sense that at least some of them were enjoying themselves and possibly getting their revenge. Some insisted the performance continued when problems arose, so they — rather than the men — were in charge. So, what was happening?

For starters, shame is a complex concept. What seemed to be an embarrassing act to middle-class male editors and commentators, often in London, was a world away from the noise and crowds of provincial streets, markets and public houses which were the centre of so many people's lives, and the sites of many wife sales.

When we think of shame, we sometimes think of Adam and Eve discovering their nakedness, but the early Quakers used nudity as a form of protest. To hippies nudity became a form of liberation, and to streakers at sports events — well, maybe you had to be there. Shame is not a one-size-fits-all concept; it depends on the person, the situation, the community at large and the motivation or need for the action. If a person chooses to do an apparently shameful act, then it is a completely different situation to that which is accidental or forced upon them.

In *The Mayor of Casterbridge*, Thomas Hardy describes a group of people from the poor part of town shaming the mayor and his former lover by carrying their effigies round the town. This, together with 'rough music', was a traditional means of expressing opposition to unacceptable social behaviour. In this case, it led to Henchard's pregnant wife being so traumatised that she went into premature childbirth and died. When Lady Abergavenny was discovered in bed with her husband's friend Mr Lydell, she pleaded with her nemesis not to betray her. She went into shock and died weeks later. Shaming could become a death sentence.[1]

This affair became famous for Lydell's betrayal of his friend Lord Abergavenny and was often cited as an example of divine and punishment and legal retribution. The injured husband sued Lydell for damages and was granted a staggering ten thousand pounds in compensation. Similarly high compensation was sometimes awarded when the betrayal was between fellow officers. This was attributed to the closeness of male bonding, but it was more than that. Members of the military have to be able to trust each other with their lives; after a betrayal, this would no longer be possible.

In order to be shamed, a person has to possess a sense of their own worth; their pride has to be injurable, so it is less common and even absent in the poor. Parson Holland wrote in 1800 of a local 'scoundrel' named Davies who reported some local people for stealing wood from the lord of the manor. The thieves paraded him in effigy, but their intended victim marched before them.[2] Davies not only failed to be hurt by this public shaming; he turned the action upside down. The parson seemed only mildly amused by the incident as he referred to them all as scoundrels.

In 2008, The News of the World tabloid printed pictures of young women in German uniforms spanking a naked Max Mosley, publicist. The shame should have destroyed his reputation, but instead he fought back and sued the paper for alleging his behaviour was Nazi-related. He won and though his name is tainted and his wife left him, he won sixty thousand pounds in damages, by changing the main story to that of a battle for personal freedom and against press corruption.

John Lydon described in his biography his arrest for assault in a Dublin pub, when he was refused bail. He claimed prison warders tried to humiliate him.[3] What should have been a shameful incident had quite the opposite effect, as Lydon claimed that he was innocent, and he had friends, family and colleagues to support him once he was released. As a man who seems to celebrate being difficult, it may have added to his fame. As with Mosley, a sense of anger, or outrage, can be a protection against attempts shame.

Until the mid-nineteenth century, all towns and villages had to maintain their machinery of punishment, i.e. the stocks, whipping posts, pillories and ducking stools in the centre of towns. Stocks were generally for drunks to sober up, the pillory for crimes that caused offence or outrage, such as publishing offensive material against church and state. The whipping post was for acts of violence, and the ducking, or cucking stool for infringements of market law, but more famously, for scolding women.

Before the Reformation, the church was the main source of

punishment for sexual misdemeanours. Their tools included forcing people to do penances or — in extreme cases — of excommunication. But these tools were lost at the Reformation. In the sixteenth and seventeenth centuries sexual misdemeanours were still reported to church courts, one of which survives in Chester Cathedral. Anyone convicted was made to confess, wearing a shift and holding a candle, in church or in public on market day in the market place, so maximising the audience. Justices of the peace could also punish adultery and fornication with whipping or the stocks.[4] Actions which today are generally seen as private matters were then seen as threats to wider society, potentially undermining the stability of neighbouring families.

By the late seventeenth century, England had lost its links with the hierarchy of Rome, had seen a king and many church leaders executed, and endured decades of debate as to faith and how people should behave, so the hierarchical structure that held society together had been disrupted; there was a widespread sense that the world had turned upside down. Even amongst the elite, church punishment seems to have carried little impact, as Mary Hampson, a respectable woman from a good family suffered years of physical abuse and financial fraud at the hands of her husband. Robert Hampson was a London barrister who lost a fortune — much of which was his wife's. He was eventually punished by the ecclesiastical courts with excommunication. But this seems to have caused him no problems in his professional or personal life, and when he died in 1688 he was buried amidst the Knights Templar and his peers in the Inner Temple Church.[5]

But Hampson was a man of high status and power, a far cry from the provincial poor, who were dependent on the lord of the manor for work and accommodation, and on local ratepayers and the parson for charity when they fell on hard times.

Punishment for sexual offences — often conception out of wedlock — was mostly for young women. This may seem to be misogynistic, but before science developed paternity tests, the man's guilt was virtually impossible to prove. Those convicted had to stand in the church porch in a white shift, i.e., their underwear. This seems far preferable to being whipped or immersed in a cold pond, but in small communities people could be incredibly cruel, and they had long memories. Many years later, a woman in Shropshire, Betty Beaman who had suffered this punishment suddenly burst into tears, explaining to a friend that paying penance had totally changed her, 'it took something out of me that'll never come back. The spirit left me', that she had lost her appetite for food, and 'somehow I 'ave a-lived like in the dust.'[6]

It seems the only way to be freed from this shame would have been to move elsewhere, but that required money, and to find work required a good reference, neither of which she was likely to obtain. If she had married her seducer, that might have resolved the matter, but it is unlikely any other man would propose to her.

In Jon Ronson's investigation of modern behaviour *So You've Been Publicly Shamed*, he describes several instances of the long-term harm that shaming can cause. He claims that in the United States, punishment by shaming died out not because it was ineffective, but that the reverse was true. One of the Founding Fathers, Benjamin Rush recommended in 1787 that the stocks, pillory, whipping post etc. should all be banned as they were too harmful.[7] Corporal punishment replaced shame within fifty years, as it was of short duration, and allowed criminals to make amends and move on, whereas there was no resolution to shaming. By destroying self-respect, it damned a person for life. This reflects the long-term damage which Betty Beaman suffered from standing in her church in a shift.

A person who has been shamed has the chance of reform, but only if their neighbours let them. If their shame was repeatedly told in the local pub, or if the person was taunted in public, their life would become a prolonged misery, and they would have to move away. But for the poor, this was seldom an option. For many people, their punishment became a life sentence

In Britain, it seems the decline of shaming was due to the rapid changes in society. Fewer people lived in small communities where shame could be applied, and many people were on the move. Shaming such as Betty suffered was limited as so many people were not part of the established — or any other — church. The draconian Elizabethan Poor Laws were little changed before the mid nineteenth century. If a man abandoned his family, he was imprisoned rather than shamed. As populations increased in the eighteenth and nineteenth centuries, public spaces declined, so there were few places where shaming punishments could happen.

A delightfully wicked example of shaming from 1751 would have delighted the late Roald Dahl. A dealer from Banbury caught a man in bed with his wife. He tied them up on a chair in front of a fire, and invited his neighbours to share tea, coffee and punch.[8] It is hard to imagine the misbehaving couple surviving such humiliation, yet the press failed to name them. It is intriguing to think what the outcome was, but the account claims the husband was content. Does that mean that the matter was closed, and that the couple were able to move on? It is less likely that the victims would have shared his belief.

At the other extreme, a woman from Wenlock, 'said to be the best abuser in the borough' was often forced to wear the scold's bridle.[9] Most people would have been terrified out of their wits by the mere threat of the bridle, so it seems this woman must have had severe mental health issues — probably the result of long-term abuse — which were of course not recognised at the time. She behaved like a punch-drunk boxer; beyond caring. Her reputation was beyond recovery; her anger outweighed whatever shame and physical pain the punishment caused, so she was in a similar state to Mr Lydon. The fact that she made money from her bad behaviour shows there was some profit for her in continuing with it, and that at least some of the locals supported her. In Wenlock, 'lawyer men' insisted on her punishment, so the pain was inflicted by people from outside the community, and was less likely to be accepted or supported by locals.

Some people were driven by desperation to indulge in shameful behaviour. In 1875, a man fled Derbyshire for America, leaving his wife and debts behind. His abandoned wife demanded part of the money raised when all his goods were sold, but when this was refused, she insisted on being included in the sale. 'There was no sale of "Lot 29"'[10]

Mothers were particular objects of shaming by the church, as they were expected to endure the ritual of 'churching' after enduring the pain of childbirth. Traditionally, it was a service of purification similar to the Hebrew practice based on the Book of Leviticus. In the sixteenth century, women were still considered unclean until this service; they were banned from touching consecrated objects, and in some churches, there were special stools to prevent them from contaminating pews with their sullied nether parts. If they refused such humiliation they were threatened with excommunication and denied communion.[11]

Some churches insisted they wear a white shift or a long veil, so echoing the practice of shaming forced on immoral women. To modern readers, comparing childbirth with prostitution is utterly bizarre and insulting, and there were women who objected to it. By the mid-eighteenth century this ritual seems to have decayed into a service of thanksgiving for their surviving the dangerous ordeal of childbirth.

It is easy to see why so many women turned against the new national church when it forced such humiliation upon them for obeying the Bible by doing their duty to propagate, but it seems this relic was a means of controlling the women, as well as an extra source of income for the priests in their increasingly empty 'steeple houses'.

The History of Myddle by Richard Gough is a seminal work of local history, describing the life of the Shropshire town in the late seventeenth century via the ownership of seats in the parish church. Gough was from an eminent local family, had trained as a barrister in London and was active in local affairs. He described many families who were ruined by drunkenness and mismanagement. He wrote of the ancient family the Bickleys, one of whom married Elizabeth

Tyler, who he describes 'was more commendable for her beauty than her chastity, and was the ruin of the family.'[12] Yet this is written as an aside. There is no sense that he was shamed. Or perhaps as a man of the world he'd seen worse.

In 1768, Anne Gibson became infatuated with an unsuitable partner, but relatives were unable to change her mind, so she married. But he soon died, and she 'retrieved her reputation for common sense'[13] by marrying a clergyman.

There were two options for church weddings: by far the most common was to have the banns read publicly in the local parish church on three successive Sundays, or to pay much more for a licence and private ceremony. But from the early eighteenth century, the former seems to have caused considerable embarrassment, motivating couples — perhaps a third of the total — and mostly of the expanding numbers of 'middling sorts' to opt for the latter.[14] This suggests the marriage ceremony was a far more boisterous and potentially embarrassing event than it is today, dad dancing and best man's speeches at the ceremony notwithstanding. Gretna Green became famous for couples wishing to marry in a hurry or free of parental intervention One source claims that the lesser-known venue at Lamberton attracted young local couples, 'still very secretive about their love affairs' who would discretely meet to cross the border and be married.[15]

Even for the gentry, discretion was an issue when marrying. When John Loveday, a gent of Wiltshire married for the third time he made plans for his fiancé and himself to arrive at the church. He wrote to her perhaps it maybe as well for you and me to travel separately to prevent bell ringing &c.'[16] And yet in his accounts, he noted payments for church bells to ring in the church where they were married and in his own parish. The '&c.' seems to be ominous.

Henry Stiles, in his book *Bundling* describes the traditional practice of young people becoming betrothed, and being allowed to share a bed in order to get to know each other before marriage. Such intimacy often happened in the presence of other people. He cites a young farmworker in Caernarvonshire in Wales who walked eleven miles every Sunday morning 'to favour his suit', and returned that night for work on Mondays. He usually arrived in time for church, then went home with his sweetheart, and they spent the following hour together in bed, 'according to the custom of the country'. Two years later, they married.

The source of this information was questioned as to the safety of this behaviour. The man claimed that in his thirty-six years in the area, where the practice was widespread, he had seen few abuses of the innocence of the practice. This belief was furthered by the fact that the young women involved were modest, and showed no embarrassment about the practice, nor did any of their parents or employers.[17] It seems it was an extension of the ancient tradition of a household sleeping together beside the fire in the depths of winter.

Such self-control was common in several of the North American colonies when religious faith was strong, and the fear of damnation kept the brakes on young passions. Stiles blamed the social traumas of mass migration, urbanisation, industrialisation for the decline of this innocent practice. These may have fed into the ultimate cause, the breakdown of closed communities of early colonists whose strict religious beliefs began to fade, causing the number of prenuptial conceptions to rise and bundling to die out. But the young people continued to court, and accidents happened.

This is probably why some of them might have been too embarrassed to marry publicly, and in some cases were in a hurry. Parson Holland of Stowey made a passing comment on a young bride being 'not so thin in the waist', but seemed unconcerned, as he had ensured the child would be born in wedlock.

Some engaged couples might have felt uncomfortable in the presence of childhood friends with whom they had shared intimate encounters. Some couples chose to have the banns read in a church some distance from their homes, but there was also the risk of various forms of boisterous rituals of the guests at the wedding celebration, which included treating, feasting, practical jokes, and ribald songs before the couple withdrew to consummate their union. Whilst private weddings were condemned for spending money on the licence, it was probably cheaper than having to fund the public celebrations. This was not just a matter of money; it was a sign of communities breaking down. It signalled that the good fortune of a couple was no longer seen to be of benefit to the wider community.

Parson Holland often complained of the struggle to find servants who were not stupid and lazy. He criticised his own servant who left the church before his banns were read to the congregation. The man stood behind him at the front of the congregation, so he made himself more conspicuous by walking out than if he had stayed in his normal place.[18]

Shame could also be used against those suspected of capital crimes, as in an incident from 1773. The practice of homosexuality was still a capital crime, but it had to be reported to the authorities. If the accused were members of the local community, this posed a problem as few people wished the death of a neighbour, though they probably felt uncomfortable about the crime itself. There was also a risk that the accused and their supporters could take revenge on their accusers, so life could become extremely unpleasant. In the case of the town of "L-y-k" (Laycock) two respectable farmers were suspected of 'an unnatural crime'. They persuaded some people to publish an order denying their guilt, but this failed to quiet rumours, so plans were made to burn the men in effigy the following market day.[19]

Instead of putting them on trial for their lives, the community subjected them to a lesser, more traditional public act of shaming. As with wife selling, this shows the local community dealing with a problem in their own way rather than resorting to the heavy hand of established law. Though it is unclear whether the men could have continued to live in the area. This shaming may have had the effect of banishment. And yet in Edinburgh in 1732, a common councilman was accused of sodomy, but he was described as being otherwise respectable, with a wife and three children. "tis supposed the matter will by some means or other be accommodated.'[20]

The alleged shame of a wife sale thus needs to be put into the context of her already having endured the shame of being married, and for mothers who attended the established church, the ritual of 'churching'. But it was still an age when the notion of privacy as we understand it was virtually unknown. The poor lived in close proximity to each other, so details of every domestic argument could spread like wildfire. Secrets were impossible to keep, at least for long. And yet this meant that there were limits on the extent to which people could be shamed. Among the better off, servants were often confidants of their masters and mistresses; many saw and heard things that should have remained secret. But this sometimes led them to become pawns in the battles between spouses which found their way to divorce courts in the eighteenth and nineteenth centuries. Complaints were sometimes made that servants blackmailed their employers, and that they exploited their powers over them when scandals erupted and/or divorce proceedings were begun.

Whilst it seems that many men in public got away with pubic misbehaviour, the adulterous Duke of Norfolk threw a great ball at his palace to coincide with the assizes in Norwich but 'the Dean of Norwich claimed it was widely boycotted as few people were prepared to risk their reputations by attending'. The Dean added that the Duke 'Carrieth himself here as cattle use to do, without shame or modesty.'[21] Thus, the use of cattle-related elements in the ritual of wife selling was not showing women were treated as beasts, but that their lack of shame attracted comparisons between them and beasts. This may seem to be a fine distinction, but it is an important one. It was a difference in how the women presented themselves, rather than how they were judged.

So, why did so many women apparently choose to be publicly humiliated by being sold in a public market? Perhaps they were already the object of neighbourhood gossip, of hostile looks, of being ignored in shops, of their businesses being boycotted. There was a whole range of behaviour that could make their daily lives uncomfortable and their employment unworkable to the point that they could be bankrupted.

They probably got fed up with all the underhanded behaviour from neighbours and decided to go public, to clear the air, to declare what everyone knew, and hopefully to move on with their lives. As most wife sales involved friends who supported them, the practice was a far cry from a young woman standing alone in her underwear in a church.

There were also several instances where the shame seems to have been suppressed by people who should have known better — and probably did. They turned a lower-class ritual into their own, such as the 'beautifully dressed woman' wearing a silk halter and lace veil at Smithfield in 1815 which was claimed to be to avert a legal process.[22] This has echoes of the fashionable paying at being commoners, as made famous by Marie Antoinette playing at being a milkmaid at Versailles, which showed how the rich had completely lost contact with the poor. Another example of a couple slumming it is from 1809 on Broadway, Westminster, when the wife was purchased by 'one of her gallants' and the troupe then went to a nearby public house to celebrate. At Bath in 1833, the woman was 'dashingly attired with a halter of silk'.

The mob often showed high levels of moral probity, as shown by the angry response of behaviour such as shouting and throwing mud etc, was in some cases noted in response to the woman allegedly showing no shame. In Bodmin, 1818 a woman was described as 'being led away in triumph', in Whitechapel 1833, 'a man with an air of bravado, and the woman with a sniff in the air'. In 1849 the woman 'departed in high glee' having 'snapped her fingers in his [the husband's] face', calling him a good-for-nothing who would not attract such a high a price. Far from being shamed, the wife was having her revenge on her husband by abandoning him for a younger spouse.

But this is not as simple as a decline in shame; it is also a shift in emphasis from the process of selling to that of purchase, from separation to marriage, as shown best in the case where the new husband gave his wife a guinea to buy a new dress and had the bells rung, and also several instances where the parties shared a meal, or the many instances where the event ended up in a pub. Unlike Betty Beaman who was forced to do penance in her shift, and whose humiliation was forced upon her by the authorities with no happy or positive outcome, there was a point to the humiliation of the sale. It allowed a resolution of a difficult or unhappy situation, a chance to have a happy ending, instead of continuing a life of misery till the death of one of the partners.

In this, the response of the mob is interesting, especially as it seems the sellers increasingly traveled out of their neighbourhoods to ensure they were not known so nobody that mattered to them witnessed their short-lived shame. They could disappear at the end of the brief event. The response of neighbours, and of the mob in general, varied widely. In the case of Rough Moey's young wife, the crowd knew her story, and the pretty young mother attracted their sympathy. The woman found the situation incredibly stressful and humiliating; she initially did her best to make light of it before she broke down, and the crowd turned against her first husband.

At the other extreme, there were many instances of the mob taking against those involved, especially those who showed no sign of distress, or shame, such as the woman labelled 'a hussy' who gaily waved her blue handkerchief, a far cry from the humiliating halter. Wife sales involved two processes: the separation which should have been shameful or sad, and then the remarriage which was a cause for celebration. So the hussy seemed to be celebrating while the crowd expected her to be sad or shamed. The wife sale was made of several parts; the sold wife and the mob were responding to different parts of it.

In several instances, such as the man who failed to sell his wife at Great Torrington market and when J. Naish put his wife up for sale in Bristol, the crowd seems to have expressed its disapproval by their silence. But in the Gloucestershire sale where a boy almost became the woman's owner, locals seemed to almost welcome the event. They were interested in it as a curiosity, a piece of street theatre.

In Sabine Baring-Gould's account of Henry Frise bringing home his bride from market, there seems to have been no sense of shame; probably because the new husband was a popular, respected member of their community. Again, this was a quiet country parish; his neighbours seem to have been curious or amused at the event. While the local authorities —Baring Gould's relatives — were probably uncomfortable about the situation, it seems they failed to take any action and he and Frise's new wife settled in to the community.

Jon Ronson's book was inspired by the rise of shaming on the internet, of the explosive outbursts, especially on Twitter that have destroyed some people's reputations and their jobs. He interviewed a Texan judge who seems to be turning back the clock by using public shame as a form of punishment, by forcing miscreants to parade in public wearing placards announcing their crimes. This makes good copy and saves the state a lot of money, but it seems a big step backwards. Fortunately for the victims, today's crowds are not the mobs of old. Ronson spoke to one of those punished, who surprisingly claimed it had improved his life. The crowds did not condemn him as the authorities expected; most onlookers wished him well and showed great kindness, which set him on the path to personal redemption.[23]

So again, the effect of public shaming and the long-term pain inflicted could produce surprisingly positive outcomes, which were largely the result of how those shamed presented themselves. The crowd seemed to see the convict as a decent person who inspired sympathy in them. As with Rough Moey's young wife, and many other couples involved in wife sales, he was given a second chance at life, unlike people who stood in shifts to confess their crimes.

Wife sales were mostly for what some called the 'middling sorts', with some money but no property. They probably had skills that they could use elsewhere, so they had opportunities to move away from any hostility the sales created with their neighbours. This same mobility may have been part of the reason for the wife sales, as they may have married with little advice or support from friends and neighbours.

Most reports of sales provide us with only the bare facts, but there was one instance which shines a light on why the women were willing to be sold, when Goward sold his wife at Nuneaton in 1787. The husband asked his soon-to-be-ex-wife if she felt shame at being sold in the open market. She claimed she did not, as she had 'got the lad she loved.' How did that make him feel? When the couple parted, they embraced and wished each other well. Her new husband celebrated by paying for a peal of church bells to be rung, so the event was much more a marriage than a separation. The article ends with: 'They spent the remainder of the day with the greatest joy possible.'[24]

This says it all: the end justified the means. The shame in the wife sale was brief and vastly outweighed by the long-term — hopefully lifelong — benefits. Scattered throughout these various accounts, we are offered fleeting glances of many lives. Some people were sad and brutal, but others were funny, clever and resourceful. Not poor, not ignorant, not immoral as has often been claimed. They had aspirations; they were not content to accept an unhappy life when there was a chance at something better. If their marriage was broken, they were prepared to fix it. These are the people we should be proud to call our ancestors. And their voices, their stories deserve to be heard.

Every happy couple was — and is — a good thing for a community. That is why traditional marriages involved so much consultation, advice and support from friends and relatives. But as Britain moved into the age of industry, when so many people were on the move, such advice was harder to obtain, and for many couples, marriage became a life sentence, a trap which the law refused to allow them to escape. Except for some of those who had the courage to find their own escape and hopefully wrote their own 'happily ever after' endings.

19
(UN)HAPPILY EVER AFTER

I am longing to be with you, and by the sea, where we can talk together freely and build our castles in the air.
  Dracula, Bram Stoker

Accounts of wife sales are mostly from newspapers rather than diaries or journals, so by their nature, they provide only a snapshot of the event, leaving readers forever wondering what happened next. Many note that the wife was already living with her purchaser, some for longer than their original marriage, suggesting the sale merely formalised an established relationship. The first marriage was probably made in haste, with little advice, so could be seen as a learning exercise, a test run perhaps, which allowed couples to discover what they liked and wanted in a relationship, like some modern couples who live together before tying the knot. Some probably embarked on the second relationship wiser, more tolerant and more realistic. Some of the women already knew they were better off than with their first husband. A few sales were celebrated with bell ringing or sharing a dinner, suggesting high hopes for their future.

The philosopher John Stuart Mill campaigned for reform of the divorce laws because marriage was increasingly seen not as a union of equals, more that of master and slave. But the institution was still supported by the state as it forced the allegedly physically stronger man to take some responsibility for the woman, so a bad marriage was preferable to no marriage. It also provided protection for any children they produced.

Mill claimed that marriage was a lottery and that happiness was not likely to be found the first time. But he also claimed that those who thought long and hard about the relationship were more likely to be disappointed when things went wrong. Mill — like many Victorians — held that sensuality in a relationship was less important than companionship and intellectual bonds. He was unlikely to have empathised with the many couples who went on a spree to celebrate the new freedoms and relationships they had chosen. Mill also claimed that there are some people who will never be satisfied, but are constantly seeking new experiences, so they are unlikely to be happy, at least for long. But in a world that is constantly changing, as was England in the eighteenth century, relationships had to be robust and flexible, and that could be asking too much of people who were struggling to cope with inner and outer chaos.

Baring-Gould recorded the story of a stonecutter who was dissatisfied with his wife so sold her to a publican he knew well. He describes the outcome:

> 'I knew the woman; she was not bad-looking. The new husband drank, and treated her very roughly, and on one occasion she had a black eye when I was lunching at the inn I asked her how she had hurt herself. She replied that she had knocked her face against the door, but I was told that this was a result of a domestic brawl.'[1]

This woman is recognisably a victim of domestic abuse. Today, her husband would hopefully be arrested and punished for it, and probably put on a register to protect women from him in future. But in this case, since the local vicar did not seem inclined to intervene, the situation probably continued till death took one of them. Being resold would have to be an improvement.

❋

Suicide was surprisingly common in eighteenth-century England, given that it meant being buried at a crossroads and denied access to heaven. It was such a horrific act that great efforts were made by coroners to avoid the term. If a man bought a rope and hanged himself, it was self-murder; if he used a rope that happened to be nearby, it was lunacy, or perhaps even an accident, hence such acts were, by modern standards, underreported.

When a gardener tried to hang himself on Chelsea Common in 1836 due to his wife being a scold, this was a truly desperate response to what must have become a hellish home life. When a carpenter sold his wife to a colleague in 1764, his decision failed to resolve his unhappiness. He seems to have regretted the agreement when he sobered up, but his wife refused to return to him, so he hanged himself. Another carpenter hanged himself in Pudsey in 1776 when his wife refused to return to him. Were they lonely without their wives, or did their wives' new happiness make them feel worthless, so driven to such desperate acts?

Sabine Baring-Gould's chapter on wife sales has the benefit of his deep local knowledge, so is a source of several outcomes. He recalled a man who had committed suicide in North Devon in 1906, as told to him by 'an old poacher and fisherman' who

> 'said casually that he could well remember having seen the dead man's grandfather leading his grandmother on a halter to be sold by public auction at Great Torrington Market. The reserve price was, in this instance, fixed at eighteen pence, but as no one would give so much money, the husband had to take his wife home again and resume matrimonial intercourse. Children were born to them, and the ultimate result was the suicide.'[2]

Eighteen pence doesn't seem like much, but this was a region that had remained agricultural and poor whilst the Industrial Revolution steamed ahead elsewhere. Rural markets in the nineteenth century were in decline with improved transport by rail, and continued emigration from the countryside to towns, so there may not have been many people there. But Baring-Gould also noted that his source 'said casually that he came of a curious family'. Was the curiosity due to the failed sale or was there something else amiss? Perhaps the woman was not sellable at any price.

Thompson cites a case from 1766 in Midsomer Norton in which the wife was better off with her new husband, but she still had to deal with her violent former partner who kept demanding more payments. In the absence of a paid police force, she and her family must have lived in fear until some means was found to control her ex, possibly when he committed a crime serious enough to remove him from the area. The woman and her new family may have been forced to move elsewhere for safety.

An unnamed woman was sold in a halter in Birmingham market for the huge sum of fifteen pounds in 1835, suggesting she was a woman of some status. Baring-Gould describes how

> 'she survived both buyer and seller, and then married again. Some property came to her in the course of years from her first husband; for notwithstanding claims put forth by his relatives she was able to maintain in a court of law that that sale did not and could not vitiate her rights as his widow.'[3]

Here we have a woman who clearly knew her rights, and was able to make full use of both the official legal system, and that of the informal folk tradition of which wife selling was part.

There is an account from about 1820 of a Gloucester man who had found his wife had been unfaithful, so approached her lover, who agreed to a public sale. The woman proved to be an excellent wife, and her new husband claimed to be fortunate to have made such a bargain. The account was reprinted forty years later when the woman had outlived both her men, so can qualify as another success story. At least for the woman.[4]

One unpleasant outcome was that a sale's lack of legal status could have later repercussions for the first husband. The main point of the sale and the various rituals and written agreements was — as with the announcement of a runaway wife — to free the husband of all future financial responsibility. But that was not always possible. Women tend to outlive men, but when the wife died, her purchaser had no legal rights to his own children, as they would become the responsibility of her first husband.

In Dudley 1849, a man was followed by mobs shouting 'who sold his wife?', which suggests neighbours showed their objections to the sales. This seems to have been the man who sold his wife to the rich Yankee. It is unlikely he had an easy life once this taunting by children began. But they were only kids, and kids get bored soon enough. Or he may have had enough and moved.

In Exeter in 1872, the woman who was sold for having too much dash moved to Plymouth with her new husband, presumably to make a fresh start without the neighbours gossiping or worse.[5] A sale in Sheffield in 1796 ended with the husband paying for the couple to move to Manchester, perhaps pre-empting any neighbourhood objections and allowing the new couple a fresh start.

The intention of a divorce of any form is to allow both man and wife to embark on a new life, on new relationships and possibly children, but there is only one instance of a man naively remarrying in a church, and being charged with bigamy and transported to Australia for seven years.

There are several accounts where the sales produced successful marriages. One example is Henry Frise, the poet who Sabine Baring-Gould saw return from market with his bought wife, who

> 'proved an excellent "wife". She was thrifty, clean, and managed a rough-tempered and tough-tongued man with great tact, and was greatly respected.'

If he had lived in property owned by the church or the squire, they could have evicted him, but his tenancy had been secure. A problem only arose when the wife died. '

> The parson insisted that he could not and he would not enter her as Anne Frise, for that was not her legal name. Then Henry was angry,

and carried her off to be buried in another parish, where the parson was unacquainted with the circumstances.'[6]

This is the only instance where the church intervened in a sale, albeit indirectly and many years later.

There is a single example of what seems to have been a very long and happy marriage, the result of a sale that happened in Halifax. Rachel Heap had believed her husband had died in the wars, so married Samuel Lumb in 1802, and they had three children together. When her first husband returned, he arranged to sell her to her new partner, but they had to wait a further twenty-five years for her first husband to die when the eighty-three-year-old Rachel was given away by her grandson in a church wedding.[7]

APPENDIX I NOTES

Ch. 1 Origins

1 pp. 437–8, Thompson, E.P., *Customs in Common*, Merlin Press, Pontypool, 2010

2 pp. liii–liv Strutt, J., *The Sports & Pastimes of the People of England*, Thomas Tegg, London, 1831

3 p.17, Anderson Graham, P., *Highways and Byways in Northumbria*, Morten Publishers, Manchester, 1973

4 John Stype, wikipedia

5 Twitter

6 p. 56, Menefee, S.P., *Wives For Sale, An Ethnographic Study of British Popular Divorce*, St Martin's Press, New York, 1981

7 p. 24, Probert, R., *Divorced, Bigamist, Bereaved? The family historian's guide to marital breakdown, separation, widowhood, and remarriage: from 1600 to the 1970s*, Takeaway, Kenilworth, 2015

8 p. 25, ditto

Ch. 2 Sources

1 p. 52, Watson, F., *The Year of the Wombat, England: 1857*, Victor Gollancz, London, 1974

2 Menefee, S.P., *Wives for Sale: An Ethnographic Study of British Popular Divorce*, St Martin's Press, New York, 1981

3 Thompson, E.P., *Customs in Common*, Merlin Press, Pontypool, 2010

4 Baring-Gould, S., *Devonshire Characters and Strange Events*, John Lane Bodley Head, London, 1908.

5 pm 58, ditto

6 p. 438, Thompson, E.P.

7 p. 390, Hibbert,C., *The English A Social History 1066–1945*, Guild Publishing, London, 1987

8 p. 8, 2003 3 August *The Sunday Times*

9 p.120 Thompson, E.P.

10 p. x, Pottle, F.A., Ed., *Boswell's London Journal 1762–1763*, The Reprint Society, London, 1952

11 p. 120, Thompson, E.P.

12 p. 7, Latimer, J., *The Annals of Bristol in the Nineteenth Century*, W & F Morgan, Bristol, 1887

Ch. 3 The Legal Position

1 p. 53, Watson, F., *The Year of the Wombat, England: 1857* Victor Golancz, London, 1974

2 1933 20 January *The Lichfield Mercury*

3 1841 27 May *North Devon Journal*

4 p. 456, Thompson, E.P. E.P., *Customs in Common*, Merlin Press, Pontypool, 2010

5 p. 452, ditto

6 pp 451–2, ditto

7 1799 1 March *Aris's Birmingham Gazette*

8 p. 56, Menefee, S.P., *Wives for Sale: An Ethnographic Study of British Popular Divorce*, St Martin's Press, New York, 1981

9 p. 129, *Punch* xvii (1849) from p. 454 Thompson, E.P.

10 p. 26, Menefee

11 p. 452, Thompson, E.P.

12 p. 327, Lovill, J., Ed., *Ringing Churchbells to ward off Thunderstorms and other Curiosities from the original Notes and Queries*, The Bunbury Press, www.bunburypress.com, 2009

13 p. 23, Martin, R.W., Ed., William Cobbett, W., *Rural Rides in the Counties of Surrey, Kent, etc.*, Macdonald Illustrated Classics, London 1958

14 pp. 87–8, Girouard, M., *The English Town*, Yale University Press, New Haven 1990

15 p. 88, ditto

16 1835 31 January *Manchester Courier and Lancashire General Advertiser*

17 1858 26 November *The Stamford Mercury*

18 p. 154, Briggs, A., *Victorian Cities*, Penguin Books, London, 1990

19 1845 22 March *The Worcester Herald* in p. 298/9 Morsley, C., *News from the English Countryside 1750-1850*, Harrap, London, 1979

20 1845 7 June *The Worcester Herald*, in p. 300 ditto

21 p. 117, Jennings, M.- L., Madge, C., Eds,. Jennings, H., *Pandæmonium 1660 : The Coming of the Machine As Seen by Contemporary Observers*, Icon Books, London, 2012

22 1937 30 January Somerset Gazette, obituary in p. 249, Menefee

Ch. 4 The Contract

1 p. 30, Menefee, S.P., *Wives for Sale: An Ethnographic Study of British Popular Divorce*, St Martin's Press, New York, 1981

2 p. 28, ditto

3 1820 14 April *West Briton*, in p. 428, Thompson, E.P., *Customs in Common*, Merlin Press, Pontypool, 2010

4 1830 10 April *The Royal Cornwall Gazette*

5 p. 432, Thompson

6 p. 65, Baring-Gould, S., *Devonshire Characters and Strange Events*, John Lane Bodley Head, London 1908

7 p. 435, Thompson, E.P.

8 pp. 421–2, ditto.

9 pp. 414 & 431 ditto

10 p. 433 ditto

11 1895 14 May, *The Daily Gazette for Middlesbrough*

12 1892 14 November, *The Birmingham Daily Post*

13 p. 435, Thompson, E.P.

14 pp. 436–7, ditto

15 p. 462, ditto

16 1822 28 December, *Bristol Mercury*, also pp. 62/3, Baring-Gould, S.

17 1883 20 November, *The Leighton Buzzard Observer and Linsade Gazette*

18 1930 27 September, *The Driffield Times*

19 1933 20 January, *The Lichfield Mercury*

20 1787 1 December, *The London Chronicle*

21 pp. 425–6, Thompson, E.P.

22 p. 425, ditto

23 1815 3 January, *The Maidstone Gazette*

24 1822 25 February, *The Newry Examiner and Louth Advertiser*

25 p. 429, Thompson, E.P.

26 p. 65, Baring-Gould, S.

27 pp. 437–8, Thompson, E.P.

28 1849 28 July, *The Preston Chronicle*

29 p. 89, Probert, R., *Divorced, Bigamist, Bereaved? The family historian's guide to marital breakdown, separation, widowhood, and remarriage: from 1600 to the 1970s*, Takeaway, Kenilworth, 2015

30 1832 7 April, *The Times*

31 1878 18 September, *The Sheffield Independent*

32 1878 8 October, *The Yorkshire & Leeds Intelligencier*

33 1789 4 September, *The Morning Post & Daily Advertiser*, from bogspot p 1

34 1885 26 September, *The Wrexham Advertiser*

35 1833 10 September, *The Limerick Evening Post*

36 p. 427, Thompson, E.P

37 pp. 156–7, Hey, D., Ed., Gough, R., *The History of Myddle*, Penguin Books, Harmondsworth, England, 1981

38 1870 9 April, *The Rochdale Observer*

39 1849 14 December, *The Doncaster Nottingham & Lincolnshire Gazette*

40 p. 29, Menefee, S.P.

41 p. 97, Jennings, P., *The Living Village: A picture of rural life drawn from village scrapbooks*, Penguin Books, Middlesex, 1972

42 1775 24 August, *The Sherborne Journal*

43 p. 448, Thompson, E.P.

44 p. 432, ditto

45 1822 2 March, *The Sheffield Independent*

46 p. 148, Stone, L., *Road to Divorce, England 1530–1987*, Oxford University Press, Oxford, 1992

Ch. 5 Crossed Wires

1 p. 52, Watson, F., *The Year of the Wombat, England: 1857* Victor Gollancz, London, 1974

2 p. 60, Baring-Gould, S., *Devonshire Characters and Strange Events*, John Lane Bodley Head, London 1908

3 p. 266, Waters, C.M., *An Economic History of England 1066–1874*, Oxford University Press, London, 1945

4 p. 30, Jordan, D., Walsh, M., *White Cargo: The Forgotten History of Britain's White Slaves in America*, Mainstream, Edinburgh, 2008

5 p. 262, Waters, C.M.

6 p. 203, Ketton-Cremer, R.W., *Felbrigg: The Story of a House*, Futura, London, 1982

7 p. 15, Menefee, S.P., *Wives for Sale: An Ethnographic Study of British Popular Divorce*, St Martin's Press, New York, 1981

8 p. 332, Martin, R.W., Ed., Cobbett, W., *Rural Rides in the Counties of Surrey, Kent, etc.*, Macdonald Illustrated Classics, London 1958

9 p. 44, Fussell, G.E., *The English Rural Labourer, His home, furniture, clothing & food from Tudor to Victorian times*, The Batchworth Press, London, 1949

10 pp. 60–1 Baring-Gould, S., *Devonshire Characters and Strange Events*, John Lane Bodley Head, London 1908

11 1853 May *The Stamford Mercury*

12 1876 29 May *The Liverpool Daily Post*

13 p. 61, Baring-Gould, S.

14 1892 14 November *The Birmingham Daily Post*

15 1932 5 May *The Hartlepool Northern Daily Mail*

16 p. 141, Tyrell, S., *A Countryman's Tale*, Century-National Trust Classics, London, 1991

17 p. 86, Morsley, C., *News from the English Countryside 1750–1850*, Harrap, London, 1979

18 pp. 60–61, Menefee, S.P.

19 p. 152, Thompson, E.P., *Whigs & Hunters, The Origins of the Black Act*, Breviary Stuff Publications, London 2013

20 p. 54, Evans, H.H., *Highways & Byways in Oxford & The Cotswolds*, Macmillan and Co., London, 1917

21 pp. 127–131, Jordan, D., Walsh, M., *White Cargo: The Forgotten History of Britain's White Slaves in* America, Mainstream, Edinburgh, 2007

22 1930 27 September, *Driffield Times*

23 p. 286, Blythe, R., *Akenfield*, Penguin Books, London, 1982

24 1903 28 November, *The Dundee Evening Telegraph*

25 1845 9 September, *The Fife Herald*

Ch. 6 Punishment

1 p. 442, Thompson, E.P., *Customs in Common*, Merlin Press, Pontypool, 2010

2 p. 427, ditto

3 p. pp. 452–3, ditto

4 p. 198 Briggs, A., *A Social History of England*, Book Club Associates, London, 1983

5 p. 413, Thompson, E.P.

6 1868 30 May, *The Staffordshire Advertiser*

7 25 January 1883, *The Hull Packet*

8 footnote, p. 453, Thompson, E.P.

9 1847 12 March, *The Stamford Mercury* in p. 417 E.P. Thompson

10 1833 10 September, *The Limerick Evening Post*

11 1865 21 January, *The Grantham Journal*

12 1818 19 January, *The Hampshire Chronicle*

13 1834 17 June, *The Stamford Mercury*

14 1835 27 March, *The Athlone Sentinel*

15 1856 16 February, *The Paisley Herald & Renfrewshire Advertiser*

16 1819 18 November, *The Cheltenham Chronicle*

17 1823 7 August, *The Birmingham Chronicle*

18 1895 14 May, *The Daily Gazette for Middlesbrough*

19 1864 26 July, *The Dundee Perth & Cupar Advertiser*

20 p. 461, Thompson, E.P.

21 1810 5 May, *Evans & Ruffey's Farmers' Journal*

22 1856 10 November, *The Glasgow Herald*

23 1849 28 July, *The Preston Chronicle*
24 1822 2 March, *The Sheffield Independent*
Ch. 7 Alternatives to Sales
1 p. 7, Rose, P., *Parallel Lives: Five Victorian Marriages*, Chatto & Windus, London, 1984

2 p. 192, Coleman, T., *The Railway Navvies: A history of the men who made the Railways*, Penguin Books, London, 1972

3 p. 192, ditto

4 p. 241, Bell, Lady, *At the Works: A Study of a Manufacturing Town (Middlesbrough)*, David & Charles Reprints, Newton Abbott, 1969

5 p. 25, Probert, R., *Divorced, Bigamist, Bereaved? The family historian's guide to marital breakdown, separation, widowhood, and remarriage: from 1600 to the 1970s*, Takeaway, Kenilworth, 2015

6 p. 240, Stone, L., *Road to Divorce, England 1530-1987*, Oxford University Press, Oxford, 1992

7 p. 291, ditto

8 p. 176, Hey, D., Ed., Gough, R., *The History of Myddle*, Penguin Books, Harmondsworth, England, 1981

9 p. 446, Thompson, E.P. *Customs in Common*, Merlin Press, Pontypool, 2010

10 pp. 41–2, Thompson, E.P., Whigs & Hunters: The Origins of the Black Act, Breviary Stuff Publications, London 2013

11 p. 449, Thompson, E.P., *Customs in Common*,

12 1734 6 June, *Grub Street Journal*, in p. 268 Menefee, S.P., *Wives for Sale: An Ethnographic Study of British Popular Divorce*, St Martin's Press, New York, 1981

13 1752 20 April *Portsmouth & Gosport Gazette & Salisbury Journal* in p. 268, Menefee, S.P.ditto

14 1753 21 July *The Oxford Journal*, p. 268 ditto

15 p. 148, Hey, D., Ed., Richard Gough,

16 p. 153, Stone, L., *The Road to Divorce, England 1530–1987*, Oxford University Press, Oxford, 1992

17 www.costwolds.info/strange-things/wfe-sales

18 1769 28 January, *Felix Farley's Bristol Journal*

19 pp. 453–4, Thompson, E.P, *Customs in Common*

20 p. 98, Torr, C., *Small Talk at Wreyland*, Adams & Dart, UK, 1970

21 1893 11 December Daily Mail, in p. 97, Menefee, S.P.

22 p. 64, Baring-Gould, S., *Devonshire Characters and Strange Events*, John Lane Bodley Head, London 1908

23. ditto

24 1827 26 July *Westmeath Journal*

25 1837 22 August *The Times* in p. 429, Thompson, E.P.

26 1849 14 December *The Doncaster Nottinghamshire & Lincolnshire Gazette*

27 1796 30 March *The Times*

28 1923 22 January Yorkshire Evening Post

29 p. 391, Hibbert, C., *The English A Social History 1066-1945*, Book Club Associates, 1987

30 p. 106, Ketton-Cremer, R.W., *Felbrigg: The story of a House*, Futura, London, 1982

31 p. 109 ditto

32 p. 124, P.J. Corfield, *The Impact of English Towns 1700-1800*, Oxford University Press, Oxford, 1982

33 1810 5 May *Evans & Ruffey's Farmer's Journal*

34 p. 443, Thompson, E.P, *Customs n Common*

35 p.190, Ayres, J., Ed., *Paupers & Pig Killers, The Diary of William Holland A Somerset Parson 1799 – 1818*, Sutton Publishing, Stroud, England, 2000

Ch. 8 Rituals

1 pp. 14–15, Cressy, D., *Bonfires & Bells: National Memory and the Protestant Calendar in Elizabethan and Stuart England*, Sutton Publishing, Stroud, 2004

2 p. 98, Jennings, P., *The Living Village: A picture of rural life drawn from village scrapbooks*, Penguin Books, Middlesex, 1972

3 p. 101, Jennings, M.L., Madge, C., Eds,. Jennings, H., *Pandæmonium 1660: The Coming of the Machine As Seen by Contemporary Observers*, Icon Books, London, 2012

4 p. 179, Cressy, D.

5 1768 9 January *Felix Farley's Bristol Journal*

6 p. 93, Barber, T., Boldrick, S., Eds., *Art Under Attack: Histories of British Iconoclasm*, Tate Publishing, London, 2013

7 p. 195, Quennell, M and C.H.B., *A History of Everyday Things in England*, Volume I 1066-1499, B.T. Batsford, London, 1963

8. p. 85, ditto

9 pp. 22–3, Torr, C., *Small Talk at Wreyland*, Adams & Dart, UK, 1970

10 1787 28 January *The Ipswich Journal*

11 1787 1 December, *The London Chronicle*

12 1850 11 May *The Carlisle Patriot*

13 1852 6 March *The Northern Whig*

14 *The Stamford Chronicle* in 1786 23 June *Felix Farley's Bristol Journal*

15 1845 9 September Fife Herald

16 p. 451, Thompson, E.P., *Customs in Common*, Merlin Press, Pontypool, 2010

17 1973 1 January, *The Guardian*

18 1815 25 July *Chester Courant*

19 1839 4 May *Jackson's Oxford Journal*

20 1970 26 November *Lancaster Gazette*

21 p. 455, Thompson, E.P., *Customs in Common*

22 plate XXXII, ditto

23 1824 21 December, *Brighton Gazette and Lewes Advertiser*

24 p. 88, Menefee, S.P.

25 1837 22 August *The Times*

26 1881 30 May, *The South Wales Daily News* in p. 456, Thompson, E.P., *Customs in Common*

27 p. 426, Thompson, E.P., *Customs in Common*

Ch. 9 Women as Victims

1 p. 271, Ayres, J., Ed. *Paupers & Pig Killers, The Diary of William Holland A Somerset Parson 1799 – 1818*, Sutton Publishing, Stroud, England, 2000

2 1848, 9 July, The Era

3 p. 47, vol. II, Southey, R., *Letters from England by Don Manuel Alvarez Espriella*, Longman, Hurst, Rees and Orme, London, 1814

4 pp. 232–3, E.P., *Customs in Common*, Merlin Press, Pontypool, 2010

5 p. 334, ditto

6 p. 313–4, ditto

7 pp. 325–6, ditto

8 pp. 43–4, Fussell, *The English Rural Labourer: His home furniture, clothing & food from Tudor to Victorian times*, The Batchworth Press, London, 1949

9 p. 333, Thompson, E.P.

10 p. 233, ditto

11 p. 7, Latimer, J., *The Annals of Bristol in the Nineteenth Century*, W & F Morgan, Bristol, 1887

12 p. 333, E.P. Thompson

13 p. 94, Williams, C., Trans, *Thomas Platter's Travels in England 1599*, Jonathan Cape, London 1937

14 p. 12, Greer, G., *John Wilmot, Earl of Rochester*, Northcote House, Tavistock, 2001

15 pp. 60–1, Stone, L., *Road to Divorce, England 1530-1987*, Oxford University Press, Oxford, 1992

16 p. 93, Rudé, G., *Hanoverian London 1714–1808*, Secker & Warburg, London, 1971

17 p. 228, Morsley, C., *News from the English Countryside 1750–1850*, Harrap, London, 1979

18 p. 309, ditto

19 p. 460, Thompson, E.P.

20 1840 21 March, *The Staffordshire Gazette & County Standard*

21 1822 28 December, *The Bristol Mirror*

22 1775 24 August, The Sherborne Journal

23 pp. 221–2, Fea, A., *Old World Places*, Eveleigh Nash, London, 1912

24 p. 476, Thompson, E.P.

25 1753 18 October, *Manchester Mercury*

26 1832 7 April The Times

27 p. 53, Menefee, S.P., *Wives for Sale: An Ethnographic Study of British Popular Divorce*, St Martin's Press, New York, 1981

28 1874 8 October, *Yorkshire & Leeds Intelligencer*

29 p. 462, Thompson, E.P.
30 Central Bristol Library Broadsides Collection
31 1810 5 May *Evans & Ruffey's Farmers' Journal*
32 1822 28 December Bristol Mercury
33 Central Bristol Library Broadsides Collection
34 1933 20 January, *The Lichfield Mercury*
35 1849 14 December *The Doncaster Gazette*
36 1841 27 May, *The North Devon Journal*
37 1892 14 November, *The Birmingham Daily Post*
38 pp. 74–5 Ketton-Cremer, R.W., *Felbrigg: The Story of a House*, First Futura, London, 1982

Ch. 10 Scolding Women

1 Osborne, *Look Back in Anger*, Act I in p. 560, Knowles, E., Ed., *The Oxford Dictionary of Quotations*, Fifth Edition, Oxford University Press, Oxford, 1999

2 pp. 421/2 Thompson, E.P., *Customs in Common*, Merlin Press, Pontypool, 2010

3 pp. 47/8, Brock, C., *The Comet Sweeper Caroline Herschel's Astronomical Ambition*, Icon Books, Cambridge UK, 2007

4 p. 398 Martin, R.W., Ed., William Cobbett , *Rural Rides in the counties of Surrey, Kent, etc.*, Macdonald Illustrated Classics, London 1958

5 p. 102, Bell, Lady, *At the Works: A Study of a Manufacturing Town (Middlesbrough)*, David & Charles Reprints, Newton Abbott, 1969

6 1794 12 June *The Derby Mercury*

7. 5 p. 50, Kermode, J., Walker, G., Eds., *Women, Crime and the Courts in Early Modern England*, The University of North Carolina Press, London, 1994

8. p. 58 ditto

9. p. 64 ditto

10 1773 15 November, *The Hampshire Chronicle*

11 ditto

12 p. 62, Jordan, D., & Walsh, M., *White Cargo : The Forgotten History of Britain's White Slaves in America*, Mainstream, Edinburgh, 2008

13. p. 60, Kermode, J., etc.

14 1775 30 October, *The Caledonian Mercury*

15 1736 7 August, *The Newcastle Courant*

16 1721 23 November, *The Caledonian Mercury*

17 1726 3 September, *The Ipswich Journal*

18 1732 6 July, *The Stamford Mercury*

19 p. 281, Fea, A., *Old-World Places*, Eveleigh Nash, London, 1912

20 1840 6 June, *The Suffolk Chronicle or Weekly General Advertiser*

21 1854 23 December, *The York Herald*

22 p. 281, Fea, A.,

23 p. 281 ditto

24 p.61, Kermode, J. etc.

25 Front cover, ditto

26 p. 59 ditto

27 p. 60, ditto

28 p. 281/2, Fea, A.,

29. p. 58, Kermode, J.,

30 p. 282, Fea, A.,

31 1846 1 May *The Tyrone Constitution*

32 p. 132, Latimer, J, *Annals of Bristol Volume 2 Eighteenth Century*, George's, Bristol, 1970

33 p.11 Footnote, Shorter, C., *Highways and Byways n Buckinghamshire*, Macmillan and Co., London, 1910

34 1726 3 September, *The Ipswich Journal*

35 1736 18 September, *The Newcastle Courant*

36 1739 20 April, *Belfast News-Letter*

Ch. 11 A Wife's Worth

1 p. 144, Morsley, C., *News from the English Countryside 1750–1850*, Harrap, London, 1979

2 p. 146, ditto

3 p. 137, ditto

4 p. 324, Markham, S., *John Loveday of Caversham 1711–1789: The Life and Tours of an Eighteenth-Century Onlooker*, Michael Russell, Salisbury, 1984

5 p. 98, Read, S., *Maids, Wives, Widows: Exploring Early Modern Women's Lives 1540–1740*, Pen & Sword, Barnsley, 2015

6 p. 200, Thompson, E.P., *Whigs & Hunters: The Origins of the Black Act*, Breviary Stuff Publications, London 2013

7 p. 56, Menefee, S.P., *Wives for Sale: An Ethnographic Study of British Popular Divorce*, St Martin's Press, New York, 1981

8 pp. 79–80, Jordan, D., and Walsh, M., *White Cargo: The Forgotten History of Britain's White Slaves in America*, Mainstream, Edinburgh, 2008

9 p. 85, ditto

10 p. 84, ditto

11 p. 135, ditto

12 p. 437–8, Thompson, E.P., *Customs in Common*, Merlin Press, Pontypool, 2010

13. p. 75, Ayres, J., Ed. *Paupers & Pig Killers, The Diary of William Hollan,d A Somerset Parson 1799 – 1818*, Sutton Publishing, Stroud, England, 2000

14 p. 195, ditto

15 p. 24, ditto

16 1769, 28 January, *Felix Farley's Bristol Journal*

17 1806 4 February, *The Times*

18 1805 12 October, *Northampton Mercury*

19 1872 14 May *The Western Times*

20 1815 25 July *Chester Courant*

21 1831 5 November, *The Newcastle Courant*

22 1833 10 September, *The Limerick Evening Post*

23 p.10, Hall, A., & Warton, A., *The History of Paradise Square*, S.C.L. Publishing, Sheffield, 1990

24 1863 24 June, *The Dundee Courier*

25 1932 23 May, *The Derby Mercury*, article titled 'From a Derby Newspaper'

26 1912 27 September, *Dorking & Leatherhead Advertiser*

27 p. 90, Probert, R., *Divorced, Bigamist, Bereaved? The family historian's guide to marital breakdown, separation, widowhood, and remarriage: from 1600 to the 1970s*, Takeaway, Kenilworth, 2015

28 p. 448, E.P. Thompson, *Customs in Common*

29 1949 14 April, *The Cornishman*

30 1848 14 October, *The Norfolk News*

31 1850 11 May, *The Carlisle Patriot*

32 1933 20 January, *The Lichfield Mercury*

33 1881 3 June *The Newcastle Courant*

34 1834 2 August, *The Caledonian Mercury*

35 1892 14 November, *The Birmingham Daily Post*

36 1870 9 April, *The Rochdale Observer*

37 1822 28 December, *The Bristol Mercury*

38 1865 29 January. *Reynold's Newspaper*

Ch. 12 Children

1 p. 176, Davies, S., *Unbridled Spirits, Women of the English Revolution 1640–1660*, The Women's Press, 1999

2 p.4, Laslett, P., *The World We Have Lost: Further Explained*, Routledge, London, 1983

3 pp. 107–8, P.J. Corfield, *The Impact of English Towns 1700–1800*, Oxford University Press, Oxford, 1982

4 Wordsworth, W., *The Prelude, Book Ninth, Residence in France*

5 1835 Liverpool Mercury

6 p. 121, Reed Stiles, H., *Bundling: its origin, progress & decline in America*, Book Collectors Association, New York, 1934

7 1856 16 February, *The Paisley Herald & Renfrewshire Advertiser*

8 p. 89, Probert, R., *Divorced, Bigamist, Bereaved? The family historian's guide to marital breakdown, separation, widowhood, and remarriage: from 1600 to the 1970s*, Takeaway, Kenilworth, 2015

9 1815 3 January *The Maidstone Gazette*

10 p. 90, Probert, R.,

11 1885 26 September, *The Wrexham Advertiser*

12 1874 8 October, *The Yorkshire Post & Leeds Intelligencier*

13 1923 22 January, *The Yorkshire Evening Post*

14 1892 14 November, *The Birmingham Daily Post*

15 1813 17 July, *The Suffolk Chronicle or Weekly General Advertiser*

16 1865 29 January, *Reynold's Newspaper*

17 1870 12 November, *The Leeds Mercury*

18 p. 443, Thompson, E.P., *Customs in Common*, Merlin Press, Pontypool, 2010

19 1857 10 October, *The Royal Cornwall Gazette, St Austell*

20 p. 65, Baring-Gould, S., *Devonshire Characters and Strange Events*, John Lane Bodley Head, London 1908

21 1870 28 April, *The Southern Reporter*

22 p. 52, Reed Stiles, H.

23 Wake, J., *Sisters of Fortune: The First American Heiresses to Take England by Storm*, Vintage Books, London, 2011

Ch. 13 Friends and Family

1 p. 51, Robinson, C.N., *The British Tar in Fact and Fiction, The Poetry, Pathos, and Humour of the Sailor's Life*, Harper and Brothers, London, 1911

2 p. 169, Hey, D., Ed., Gough, R., *The History of Myddle*, Penguin Books, Harmondsworth, England, 1981

3 p. 264, Stone, L., Road to Divorce, England 1530–1987, Oxford University Press, Oxford, 1992

4 pp. 218–9, ditto

5 pp. 228–9, Hudson, W.H., *A Shepherd's Life*, Macdonald Futura, Aylesbury, 1981

6 p. 28, P.J. Corfield, P.J., *The Impact of English Towns 1700-1800*, Oxford University Press, Oxford, 1982

7 1892, 14 November, *The Birmingham Daily Post*

8 p. 28, ditto

9 p. 32, ditto

10 p. 28, ditto

11 p. 432, Thompson, E.P., *Customs in Common*, Merlin Press, Pontypool, 2010

12 1850 11 May, *The Carlisle Patriot*

13 1831 5 November, *The Newcastle Courant*

14 Bristol Broadside Collection, Central Bristol Library

15 p. 89, Probert, R., *Divorced, Bigamist, Bereaved? The family historian's guide to marital breakdown, separation, widowhood, and remarriage: from 1600 to the 1970s*, Takeaway, Kenilworth, 2015

16 p. 65, Baring-Gould, S., *Devonshire Characters and Strange Events*, John Lane Bodley Head, London 1908

17 p. 436, Thompson, E.P., *Customs in Common*,

18 1857 10 October, *The Royal Cornwall Gazette St Austell*

19 1835 31 January, *The Manchester Courier and Lancashire General Advertiser*

20 p. 99, Stone, L., *Road to Divorce, England 1530–1987*, Oxford University Press, Oxford, 1992

21 p. 124, Morsley, C., *News from the English Countryside 1750–1850*, Harrap, London, 1979

22 p. 360, ditto

23 p. 285, ditto

Ch. 14 Missing Men

1 p. 327, Lovill, J., Ed., *Ringing Churchbells to ward off Thunderstorms and other Curiosities from the original Notes and Queries*, The Bunbury Press, 2009

2 1784 13 September, *The Sherborne Mercury* in p. 443, Thompson, E.P.

3 1785 20 August, *Jackson's Oxford Journal*

4 1815 28 May *The Independent Whig* in p. 443, Thompson, E.P.

5 p. 443, Thompson, E.P.

6 p. 60–1, Menefee, S.P., *Wives for Sale: An Ethnographic Study of British Popular Divorce*, St Martin's Press, New York, 1981

7 1859 26 November, *The Birmingham Journal*

8 p. 15, Norway, A.H., *Highways and Byways in Yorkshire*, Macmillan and Co., London, 1911

9 p. 443, Thompson, E.P.

10 p. 26, Menefee

11 1889 2 March, *The Sheffield Evening Telegraph*

12 1892 14 November, *The Birmingham Daily Post*

13 Plate facing p. 185, Briggs, A., *A Social History of England*, Book Club Associates, London, 1983

14 p. 21, Blythe, R., *Akenfield*, Penguin Books, London, 1982

Ch. 15 Mobs and Crowds

1 pp. 450–1, Thompson, E.P., *Customs in Common*, Merlin Press, Pontypool, 2010

2 1870 12 November, *The Leeds Mercury*

3 p. 451, Thompson, E.P.

4 1865 29 January, *Reynolds Newspaper*

5 p. 455, Thompson, E.P.

Appendix I Notes

6 p. 22, Hey, D., Ed., Gough, R., *The History of Myddle*, Penguin Books, Harmondsworth, England, 1981

7 p. 41, Hill, C., *The World Turned Upside Down, Radical Ideas During the English Revolution*, Penguin Books, London 1991

8 p. 279, Schmiechen, J., Carls, K., *The British Market Hall: A Social and Architectural History*, Yale University Press, New Haven, 1999

9 1845 9 September, *The Fife Herald*

10 1852 7 May, *The Leicester Journal*

11 1847 29 January, *The Exeter Flying Post*

12 p. 92, Menefee, S.P., *Wives for Sale: An Ethnographic Study of British Popular Divorce*, St Martin's Press, New York, 1981

13 p. 94, ditto

14 1830 10 April, *The Royal Cornwall Gazette*

15 1829 12 September, *The Worcester Herald*

16 1870 9 April, *The Rochdale Observer*

17 1834 27 June, *The Stamford Mercury*

18 1828 25 July, *The Morning Chronicle*

19 p. 126, Menefee, S.P.

20 1796 30 March, *The Times*

Ch. 16 Beyond Smithfield

1 p. 11, Girouard, M., *The English Town*, Yale University Press, New Haven 1990

2 p. 419, Thompson, E.P., *Customs in Common*, Merlin Press, Pontypool, 2010

3 p. 123, Latimer, J., *The Annals of Bristol in the Nineteenth Century*, W & F Morgan, Bristol, 1887

4 p. 26, Girouard, M.

6 1763 26 July *The Leeds Intelligencer* in p. 47, Morsley, C., *News from the English Countryside 1750–1850*, Harrap, London, 1979

7 pp. 67–8, Ketton-Cremer, R.W., *Felbrigg: The Story of a House*, Futura, London, 1982

8 p. 8, Davies, S., *Unbridled Spirits, Women of the English Revolution 1640-1660*, The Women's Press, 1999

9 www.legendary.dartmoor

10 p. 129, Sutton, A., Ed., Leech, J., *Rural Rides of the Bristol Churchgoer*, Nonsuch, Stroud, 2004

11 1865 21 January, *The Grantham Journal*

12 1827 26 July, *The Westmeath Journal*

13 1831 5 November, *The Newcastle* Courant

14 1809 1 November, *The Bury and Norwich Post*

15 p. 243 Menefee, S.P., *Wives for Sale: An Ethnographic Study of British Popular Divorce*, St Martin's Press, New York, 1981

16 1859 1 October, *The Leicestershire Mercury*

17 1874 8 October, *The Yorkshire & Leeds Intelligencier*

18 p. 172, Villers, A.J., *Convict Ships and Sailors*, Philip Allan & Co., London 1936

Ch. 17 Extraordinary Cases

1 1837 22 August, *The Times*

2 p. 51, Menefee, S.P., *Wives for Sale: An Ethnographic Study of British Popular Divorce*, St Martin's Press, New York, 1981

3 1852 7 May, *The Leicester Journal*

4 1806 4 February, *The Times*

5 1852 6 March, *The Northern Whig*

6 1874 8 October, *Yorkshire & Leeds Intelligencer*

7 pp. 414 & 431 Thompson, E.P., *Customs in Common*, Merlin Press, Pontypool, 2010

8 1865 25 February, *The Newry Examiner & Louth Advertiser*, 29 January *Reynolds Newspaper*

9 1933 20 January, *The Lichfield Mercury*

10 1859 3 December, *The Oxford Chronicle & Reading Gazette*

11 1864 10 August, *The Birmingham Post*

12 1775 23 December, *Jackson's Oxford Journal*

13 p. 64, Baring-Gould, S., *Devonshire Characters and Strange Events*, John Lane Bodley Head, London 1908

14 1864 26 July, *The Dundee, Perth & Cupar Advertiser*

15 1903 28 November, *The Dundee Evening Telegraph*

16 1815 22 August, *The Cumberland Pacquet & Ware's Whitehaven Advertiser*

17 1888 12 January, *The Birmingham Daily Post*

18 1855 25 July *The Ulsterman*, from *The Stockton Mercury*

Ch.18 On Shame

1 p. 268, Stone, L., *Road to Divorce, England 1530–1987*, Oxford University Press, Oxford, 1992

2 p. 27, Ayres, J., Ed. *Paupers & Pig Killers, The Diary of William Holland A Somerset Parson 1799 – 1818*, Sutton Publishing, Stroud, England, 2000

3 p. 256, Lydon, J., *Anger is an Energy*, Simon & Schuster, London, 2015

4 p. 232, Stone, L.,

5 p. 103, Malay, J.L., *The Case of Mistress Mary Hampson Her Story of Marital Abuse and Defiance in Seventeenth Century England*, Stanford University Press, Stanford, 2014

6 p. 502, Thompson, E.P., *Customs in Common*, Merlin Press, Pontypool, 2010

7 p. 51, Ronson, J., *So You've Been Publicly Shamed*, Picador, London, 2015

8 p. 241, Stone, L.

9. p. 502, Thompson, E.P.

10 1889 2 March *The Sheffield Evening Telegraph*

11 pp. 117–8 Davies, S., *Unbridled Spirits, Women of the English Revolution 1640–1660*, The Women's Press, 1999

12 p. 206, Hey, D., Ed., Gough, R., *The History of Myddle*, Penguin Books, Harmondsworth, England, 1981

13 p. 451, Markham, S., *John Loveday of Caversham 1711–1789: The Life and Tours of an Eighteenth-Century Onlooker*, Michael Russell, Salisbury, 1984

14 p. 100, Stone

15 p. 17, Anderson Graham, P., *Highways and Byways in Northumbria*, Morten Publishers, Manchester, 1973

16 p. 408, Markham, S.

17 pp. 26–7, Reed Stiles, H., *Bundling: its origin, progress & decline in America*, Book Collectors Association, New York, 1934

18 p. 217, Ayres, J., Ed.

19 1773 23 October, *Felix Farley's Bristol Journal*

20 1732 10 January, The Caledonian Mercury

21 p. 315, Stone, L.,

22 1815 25 July, *The Chester Courant*

23 p. 83, Ronson, J., *So You've Been Publicly Shamed*, Picador, London, 2015

24 1787 1 December, *The London Chronicle*

Ch. 19 (Un)happily Ever After

1 p. 61, Baring-Gould, S., *Devonshire Characters and Strange Events*, John Lane Bodley Head, London 1908

2. p. 65, ditto

3. p. 68, ditto

4. 1863 30 October, *The Royal Cornwall Gazette*

5 1872 14 May, *The Western Times*

6 p. 60, Baring-Gould, S.

7 p. 443, Thompson, E.P., *Customs in Common*, Merlin Press, Pontypool, 2010

APPENDIX II TIMELINE

1553 Parson Chicken sold wife to a butcher
   1584, 1585, 1613, 1638, 1696 mentioned in ecclesiastical courts
   1640s Warwickshire yeoman
   1692 Sale in Tipton
   1696 Chinnor, Oxon, wife sold for 2 pence per pound
   1720's South Staffordshire 5 shillings
   1735 London wife returned on day of sale
   1741 Churchwarden paid 40 shillings for women to marry out of Shoreditch parish, London
   1745 Woman sold by deed — case before Lord Hardwicke, London
   1748 Forced marriage at Stogumber. 1784 wife sold to father of her children
   1751 Woman scolded husband in ale house so sold for tankard of beer & half crown
   1760 Couple married Gloucester, soon parted and woman sold. Went to Bath to be married by 'lawless minister'
   1763 Lord Mansfield condemned sale in chancery where seller prosecuted on the grounds of against public decency and good manners

1764 Woman with halter round neck sold Parham fair for bullock which later sold for 6 guineas

1764 Wife sold but carpenter husband regretted it. No price recorded. Husband committed suicide.

1766 Midsomer Norton sale 6 guineas. Problems later caused by violent ex-husband

1767 Sale Marylebone London for ¼ guinea and gallon of rum. Woman inherited legacy, new husband married her to obtain it.

1767 Two women and man asked Bristol magistrate to attest husband changing wives of 10g. Told this was invalid, so went to publican to officiate and celebrate.

1767 Deputy workhouse keeper in Oxford taken before Mayor of London for luring girl to London to sell her abroad

1768 Cordwainer failed to buy his landlord's wife so married old sweetheart instead

1772 Sale Derby Market Place with halter round waist, 18 pence

1783 Entry in Edgbaston Toll Book wife sale, 6 people involved, market toll paid

1774 Hull, sold for 20 guineas

1774 Leeds Town Crier announced sale of husband, carpenter. Sold for 5 shillings and gallon of gin

1775 Procession by farmer dressed as cuckold. Sold for 20 guineas, huge crowd.

1775 December: Swindon Fair, sale arranged for £50 but sellers vanished

1776 Carpenter at Pudsey hanged self when wife refused to return to him.

1777 Witham: sale of wife, child, fowl, 11 pigs and 6 guineas

1775 Derbyshire's most notorious case. Farmer sold wife for 18 pence, with written agreement. She was delivered in Derby Market Place with witnesses.

1782 Purleigh Essex baptismal register child of wife bought in a halter

1784 Wife sold by husband returned from years abroad

1785 Wife sold by returned sailor, Liverpool

Appendix II Timeline

1786 June: Stamford wife sold for 5 shillings, delivered in halter. Written document with 3 witnesses then celebratory dinner

1786 August: London sale for 5s with halter round her neck. But purchaser soon tired of her so gave her to another.

1787 January: Ipswich farmer sold wife to neighbour. Purchaser so pleased he bought her a new gown and rang church bells.

1787 December: Woman with halter round her sold at Nuneaton market for 3 guineas. Purchaser rang church bells

1788 June: Woman sold 12 shillings, husband insisted on new shillings as never had anything but bad from her.

1789 Canal navvy tied rope round wife's waist, handed rope over to new husband for 3 shillings.

1789 October: Wife sold with halter round neck for 1 shilling. Seller announced in press he was no longer responsible for her bills.

1790 Young girl in Oxfordshire sold her hair to provide fifty pound dowry

1789 September: Woman sold at Yarlington Fair for 5 shillings, Delivered as custom with large cord, paid 6 pence deposit.

1790 January: Man sold wife 2 or 3 years earlier but thought contract unsound so led her on string to Thame market. Sold for 2 shillings 6 pence and paid 4 pence toll

1790 Woman was sold by overseers of poor at Burton fair. Husband absconded. Sold for 2 shillings less halter in which she was delivered. In toll book.

1790 February: Wife delivered in the usual way, though paper declared it was illegal and void.

1790 March: Warnings in Birmingham that sales were covers for adultery.

1796 August: Woman advertised for sale for 5 shillings, hard worker but needs tight rein. Husband parted with her as she was too much for him. Her clothes included.

1796 March: Man sold wife for 6 pence in Sheffield. He paid 1 guinea for coach to take couple to Manchester.

1797 Yorkshire blacksmith sold pregnant wife to workman for 2 guineas, 'sold to right father'.

1797 July Butcher put wife on sale Smithfield market with halter round neck and another to tie her to railings. Sold for 3 guineas and a crown (probably bowl of punch).

1797 Hosteller's wife sold for 25 guineas. Rumour of wife sale at Christies. 1797 December poor show at last wife sale though plenty of bidders.

1799 Baptism, Formby Catholic Register daughter of woman sold at Formby Cross for 15 shillings and crown bowl of punch

Towards the end of the eighteenth century, Manchester, sale of husband. Treated as joke, the man played flute and made boots. Sold for a guinea, a pair of fowls and a new dress.

1800 February: Parish sold wife, Oxford.

1800 February: Wife sale Stafford market. Many bids, from 1 pence, sold at 5 shillings, 5 pence. No halter

1801 January: West Luton wife sold for 5 shillings, with half returned. Sold Saturday, delivered Monday.

1801 September: Pig butcher offered wife with halter round neck, Smithfield market. Seafarer paid 1 guinea, couple left in coach.

1802 March: Chapel-en-le-Frith man sold wife, child, furniture at market cross for 11 shillings

1802 Hereford butcher sold wife for 24 shillings and a bowl of punch drank by those involved.

1803 Wife sold in Sheffield market. Led her with halter round neck, sold fro 1 guinea.

1803 March: Man sold unfaithful wife at Smithfield for 2 guineas.

1803 Wife from Ferry Bridge sold Pontefract. Bidding began at 12 pence, sold 11 shillings. Purchaser led her away by halter, pelted with mud and snow.

c.1805 Returned soldier sold wife at Halifax cross to father of her 3 children. Couple married 25 years later when husband died, was given away by her grandson.

1805 Man sold wife and child at Tuxford market place, 5 shillings for both.

1805 October: Man exposed good looking woman wearing halter at Smithfield market. Opened at 50 guineas but settled for 2. Sale entered in market books.

Appendix II Timeline

1806 Valentine's Day woman put on sale Hull market but drew huge crowd so deferred. She was later sold for 20 guineas and delivered to lodger.

1806 May: Labourer sold wife with halter round neck to butcher for 5 guineas and half crown bowl of punch.

1807 Man purchased innkeeper's wife, Grassington for 100 guineas, with 1 guinea deposit. Next day wife refused, man lost deposit.

1807 Warwick man indicted for causing riot by putting wife for sale with halter round her neck. Buyer and seller in gaol till provide sureties to attend next sessions.

1807 Wife sold Knaresborough for 6 pence plus quid of tobacco

1809 Woman was exposed wife on Broadway, Westminster, demanding 3 guineas, offered 2 by one of her gallants. New couple left with friends to celebrate in pub.

1810 May: Couple in Bewcastle fell out, so tried local sale, then went to Newcastle where husband was taken by press gang.

1810 Wife sold at Hull for 20 guineas

1811 Woman was led by halter to Sittingbourne, sold to highest bidder. Sale included 5 children, horse and cart, all household furniture.

c.1812 Man sold wife, Cornwall petty sessions

1814 Parish sale, Surrey: forced marriage of woman to father of illegitimate child. Marriage failed, woman sold again, but second husband abandoned wife as believed marriage not legal.

1814 Man led wife to Hailsham market in halter. Sold for 5 shillings.

1815 January: Sale of wife and a child for 1 pound at Maidstone. Deed and conveyance signed.

1815 January: Wife sale St Thomas's market, Bristol. Woman led in new halter round her middle. Offers made for her, 3 children, furniture but proxy so argument broke out.

1815 April: Man exposed wife in halter for sale at York market cross. He accepted 25 shillings.

1815 July: Sale of well dressed young woman arrived in coach with silk halter covered by lace veil. She was sold for 50 guineas plus horse.

1815 August: Manchester man sentenced to pillory for wife sale, will also be in prison 3 months.

1815 Woman sold husband in a halter at Dewsbury market for 6 pence. 1815 man offered wife Pontefract for 1 shilling, sold for 11.

1817 Man tried to place halter round neck of beautiful young woman at Smithfield market. Crowd and constables intervened. Husband claimed she had been unfaithful.

1817 April: Sale on public quay, Dartmouth

1871 May: Wife sold Preston obelisk

1817 June: Wife sale Market Drayton Fair

1817 Wife sold for 3 farthings at Boston. Husband provided shoulder of mutton etc.

1818 January: Man on bail, Andover for wife sale. He claimed to be ignorant that it was an offence

1818 July: man sold unfaithful wife in Penzance market for ½ guinea

1818 November: Wife sold to a discharged soldier at Bodmin market

1819 February: Rutland sessions punished man as an example for buying a wife.

1819 February: Dispute between 2 parishes over maintenance of 3 children, by man who purchased wife, entered in parish register as legitimate.

1819 November: Man sentenced to 6 months' prison for offering wife for sale Leominster market.

1819 December: Woman sold in Redruth market for 2 shillings and 6 pence. Declared to be the first of its kind there.

1820 Man led wife to cattle market, Canterbury hired pen, paid toll, led wife in halter. She was sold for 5 shillings.

1821 December: Wife who had been sold in Lincolnshire sent to house of correction for threatening arson of former husband's property.

1821 December: Wife sold to former housekeeper of buyer.

1822 Wife sold in public house, Derbyshire for 4 pence.

Appendix II Timeline

1822 Wife sale at Caerleon for 3 pence, offered to take her back after 3 weeks and return half the sale price.

1822 March: Woman sold Retford market, quickly purchased by paramour for 7 shillings. Buyer tried to sell halter in market.

1822 March: Man took wife to Mansfield market to sell her but changed his mind, claims made that it was a mock auction.

1822 November: Shoemaker assaulted wife for some time, so wife agreed to sale in Bristol Opened at half crown, sold for 1 pound. Buyer bought her new clothes.

1822 December: rich young woman separated from husband arranged proxy to buy herself.

1822 Man sold wife at Paradise market, Sheffield, for 5 shillings & watch.

1822 December: Wife selling extraordinary. Plymouth woman sold herself via proxy, £2 deposit with remainder £17. Couple taken to magistrates. Did not understand what was wrong as they had followed accepted practices.

1823 May: Wife sold for 6 pence, but changed his mind, woman refused to be re-sold unless magistrate ordered, so left with her mother

1823 August: Wife sold to her own mother

1823 August: Abused wife sold to her own brother. Husband married in church, convicted of bigamy, transported 7 years

1823 Husband tracked down wife to Liskeard, announced sale by bellman, put rope round wife's neck but police stopped sale.

1823 Husband repeatedly threatened to sell wife before doing so. Purchaser abducted her in advance, purchaser in prison as warning to others

1824 Town crier announced sale Wenlock market. She wore halter round waist, sold 10s plus pint of ale. Sale price spent celebrating.

1824 June: Manchester sale for 5 shillings but wife unhappy with buyer so resold for 3 shillings and quart of ale

1825 Wife sold Horsham market for 2 pounds, 5 shillings including 1 of their 3 children.

1825 Sale Horsham Colt Fair.

1826 February: Sale at Loughborough market cross, with halter. Eventually sold for 1 shilling, but parties were arrested and sent to treadmill.

1826 May: Sold Lodesworth for 30 shillings plus 1 shilling toll. Tollkeeper claimed she was any article not listed, applied.

1826 August: Man put notice on his house advertising wife for sale. Wife sought help. Not an offence.

1826 December: Sale in Reading attracted great crowd, magistrates intervened, sale stopped. Woman left with intended buyer.

1827 June: At Longtown fair, wife sold to mother for 5 shillings

c.1828 Sale at Bridlington claimed to be similar to one a decade earlier.

1828 February: Sale at Anstey, Leics. But when seller saw her working happily, aimed a loaded gun at her.

1828 April: Sale at Smithfield, but when bidding reached £2 husband realised her value, changed his mind so kept her.

1828 Messy domestic arrangements: lodger in poor law cottage became wife's lover. Overseers intervened, all three sent to prison.

1828 Tintagel: Man forced to support wife he had sold 7 years earlier, plus children of purchaser or be sentenced to the treadmill.

1829 Bristol: Woman sold wife for a donkey

1829 June: Yorkshire man paraded wife with new sixpence halter round her neck. Purchaser appeared, 18 pence agreed, which they spent in pub.

1829 September: One legged cobbler sold wife Garnet Fair. Bids rose to 5 shillings, but wife rejected buyer, resold for 3 shillings 6 pence and quart of ale. Trio pelted by crowd, woman left behind.

1829 Wife sold Stamford for 4 shillings

c.1830 Black Country wife sale. Old Rough Moey sold young wife with child via street theatre.

1830 February: One of 1st sales in new St Thomas's market, Bristol was a wife sold for 5 pounds 10 shillings.

1830 April: Cheltenham Corn Market man offered wife for sale, offered 6 pence as a joke by a sweep. Wife lured into market so fled, husband fled dousing at the pump.

1830s Wenlock market. Husband lost his nerve but wife insisted on sale as she wanted a change.

1831 Wife sold at Tong Moor-gate, Bolton for 3 shillings 6 pence and gallon of ale to couple's lodger. Delivered by husband and bellman announced he would no longer pay her debts.

1831 October: Wife sold Stockport market for 2 shillings 6 pence to her father, 1 shillings 6 pence returned for luck.

1831 November: Woman sold York Pavement with halter round neck for 60 guineas. Crowd cheered.

1832 April Joseph Thompson of Carlisle gave humorous speech about why he and wife were unsuited. Sold her for 20 shillings and a Newfoundland dog. Halter transferred from wife's neck to the dog.

1832 November: Man charged with bigamy claimed he had separated from wife via agreement written by a clergyman; who was living in adultery with same clergyman. First wife gave him 2 pounds to marry.

1833 Sale at Bolton after market. Three parties exchanged stamped receipt in hostelry after money exchanged. Parties came from same village and shared a meal and drinks afterwards.

c.1833 Sale outside Whitechapel pub, landlord auctioneer, sold to highest bidder

1833 March: Epping Workhouse master sold wife to help couple to prevent her becoming dependent on parish.

1833 September: Man offered highly praised wife for sale for 50 pounds at Falmouth. He sold her as he preferred wine to women. Asked 10 shillings, accepted 5.

1833 August: Woman sold to mother, Halifax

1833 September: Couple attempted sale Melksham market held on bail. Purchaser put in jail in default of bail.

1833 September: Wife sold Lansdown Fair, Bath for ½ crown, but not considered legal so arrested so tried in market but were arrested. Reprimanded by mayor but there was no prosecutor so husband was freed. Purchaser already had a wife.

1834 Wife sale, Birmingham: similar to Canterbury 1820.

1834 June: Magistrates in session when sale at Hertford market. Husband was absent, woman and chosen buyer arrested when fleeing. Husband appeared, gave surety not to re-offend. Abused by crowd, the woman became ill.

1834 August: Couple arrested for being drunk and disorderly in Gorbals pub. Publican had sold woman for 7 shillings 6 pence. Disturbance caused by argument as to how to spend the sale money.

1834 March: Man led wife by halter to Birmingham market place, sold her for 15 pounds. She outlived both men, gained inheritance from late first husband.

1835 January: Wife sold at gas pillar, new market place at Manchester. Paid money in pub and receipt stamped,

1831 January: Wife sold at Haverside near Manchester to brother-in-law whom she had cohabited 4 years. Both sacked from work out of disgust.

1835 February: Crowd at Bolton prevented authorities intervening in sale. Similar to incident at Ashburn Derbys., when JP intervened but crowd pelted constables.

1835 February: Woman sold to own mother, unclear where.

1835 March: Confused scene at market hall, Suffolk. Wife for sale with halter round waist amidst jeering onlookers. Jokers bought her for 6 shillings, 6 pence. Husband pelted with water. Trio fined at guildhall. Rioted proceedings got husband re-arrested.

1835 May: Wife sold Bolton Obelisk

1836 Date unknown: Cornishman sold wife with halter round waist. Little interest, sold to pair of tinkers for 4 pence. Husband paid penny market toll, i.e. as for pig

1837 February: Wife sold at butter market, Bradford. Wife interested in man who sometimes dined with them. Only bid a sovereign, accepted.

1837 May: Halifax common site for sales. Wife sold to married man for half a crown.

1837 June: Man in West Riding sentenced to 1 month in prison with hard labour for selling his wife.

1837 August: Wife eloped, couple tracked down by husband to demand public sale, handing over halter. Ring delivered and paid 3 sovereigns and 3 shillings 6 pence.

1837 October: Wife sale Wolverhampton with halter round neck and middle for 2 shillings 6 pence. She had been living with purchaser 3 years.

1838 Gloucestershire market countryman sold wife in halter after cattle sales. Sold for 18 pence.

1838 February: Woman sold at Smithfield

1838 Wife sale, Bakewell fair

1838 November: Wife sale Bridlington similar to one a decade earlier.

1838 November: Wife sold by husband who returned from transportation.

1839 Wife sold for tub of swedes, Lincolnshire

1839 Wife offered for sale Dudley, for 3 ½ pence, sold for 6 pence

1839 May: Wife led 3 times round market place followed by crowd. Woman shamelessly waved handkerchief.

1839 September: broadside of sale at Thetford market. Sold for 5 pound, handkerchief round woman's neck handed over to former lodger. Husband danced and sang to be free of her, descended into argument.

1840 March: woman sold to soldier at Loughborough was so keen to be sold put rope round her own body.

c.1841 Gloucester man sold wife to wife's paramour. Woman led to market in new bonnet with halter round her neck. Sold for ½ crown. She outlived both men.

1841 Unwilling wife tied to pen by halter was sold Smithfield for 30 shillings. She was warned by magistrate of legal dangers if she consorted with purchaser.

1840s Farmer by side of road in Devon offered wife for sale with rope round her neck, wearing a shift. Eventually was sold for 10 shillings.

1841 August: Dissolute man led wife to Penkridge with halter round her body. Paid toll, led her round market, sold for 18 pence and quart ale.

1841 August: Wife sold for 10 shillings 6 pence at Retford public market.

1842 November: Wife offered for sale at Inn, Boston. Auctioneer provided with writing materials, but police intervened.

1842 December: Wife sold to former housekeeper, Lincoln.

1844 Unfaithful wife in Glamorganshire called on her paramour and they agreed a sale, for 2 shillings, 6 pence, paid for by wife.

1844 June: Wife sold Chelmsford market for 15 shillings, having failed to sell previous day.

1844 Wife sale Horsham Colt Fair

1845 September: Woman for sale Banbury market place to man she was already living with. But they were stopped by police, told to go further away.

1846 January: Wife for sale Callington market place, but riot threatened, so decoy couple appeared and sale was completed for half a crown.

1847 January: Man forced wife to be sold.

1847 Crier announced sale at Barton market place of woman in new halter round her waist. Noisy crowd but sold for 1 shilling, with 3½ pence returned for luck. But purchaser refused to honour new wife's debts.

1848 October: man offered wife for sale Mansfield market. Woman with halter round waist was sold for 1 shilling 6 pence.

1848 November: wife sold Bradford with pink ribbon round neck, but arrested.

1848 June: Sale at Witney, wife led by haler to market by husband wearing huge horns.

c.1848 Man married woman at Shepton Mallet for her house, then tried to sell her but rescued by neighbours.

1849 Monkswearmouth man offered wife for sale.

1849 December: Woman eloped when husband in infirmary, so agreed to sale for 5 shillings and 9 pence.

1850 May: 'Dutch Auction' at Knott-mill of wife with rope round waist. She addressed man in crowd, who agreed to buy her for 19 shillings, 6 pence.

ABOUT THE AUTHOR

Barb Drummond climbs mountains to see past times. She burrows for hidden stories and lures them into the open to reveal their secrets. She asks why things happened, who was involved, how could they think it was a good idea. Sometimes she finds diamonds, or dust of things that mattered. She finds a single name, or a sentence, that lights up the sky like fireworks. Or she finds silence, which can also bear great meaning. She seeks patterns, themes, traces. Or shapes left by them. Sometimes she uses guesses to patch what is missing, but she makes it from the best possible material.

www.barbdrummondcurioushistorian.com
Twitter: @Barb_Drummond
Facebook: Barb Drummond

UNTITLED

www.ingramcontent.com/pod-product-compliance
Lightning Source LLC
Chambersburg PA
CBHW071337080526
44587CB00017B/2865